ALSO BY STEVE MILLWARD:

*From Blues To Rock: An Analytical History Of
Pop Music* – with David Hatch (Manchester
University Press)

Changing Times: Music And Politics In 1964
(Matador)

DIFFERENT TRACKS

Music And Politics In 1970

Steve Millward

Matador
9 Priory Business Park,
Wistow Road, Kibworth Beauchamp,
Leicestershire. LE8 0RX
Tel: (+44) 116 279 2299
Fax: (+44) 116 279 2277
Email: books@troubador.co.uk
Web: www.troubador.co.uk/matador

ISBN 978-1783064-762

British Library Cataloguing in Publication Data.
A catalogue record for this book is available from the British Library.

Typeset by Troubador Publishing Ltd, Leicester, UK
Printed and bound in the UK by TJ International, Padstow, Cornwall

Matador is an imprint of Troubador Publishing Ltd

For my friends

Preface

In June 1970 I was one of the first generation of eighteen-year-olds able to vote in a UK General Election and duly went off to the polling station in my school uniform. The following month I left school and moved with my family from Worcester to Leicester. I spent the summer listening to records, going to see bands like Derek and The Dominos at the De Montfort Hall and watching the World Cycling Championships. In September 1970 I went to university. At school my favourite bands had been The Beatles, The Who and Cream, but now I was introduced to a variety of new music – Fairport Convention, Love, The Soft Machine, Crosby, Stills and Nash, James Taylor and many others. Like most students of the era, I participated in marches, demos and sit-ins. Yet at the same time there was an uneasy feeling that things were not quite as good as they had been in the glory days of the 1960s.

I mention these autobiographical details to illustrate how much I understood about 1970 at the time, and also how little. While I can claim that many of the arguments contained in this book stem from direct experience, I would be the first to admit that it is only in retrospect that the real significance of the year began to dawn on me. Those who have read my last book will know that in my view the year 1964 marked the beginning of so much that was important in the 'swinging sixties'. In 1970 most of it came to an end. Yet that enabled new ideas to flourish, unencumbered by the precepts of the previous generation. Not all of these developments were beneficial, constructive or desirable but in nearly every case they determined the political and musical undercurrents of what was to be a very different decade.

Deciding just what comprises the music of 1970 is no easy task. LPs (long-playing records, for those too young to recognise the term) had taken over from singles as the preferred format of the leading artists in rock, the most creative, and popular, musical idiom of the period. But the huge amount of time often involved in producing them meant the interval between commencement and eventual release might span two calendar years. For the purposes of this book I include any item both recorded and issued within the year, plus any item made in 1969 (or earlier) and released in 1970 – on the obvious basis that its impact could only date from when it became available. For the same reason I have tended to omit records made in 1970 but not released until later unless specific events from 1970 influenced their creation.

Many people have helped me write *Different Tracks*. Some loaned records, films, books or periodicals; others gave interviews or offered advice, comment and feedback. So my grateful thanks go to Nicky Crewe, Julie Downing, Dave Driver, Tim Gausden, Simon Harmsworth, Beverly Howbrook, Louise Hunt, Chris Lee, Matt Luheshi, Jackie Marsh, Mary Millward, Matthew Millward, Tom Millward, Linda Moore, Rich Page, Julia Polyblank, Jim Rafferty, Jennie Singer, Jenny Slaughter and Sid Toole. Special mention must be made of John Greenway and Pete Newton who gave me access to their extensive collections of material from the period; Pete also contributed valuable facts and suggestions concerning the ECM label. Finally I should like to express my gratitude to Naomi Green and the team at Troubador for their patience, guidance and support.

Contents

CHAPTER 1

All Things Must Pass

On 31 December 1969 Jimi Hendrix took his group, Band of Gypsys, into the Fillmore East, New York City. The two sets they played that night and the two a day later thus straddled the turn of the decade. As well as their temporal significance, Hendrix's shows also had a musical importance. His first three albums had balanced aggression with gentleness, yet here was a uniformly violent music, protesting not only the Vietnam War but racial injustice. In his spoken introduction to 'Machine Gun', an epic performance in which the band simulate the rapid fire of the eponymous weapon, he dedicates the piece to 'all the soldiers that are fighting in Chicago, Milwaukee and New York ... oh yeah, and all the soldiers fighting in Vietnam', thus equating the conflict in South East Asia with the civil rights demonstrations taking place in cities across America. His two colleagues in the band, Billy Cox and Buddy Miles, were both African-Americans, having replaced the white musicians Noel Redding and Mitch Mitchell, his partners in The Jimi Hendrix Experience.

But Hendrix's appearance at the Fillmore East also symbolised a cultural shift, away from the carefree hedonism of the 1960s and towards the brutish uncertainties of the 1970s. The wind was now blowing in a different direction and the atmosphere was changing. Insurrection, revolution and terrorism were rife while the suppression of legitimate protest was allowing an illegitimate variant to flourish. And the war in Vietnam still dragged on, spilling over into neighbouring Cambodia.

Just as the creative energy of the mid-1960s had been ignited by the explosive music of The Beatles, so it was that a concert on 6 December

1969 by their friends and rivals, The Rolling Stones, seemed to extinguish it. At the Altamont Speedway Free Festival, organised and headlined by the band, there were four deaths. Three of them were accidental but one, shockingly, was not: Meredith Hunter was stabbed to death by one of the Hell's Angels allegedly policing the event. Later it transpired that Hunter was carrying a gun and high on amphetamines, and his assailant, Alan Passaro, was acquitted of murder. Nevertheless, Altamont was a sharp contrast to the peaceful Woodstock Festival, held only three months earlier and attended by a much larger audience.

Jimi Hendrix was doing no more than confirming what Altamont had signalled: the end of a dream and the start of a new reality. Within nine months he himself was dead, his demise symbolic of the passing of an era: for 1970 saw the decline and death of many things – not only in music but also in the world of politics, and in society more widely. What came next rose from the ashes and heralded, or indeed constituted, a revolution.

★ ★ ★ ★ ★

For most of 1969 there was little hint that change was on the way: in fact it might be argued that the last year of the 1960s was in many respects its most stable, at least in the Western world. President Richard Nixon, for example, seemed to be convincing the American people that he was dealing competently with the Vietnam War. The first troop withdrawals began in early July and later in the month he was able to bask in the reflected glory of the Apollo 11 moon landing. During the year Nixon's approval rating did not fall below 56%, while his disapproval rating never exceeded 29%. Contrast that with 1970, when he fell below 56% approval nine times and exceeded 29% disapproval on no fewer than eleven occasions.★

In the UK, the early part of the year had proved difficult for Prime Minister Harold Wilson, but he restored order (at least temporarily) after

---

★Source: Gallup statistics, held at The University of Connecticut, Roper Center for Public Opinion Archives.

the August riots in Northern Ireland by deploying soldiers to protect the Catholic minority. By the autumn, the economy had improved, with excellent trade figures caused by a boom in exports. Elsewhere in Europe, there were new governments for both France and Germany. The latter was a coalition of the Social Democratic Party and the Free Democrats and was led by Willy Brandt, a courageous and popular politician who was keen to see a rapprochement with the Eastern Bloc. Untainted by any association with Nazism (just the opposite: he had been vehemently opposed to Hitler), Brandt seemed to be leading his country in a productive direction.

1969 was an uncharacteristically settled year across the major countries of South America. Military governments were operating in Argentina, Brazil, Paraguay and Peru; Ecuador, Chile and Venezuela were under Conservative/Christian Democrat control; while Colombia was ruled by the National Front coalition of Conservatives and Liberals. Only in Bolivia and Uruguay was there any instability. Furthermore few of these regimes were showing any frailty, except perhaps in Chile, where President Frei was struggling to make good his promises of far-reaching reforms.

It was almost as if the West was having a breather after the turmoil of 1968, which had seen the assassinations of Martin Luther King and Robert Kennedy, violent student protests at the Sorbonne University in Paris, and riots at the Democratic Convention in Chicago – let alone the Soviet invasion of Czechoslovakia where the 'Prague Spring' had flowered all too briefly. Looking at the decade in total, a pattern emerges whereby years of tension and uncertainty were interspersed with phases of confidence and creativity. Thus the escalation of the Cold War in 1960, when the US spy plane piloted by Gary Powers was shot down over the Soviet Union, and 1961, with the Bay of Pigs crisis and the construction of the Berlin Wall, was followed by a more positive period (albeit bisected by the death of President Kennedy and the intensification of the Vietnam War) which peaked in 1964 with an explosion of innovation in music, art, fashion, science and technology. 1965 and 1966 were years of consolidation and 1967 was illuminated by the Summer of Love, an illusory prelude to the *annus horribilis* that followed. After 1968, things couldn't get worse, and they didn't.

Admittedly, student protests continued into 1969 (there was even a sit-in at Harvard University on 9 April) but they were now so routine they ceased to shock. One event that did make the headlines took place on the weekend of 9-11 May when 3,000 young people descended on the small town of Zap, North Dakota. They came at the invitation of students from UND (University of North Dakota) who were trying, with the slogan 'Zip to Zap', to create their own version of the spring festivities held in the warmer climes of Fort Lauderdale, Florida. Unfortunately Zap's resources were insufficient to cope with such an influx and though most of the visitors left following entreaties from local residents, those who remained – disaffected by inflated beer prices and freezing temperatures – started to make a nuisance of themselves. The National Guard were immediately called in to disperse them, something of an overreaction and symptomatic of the increasingly heavy-handed response by the authorities to gatherings of young people.

At the same time there was genuine cause for concern in the larger centres of population. Instances of terrorism, sporadic since the late 1940s, were becoming more frequent. Employing a similar model to that of the Basque separatist organisation, ETA, who had begun a campaign of violent action the previous year, the FLQ (Front de libération du Québec) bombed the Montreal Stock Exchange on 13 February 1969, killing 27 people; on 28 September, they planted a bomb in the home of the city's mayor, Jean Drapeau. Earlier in the month, the Marxist group MR-8 had kidnapped the US Ambassador to Brazil, Charles Burke Elbrick, in Rio de Janeiro. In February, Palestinian terrorists attacked an El Al aircraft at Zurich Airport and exploded a bomb in a Jerusalem supermarket; in August, led by Leila Khaled, they hijacked a TWA plane following take-off from Rome. In December, seventeen people were killed by a bomb detonated in the National Agrarian Bank, Milan; the identity of the group responsible has remained a mystery to the present day.

Even so, an upbeat mood pervaded 1969 and right across the musical spectrum it was a year of plenty, the culmination of five years' worth of rapid, sustained progress. Rock, in particular, was soaking up influences –

not only from other forms of Western music, but from around the world – and a new term, 'fusion', was coined to describe the outcome. Thus there were fusions of rock with:

- Jazz – The Electric Flag, Chicago, Blood, Sweat And Tears, John Mayall, Colosseum, The Soft Machine
- Classical music – The Nice, Procol Harum, Deep Purple, Renaissance
- Folk – Fairport Convention, Steeleye Span
- Indian music – begun by The Beatles, continued by Quintessence and The Third Ear Band
- Latin – Santana
- Country music – Bob Dylan, The Byrds

Musicianship and production values reached new standards of excellence and there was a flood of high quality albums from both new and established bands. Among the newcomers were such diverse acts as Led Zeppelin, The Stooges, King Crimson, Thin Lizzy, Yes, Black Sabbath and The Carpenters, all of whom, in their various ways, were to have a big impact on the 1970s. Nevertherless it was the big names of pop music who consolidated their position at the head of the hierarchy. The Beatles, for example, recorded and released *Abbey Road*, considered by most critics to be among their finest albums. Coming after *The Beatles* (widely known as *The White Album*), which felt like the work of four individuals rather than one band, it was a surprisingly coherent and unified effort, overflowing with memorable melodies. Immaculately produced by George Martin, it drew back from the relentless experimentation of the previous three years, resulting in their purest pop product since *Rubber Soul*. It was also pleasing to discover that the best two tracks were both George Harrison compositions – the catchy, optimistic 'Here Comes The Sun' and the ballad 'Something', described by Frank Sinatra as the best love song of the 20th century.

Of comparable calibre, but very different in ambience, was The Rolling Stones' *Let It Bleed*. Issued the day before Altamont, it starts with the appropriately apocalyptic 'Gimmie Shelter', which builds from a tentative, eerie opening to become a pulsating rocker laced simultaneously with doom and defiance. A similar formula is followed for 'You Can't Always Get What You Want', though the tracks in between, notably 'Live With Me' and 'Midnight Rambler', convey unadulterated menace.

Blind Faith, who made their live debut in front of 100,000 people in Hyde Park, London, were a much-vaunted 'supergroup', consisting of Stevie Winwood, who had recently left another all-star band, Traffic; ex-Cream stalwarts Eric Clapton and Ginger Baker; and Ric Grech, late of Family. As is sometimes the case with such line-ups, they went rapidly from being overrated to being underrated. Although their eponymous album, released in August, is far from perfect, it does contain some exceptional tracks, none better than 'Had To Cry Today' with its thrilling guitar duet between Clapton and Winwood and a solo by Clapton that uncoils in extravagant fashion.

Another of the year's outstanding albums came from Clapton's erstwhile employer, John Mayall, who broke new ground with his live recording, *The Turning Point*. At a time when most bands were getting louder, Mayall's group was a refreshing departure. He dispensed with the quintessential rock sounds of heavily amplified guitar and drums, using instead the saxophone and flute of Johnny Almond and the delicate acoustic guitar of Jon Mark. This format worked so well that Mark and Almond built their own group around it the following year. In the meantime, Fairport Convention were heading in the opposite direction. After three mellow, eclectic folk-rock albums, Fairport gave greater definition to each of the central components of their music on *Liege And Lief*. The folk element was emphasised by the presence of fiddler Dave Swarbrick and a selection of traditional material including the ancient ballads, 'Matty Groves' and 'Tam Lin'; thumping bass, resonant electric guitar and – in particular – the crisp propulsion of drummer Dave Mattacks convert them both into rock classics. *Liege And Lief*, released in December 1969, proved to be a seminal record – as Rob Young has written, 'a high-water mark for Fairport Convention and for the whole notion of British folk-rock' (*Electric Eden*, p. 264). It proved that, even after five years of untrammelled creativity, there were new dimensions to be found in rock, that apparently most basic of musical idioms.

Released on 23 May 1969, The Who's double album *Tommy* was heralded as the first-ever rock opera (even though there were precedents in the work of The Pretty Things and, indeed, The Who themselves). On closer examination, it had many flaws: some critics seized on the thin storyline and the inconsistencies of the allegory while others viewed it as an artistic dead-end. Yet *Tommy* was evidence both of the maturity of rock as an art form and of its apparently inexhaustible malleability. More importantly, it showed that seasoned pop songwriters like Pete Townshend were still willing to try something new.

Away from the rock mainstream there was still greater evidence of innovation. Holger Czukay's 'Boat Woman Song' was, for example, one of the earliest compositions – possibly *the* earliest – to use sampling: an extract from a piece by the thirteenth century French musician Adam de la Halle is overlaid by a chorus of Vietnamese voices to spine-chilling effect. Czukay was also making experimental music with his band, Can, whose debut album, *Monster Movie*, was also released in 1969; its radical mix of free jazz, psychedelic rock and contemporary classical music of the type pioneered by Czukay's mentor, Karlheinz Stockhausen, distanced it from the UK/US hegemony, thus ensuring, for a while at least, commercial oblivion.

Elsewhere in West Germany, there were moves in a very different musical direction. For 1969 was the year that Bavarian bass-player Manfred Eicher founded ECM Records which, before very long, became one of the most renowned labels in jazz. Again, there was a clear distinction between Eicher's agenda and what his counterparts in America and Britain were trying to achieve. Tending towards the tranquil and cerebral with sleeve designs as minimalist as the music inside, ECM's artists – among them Jan Garbarek, Eberhard Weber, Terje Rypdal, Ralph Towner, Egberto Gismonti and John Surman – specialised in exploring their own folk traditions and those of other cultures, thus making the label one of the first champions of what came to be known as 'world music'.

Something of ECM's methodology emanated from Miles Davis who in 1969 was still the foremost musician in jazz. His quintet had dominated the previous five years yet, though successful aesthetically, its appeal was restricted to an audience comprising, at least in Davis's eyes, white middle-class record-buyers. His album *In A Silent Way*, recorded on 18 February and released on 30 July, returned the rhythm section to a central role in jazz; and now the pulse was not only derived from rock but provided by its key instruments – electric guitar, electric piano, bass guitar and drums. It was thus instantly accessible including, crucially, to a younger generation of listeners who were buying albums in huge quantities. It also presented a new sound: cool, contemplative, open-ended and thus a complete contrast to the free jazz maelstrom that had engulfed the mid-sixties.

All of these undercurrents were to prove important for the decade ahead but, at least as far as the world of popular culture was concerned, 1969 meant celebration and good vibes. A month after the Blind Faith event, The Rolling Stones also played for free in Hyde Park, this time to an audience of a quarter of a million; the concert acted as something of a catharsis following the death of former band member Brian Jones two days before. Then in August came 'An Aquarian Exposition' presented by the Woodstock Music and Art Fair, more commonly known as Woodstock, a mammoth three-day rock festival in New York State attended by 450,000 and featuring such artists as Jimi Hendrix, The Who, Santana, The Band, The Grateful Dead, Sly and The Family Stone, Joan Baez, Janis Joplin and Crosby, Stills, Nash and Young. Though not without incident, the festival passed off peacefully and is now regarded as one of the defining events of both the 1960s and the 20th century as a whole. Only later did it emerge that the organisers had persuaded the Governor of New York, Nelson Rockefeller, not to send 10,000 National Guardsmen to the site.

On a smaller scale, yet no less newsworthy, were the pop star weddings that punctuated early 1969. 12 March saw the wedding of Paul McCartney and Linda Eastman; eight days later John Lennon married Yoko Ono in

Gibraltar, a prelude to their much-publicised 'bed-in' in the Hilton Hotel, Amsterdam, an event that contrived to combine serious intent with surrealism and high comedy. The previous month Lulu had married Bee Gee Maurice Gibb and she hit the headlines again on 29 March when, representing the UK, she was part of an unprecedented, and farcical, four-way tie in the result of the Eurovision Song Contest: her 'Boom Bang-A-Bang', one of the least distinguished British entries ever – at least, prior to those of the 2000s – attracted the same number of points (eighteen) as those from the Netherlands, Spain and France. Never mind: it all added to the impression of a thriving, ebullient pop scene, the commercial counterweight to the great events going on in rock music. But in retrospect, it was the death on 3 July 1969 of Brian Jones who, having ingested a prodigious quantity of drugs and alcohol, drowned in his own swimming pool, that seems a more accurate harbinger of the year to come.

★ ★ ★ ★ ★

By the end of 1969, there were gloomy portents, too, for the Labour Government. At the by-elections on 30 October the Conservatives captured the constituency of Swindon and Labour only narrowly held on to Paddington North, Islington North, Glasgow Gorbals and Newcastle-under-Lyme. The average swing to the Conservatives on the day was just over 10%. On 4 December the Tories took Wellingborough from Labour with a swing of nearly 10% and held Louth with a swing of 14%. The first in a series of teachers' strikes was held in November; on 8 and 9 December there were backbench revolts over the Biafra and Vietnam Wars. And on 17 December the Government suffered one of its lowest majorities of the session when 30 Labour MPs voted against its prices and incomes policy.

Yet on Northern Ireland – both a major domestic issue and, increasingly, the focus of international attention – Wilson seemed to be making encouraging progress. In November the Ulster Defence Regiment and Police Bills were given their second reading, the effect of which was to separate the military from the police in Northern Ireland, thus providing for the abolition of the Ulster Special Constabulary (also known as the 'B' Specials), whose activities so enraged the Catholic minority. On 17 November, Bernadette Devlin, the Independent Civil Rights MP for Mid-Ulster and a fierce republican, protested in the Commons that recruitment was taking place before the Ulster Defence Regiment Bill had become law, but five days later she was sentenced to six months' imprisonment for causing incitement to riot during the August 'Battle of the Bogside' riots in Derry. Thus, for a short time at least, the tension in Northern Ireland was defused by a few degrees.

The New Year of 1970 saw more milestones in Labour's programme of reform which had commenced at their accession to power in 1964 and been given renewed impetus at their re-election, with an increased majority, two years later. Thus on 9 February 1970, the Equal Pay Bill received an unopposed second reading: this meant that legislation would follow to outlaw different rates of remuneration for men and women doing the same job, although this would not be accomplished fully until 1975. In May there was the publication of the White Paper, *The Protection Of The Environment: The Fight Against Pollution*; reluctant local authorities were compelled to introduce comprehensive education; and, just before the General Election, the Chronically Sick and Disabled Persons Bill became law, the first legislation anywhere in the world to recognise and give rights to people with disabilities.

Labour held a consistent lead over the Conservatives in the opinion polls. On 12 May it stood at 7.5% and exactly one month later, less than a week before the election, Labour were eleven points ahead. Yet for all their apparent primacy and the success of their social legislation there was still scope to defeat Labour. Their vulnerability lay in some of the issues most important to British voters including law and order and unemployment. The Conservatives had held a conference for the upper echelon of the Party at Selsdon Park, near Croydon, in late January. One issue which excited, and united, delegates was the apparent crime wave which was being ignored – tantamount to being condoned – by the Labour Government. Although the evidence for any such calamity was at best inconclusive, an increase in policing and tougher legislation would be a popular response to the seemingly constant round of civil disobedience. On 23 April it was announced that the jobless figure in the UK was now 616,660, the highest since 1940, calling into doubt the Government's suite of economic policies on industrial relations and prices and incomes.

The Tory leader, Edward Heath, was also coming across as a credible alternative to Harold Wilson. The two men had a good deal in common – both were born in 1916 into lower middle-class families and both won scholarships, first to grammar school, then to Oxford. However their political paths diverged, largely due to the influence their fathers' very different experiences had exerted upon them. Herbert Wilson was a vocationally-educated industrial chemist who became unemployed in 1930 and then, lacking the cachet of a university degree, struggled to find work. It is easy to trace the impact this had on his son, from the egalitarian tone of the 1964 Labour manifesto to the creation of the Open University in 1969. William Heath, on the other hand, left school at twelve and became a successful builder who ran his own firm and profited by the post-war construction boom. Although some of his habits embarrassed his son – Heath's biographer, Philip Ziegler, quotes a female family friend as describing him as 'a great hugger and a kisser, even a bottom-pincher' (*Edward Heath*, p. 2) – he inherited his father's energy, ambition – and politics.

Nevertheless Heath was not a stereotypical Tory. His wartime service, when he witnessed first-hand the devastation wrought by Nazism, convinced him that a federation of European states was essential for both political and economic reasons. As Lord Privy Seal he was responsible for Britain's relationship with Europe and led negotiations for its entry to the European Economic Community. As it turned out, this initiative foundered but with the resignation in April 1969 of the principal obstacle to UK membership, President de Gaulle of France, Heath – by now the Leader of the Opposition – led his Party to a pro-European position.

He also had liberal views on overseas aid, capital punishment and, at least in his early career, industrial relations. All of this enhanced his image as a progressive Party Leader who could be trusted not to unravel the social reforms of the late 1960s while at the same time reassuring the public he would have no truck with criminals, layabouts and belligerent student demonstrators – categories conflated in the minds of many voters. Furthermore, in the run-up to the Election he refrained from being too specific on highly controversial issues such as Rhodesia and prices and incomes.

One controversy he could scarcely avoid, however, was immigration. His contemporary and former contender for the Party leadership, Enoch Powell, was prone to denounce the influx of Commonwealth citizens (many of them British passport holders) into the UK, using terminology that was barely short of racist. Of course, this endeared him to a small but significant portion of the electorate, even if such views were repugnant to the majority. After one especially inflammatory speech in April 1968, Heath dismissed him from the Shadow Cabinet. Yet Powell remained within the Party and was always careful to express his support for it, so that at the 1970 General Election Heath was able to retain the votes of both the pro- and anti-Powell factions.

The Election took place on 18 June 1970 and – literally against all the odds – the Conservatives were victorious, with an overall majority of 30. Much of their success was directly attributable to Heath, who had run a quasi-Presidential style campaign, comprising slogans, sound bites and consistent personal visibility. Certainly he was assisted by some good fortune. In May it was announced that the trade figures were showing a £31 million deficit and the sense of depression was deepened just four days before the Election when England lost to West Germany in the quarter-final of the World Cup in Mexico. One can only wonder at the effect a decisive England victory would have had on that other battle of the giants, five-and-a-half thousand miles away. But in the event, the game in Léon signified more than the death of England's football supremacy; it seemed to symbolise the end of a halcyon era.

* * * * *

The 1970 General Election was the first in which eighteen-year-olds were able to vote. Edward Heath, however, had shown no real affinity with young people. He was seen as equivocal at best on the sort of issues that interested them, such as immigration and the troubles in Northern Ireland and, unlike Wilson, he had made no attempt to consort with pop stars or other figures from popular culture; though he was an extremely capable musician his interest lay in classical music, anathema to most teenagers. He had no sympathy with those who protested against the Vietnam War and, what was worse, he intended to reform the law of trespass to cover demonstrations. It was felt that this would also affect pop festivals, which were growing in size on the American model. Fiery Creations, the organisers of the mammoth Isle of Wight Festival of 1970, even billed it as 'The Last Great Event'.

Over 600,000 people (of whom the author was one) attended the festival, making it bigger than Woodstock. It lasted longer, too, from Wednesday 26 to Sunday 30 August. However the benign atmosphere that had permeated the American event was largely absent at the Isle of Wight. There was trouble as early as Day One when the crowd, unable to hear Kris Kristofferson, booed him off stage, but a greater problem was the massive gantry housing a camera crew and their equipment. Located right in the centre of the arena, it blocked the view of thousands, though most bore it without complaint, imagining that the resultant film would appear promptly: as it was, we had to wait 26 years for the release of *Message To Love*.

The location at East Afton Down meant that large numbers of spectators could watch from the adjacent hill; others congregated at its foot, near the corrugated iron fences that surrounded the arena – this became known as 'Desolation Row'. Most of those who gathered in these areas had not paid to come to the festival and had no intention of doing so – in fact, some of the more belligerent elements decided to vent their frustration with the organisers, and hence the System, by breaking down the fences and converting the event into a free festival.

On Saturday, Joni Mitchell's set was interrupted by Yogi Joe, a Greek hippie actually known to her, who, after joining in on congas, seized the microphone and said, 'I have an announcement that I've been asked to make. Desolation Row is this festival, ladies and gentlemen' – whereupon he was manhandled off the stage. This, in effect, was the defining moment of the entire Isle of Wight event. Sympathies were divided between Joe and a visibly-upset Mitchell: it thus encapsulated the tension between those who wanted a free festival and those who had bought tickets; between fans experiencing all the privations of an event of that kind and the musicians, many of whom had arrived in expensive cars and, in some cases, by helicopter; and more widely, between and the hippie ethic and the forces of the Establishment. But *these* hippies were no longer prepared to settle for passive expressions of peace and love: they favoured positive action. And at the Isle of Wight they won the day.

Fiery Creations had come up with a range of strategies to make the event work, from berating the audience for booing Kris Kristofferson to funding *Freek Press*, a newsletter produced on the spot by writers from the magazines *Friends* and *Oz*; alongside helpful advice and information for festival-goers were statements by Fiery Creations explaining their financial obligations to the acts and why, because of agreements with the National Trust and the local golf club, they would have to clear the hill. Yet it was all to no avail. On Sunday, when it was clear they could no longer break even, Fiery Creations declared their Festival free.

By then, in spite of all the trials and tribulations, there had been some exhilarating moments. Whether through chance or inspired programming, Saturday afternoon was unforgettable. After Joni Mitchell, it was time for Tiny Tim, who lifted the mood so high that by the end of his set he had the crowd on their feet singing along to 'There'll Always Be An England' and 'Land Of Hope And Glory' – and they stayed there throughout the DJ set that immediately followed, dancing to Otis Redding's 'Respect' and Free's 'Alright Now' and making the peace sign to two balloonists flying overhead. Next came Miles Davis, whose stage persona was as dense and impenetrable as his music: no announcements, one hour, one number, 'Call It Anything'. Orthodox rock music returned in the evening and continued into the night with exceptional sets by The Doors and The Who. Sunday, however, was more downbeat. The realisation was setting in: this was the Last Day of the Last Great Event. Poor sound and a preponderance of acoustic acts didn't help and even Jimi Hendrix was uncharacteristically tentative and subdued.

Less than three weeks later, Hendrix was dead; seventeen days after that, Janis Joplin died, too. Both were victims of drug overdoses. On 25 November, the body of the visionary saxophonist Albert Ayler – far less famous but just as gifted as the other two – was found in the East River, New York City.

* * * * *

Joplin had given her fans something to remember her by – an excellent album, *Pearl*, completed just before her death and showing off her anguished, at times uncontrolled, vocals to great advantage on a range of material that encompassed the driving 'Move Over', deep soul numbers like 'Cry Baby', and 'Mercedes Benz', an unaccompanied sardonic comment on materialism that she had given to John Lennon as a birthday present. Given the circumstances, it was tempting to read more into titles like 'Get It While You Can' and 'A Woman Left Lonely' than was, probably, intended. Ayler, in contrast, had been lacking in direction – although his 1968 album, *New Grass*, was accurately titled, its bow to rock music was more parody than paean and he had struggled to follow it up. So in some ways Ayler's death, presumed to be suicide, was not surprising.

But when Jimi Hendrix died it was more than a surprise: it was devastating. His radically original songs and phenomenal guitar playing had seemed to embody the spirit of freedom that enriched popular culture in the late 1960s. Indeed such was the vitality of his music that it was almost impossible to imagine such a man ever dying. True, he had a fascination with mortality – references to his own death, and that of others, recur throughout his work – though even in the last weeks of his life he was looking ahead with enthusiasm:

'Then I started thinking. Thinking about the future. Thinking that this era of music – sparked off by the Beatles – had come to an end. Something new has got to come, and Jimi Hendrix will be there. I want a big band ... we are going to give them something that will blow their mind, and while it's blown there will be something there to fill the gap.' (*Melody Maker*, 5 September 1970, p.7)

Hendrix's passing was the second seismic shock suffered by the pop world in 1970 – most fans had only just got over the break-up of The Beatles five months earlier. Rumours about the split had been circulating for some time, fuelled by the side projects that each member of the band was engaged in and the bleak prospect afforded by the *White Album*, where very few tracks seemed to involve them all, at least at the same time, and during the recording of which Ringo Starr did actually leave the group temporarily.

Abbey Road seemed to offer some hope but the signs were clear that The Beatles were not getting on with each other on a business, musical or personal level. A lot of the problems came to a head while *Let It Be* – film and album – were being made in January 1969, though in truth things had been going awry since 1966, when it became abundantly clear that touring had ceased to be fun. A disastrous visit to the Philippines was the prelude to a stressful American tour, plagued by hostility to John Lennon for his remarks on the relative popularity of Jesus Christ and The Beatles, and their appearance at Candlestick Park, San Francisco, on 29 August, proved to be their last. Reviewing The Beatles' press conferences from their first flush of fame in 1963 to that terrible summer of 1966, it is easy to trace their changing demeanour, from cheery, cheeky Liverpudlians to four serious adults beset by their own, and the world's, problems. The Beatles were growing up and they didn't always like what they saw.

The end, when it came on 10 April 1970, was curiously anti-climactic – a media pack from Paul McCartney enclosing his new album and a written Q&A brief confirming that The Beatles were no more. Yet it led to headline news throughout the world and outbursts of angst from their fans which were scarcely extinguished by the release of *Let It Be* exactly four weeks later. It says something for this disjointed album – some tracks unfinished, others finished too much – that despite its flaws it came in at number 86 in the *Rolling Stone* poll for the 500 Greatest Albums of All Time, conducted in 2005. Admittedly it ranked below seven of their other albums but it was ahead of much-praised releases like Pink Floyd's *The Wall*, *Tommy*, Radiohead's *The Bends* and *Hunky Dory* by David Bowie.

Some idea of how the album would have sounded without the overdubs carried out by Phil Spector can be gained by listening to *Let It Be ... Naked*, released under the supervision of McCartney whose objections to the involvement of the American producer had been one of the causes of the split. Yet by that time listeners were very well accustomed to the version issued in 1970, so much so that 'The Long And Winding Road', shorn of its lavish orchestration, seems to lose both its drama and its sweeping romanticism. Similarly, the pared-down 'Across The Universe' is devoid of the cosmic trappings which Spector's layers of sound provided so aptly.

However the project, at least when it started, was intended to be a return to basics – its working title had actually been *Get Back* (though in the end, given the furore that surrounded the split, *Let It Be* proved far more appropriate) and the song of that name is one of the highlights. Ebullient and infectious, its lyrics are laden with in-jokes, and barbs, despite the insouciance of McCartney's vocal delivery. He excels, too, on the title track, offsetting the inherent sentimentality of the words with the profound melodic cadences of gospel.

Lennon's singing on 'Don't Let Me Down' verges at times on the comic, almost as if he were parodying the emotional outpourings of the song's antecedent, 'You Can't Do That'; yet it is tempting, too, to see more contemporary implications in its words. The same is true of 'Two Of Us', supposedly about McCartney's relationship with Linda Eastman but open to other interpretations: could the protagonists be Lennon and McCartney and the song a dreamlike vision of a return to the innocent companionship of earlier years? Certainly there are two collaborations between them – by now something of a rarity – elsewhere on the album, one ancient, one modern. The rocker, 'One After 909', was one of the first numbers they wrote together and exudes exuberance, while 'I've Got A Feeling' is notable for its clever song-within-a-song and soulful performance by the band, enhanced, as on many other tracks, by Billy Preston on electric piano. Of the two Harrison songs, 'I Me Mine' is superior, a savage diatribe against the selfishness surrounding him.

As far as quality goes, that was about it, yet eight excellent tracks out of twelve was a pretty good ratio – far better, in fact, than most contemporary bands could boast. There was no escaping the elegiac aspects of the album even if they were twisted up with the bitterness that had dominated the sessions, stretching back to the previous January, at which it was made. As if further proof of the rancour were needed, it came with the *Let It Be* film which was released later in the month. Here the breakdown in relations between McCartney and Harrison and between McCartney and Lennon was exposed for all to see; Starr tended to bear it all with stoicism. The convivial rooftop concert that closed the film came as a complete and welcome relief – there was something both touching and uplifting about Lennon's mock vote of thanks at the end of the set: 'I'd like to say thank you on behalf of the group and ourselves, and I hope we passed the audition'.

One of the main reasons that the break-up of The Beatles seemed so catastrophic was that no other band had come into the pop music mainstream to replace them when they progressed to more complex and ambitious territory. One look at the UK number ones in late 1969/early 1970 proves the point conclusively – the artists concerned being, from 1 November – 21 March inclusive, The Archies, Rolf Harris, Edison Lighthouse and Lee Marvin. True, Simon and Garfunkel were at the top of the chart in the week The Beatles split, but they, too, were soon to go their separate ways. In the months following the break-up, the acts reaching number one included Dana, Christie and the England World Cup Squad.

Furthermore, although contemporaries like Bob Dylan, The Rolling Stones and The Who were still around, 1970 was a fallow year for them all. The latter two bands released only live albums and Dylan's *Self Portrait* and *New Morning* were among the worst records of his career. So the spotlight fell again on the (now former) Beatles: how well would they fare as solo artists?

★ ★ ★ ★ ★

In a year of so many endings, most of them unhappy, it was widely hoped that 1970 would also see the conclusion of the Vietnam War, which had been raging for over ten years. Instead, what came to an end was any immediate prospect of peace. The war had already destroyed the Presidency of Lyndon Johnson who, almost without realising, had allowed it to engulf his domestic programme and divert him from the creation of the 'Great Society', his Utopian vision for a better America.

Johnson decided not to stand for re-election in 1968 and it is some measure of the uncertainty that war engendered amongst voters that the Presidential race turned out to be almost as close as that of 1960, when John F Kennedy had won by the narrowest margin of the century thus far, 0.17%. The loser on that occasion, the Republican Richard M Nixon, was the victor in 1968, even though he obtained fewer votes than he had eight years previously. In fact, had Spiro Agnew, who delivered five Southern States, not been his running-mate, he may not have won at all; as it was, the Democrats retained control of both the Congress and Senate. Nixon's comeback was a remarkable story and speaks volumes for his tenacity that he made it to the White House after his career had seemed all but over when he followed up his defeat by Kennedy with a failed attempt to become Governor of California in 1962. Unfortunately the qualities that sustained him through his years in the political wilderness brought about his eventual downfall. More immediately, they led to his mishandling of the war.

Nixon was an implacable enemy of Communism. He had entered Congress in 1947 by denouncing his opponent, Jerry Voorhis, as a Communist sympathiser and soon after became a prominent member of the House Committee on Un-American Activities, pursuing, almost singlehandedly, the case against the former State Department employee Alger Hiss, (perhaps there was something about surnames with 'his' in them that he didn't like). The Hiss affair became a *cause célèbre* and when he was convicted for perjury it made Nixon into a nationally-known figure. It was no surprise when, running for Senate in 1950, he beat the former Broadway star Helen Gahagan Douglas by highlighting her apparent Communist tendencies – he was no doubt aided, too, by China's intervention in the Korean War just before the election. Two years later, he rebuffed accusations of financial irregularities as a Communist smear campaign, stating in front of a TV audience of 58 million, at that time the largest in history, that the only gift he had received was a little spotted dog which his daughter had named 'Checkers'. In his second term as Eisenhower's Vice-President he was able to build up his expertise in foreign policy, taking every opportunity to advance the cause of right-wing, anti-Communist regimes.

As President, and hence commander-in-chief of the US forces in Vietnam, he therefore had no ideological problem with fighting the Communist North Vietnamese. Yet during the election, Nixon had promised to achieve 'peace with honour', implying that the war could not be won, at least by the United States. Now, he was in dread of losing it and to authorise the immediate wholesale withdrawal of American forces would look very much like defeat.

So Nixon hit upon the strategy of 'Vietnamisation' – the transfer of responsibility for the war to the South Vietnamese. This entailed bringing ground troops home, a popular measure with a public starting to become sceptical that progress was being made. At the same time he would continue the bombing and, moreover, extend it – secretly – into neighbouring Cambodia which, though neutral, was being used both as a base and a transport route by North Vietnam and the Viet Cong.

Vietnamisation might have been effective except for the fact that the South Vietnamese were by no means keen to prosecute the war alone, knowing that without the US they would certainly be defeated and surmising, correctly, that while the War continued the US would never back out entirely. It also dealt a blow to the peace negotiations, since any American retreat would lead to almost certain victory for the North Vietnamese: there was therefore no need for them to make any concessions. Nixon's response was to try to bomb them into submission, a tactic that only made them more resolute and caused further disquiet among the American people. At the beginning of 1970 peace with honour, indeed peace of any kind, was looking a remote prospect, but Nixon stuck to his guns, literally and metaphorically. Angered by criticism, especially, from the press, he became by turns paranoid, aggressive and obsessive about the war. In short, he began to sink into the same quagmire that had swallowed Johnson.

In spring, the situation in Cambodia deteriorated rapidly. While its ruler, Prince Sihanouk, was in Paris he had been deposed by General Lon Nol, who abandoned the policy of neutrality to side firmly with the USA and South Vietnam. North Vietnamese troops, pushed inland by the South Vietnamese, were now not far from the capital, Phnom Penh, thus increasing his anxiety. He was also facing a backlash from supporters of Sihanouk who now allied themselves with the, at that stage, small Communist group, the Khmer Rouge. Armed clashes between the factions followed and by late March Cambodia had plunged into anarchy, on the brink of a civil war.

Nixon's response was to invade Cambodia. Although on a national TV broadcast on 30 April he had described it as an 'incursion', there is no doubt that he wanted to take a momentous, decisive step to end the conflict and signal to the North Vietnamese that he still meant business in the region. It is perhaps indicative of his state of mind that he somehow believed such an action was consistent with peace. Thus Stanley Karnow writes,

On April 20, 1970, Nixon announced the withdrawal of another hundred and fifty thousand US troops from Vietnam within a year – adding that "we finally have in sight the peace we are seeking." Two days later, at five o'clock in the morning, he dictated a memorandum to Kissinger declaring that "we need a bold move in Cambodia to show that we stand with Lon Nol" ... He wanted to stage "the big play" – going for "all the marbles," since he expected " a hell of an uproar at home" whatever he did. (*Vietnam: A History*, p. 608)

In the latter respect, at least, his judgement was correct.

★ ★ ★ ★ ★

Throughout the latter part of the 1960s rock music had been the major channel of protest against the war in Vietnam, more consistent in its opposition than even the news media, where the position of the Administration had to be reported and where there were even the occasional pockets of support. But in rock there was only one point of view. Song lyrics denounced the war, both implicitly and explicitly, and musicians were always ready to make their disapproval known whether from the stage or in interview. And of course rock was the main leisure pursuit for millions of young people including those who attended demonstrations, marches and the outdoor festivals that served to reaffirm their antagonism to the war and to those in the US Government who were conducting it.

In 1970, however, there was a widespread disintegration of the essential medium through which most rock and pop music was transmitted: the group. The demise of The Beatles was the major story, but even before that, Band Of Gypsys had split. Less than a month after the Fillmore shows, they made a disastrous appearance at Madison Square Garden where Hendrix insulted a woman in the audience and left the stage after just two numbers, thus ending the brief existence of a band who had promised so much. Before the year was out they had been followed by such diverse outfits as The Mothers Of Invention, Diana Ross and The Supremes, Simon and Garfunkel, Brian Auger and The Trinity, Spirit, The Liverpool Scene and The Velvet Underground. As noted above, there were no studio albums from The Rolling Stones or The Who (although both bands came back with a bang in 1971).

At the same time questions were being asked about the nature of the music itself. In August, for the first time ever, a rock band – The Soft Machine – played at the prestigious Henry Wood Promenade Concerts (more popularly, 'The BBC Proms'), an annual festival of classical music held in London's Royal Albert Hall . Was this a good thing? Was it overdue recognition of rock or a dilution of its identity? And what about use of jazz in rock, and rock in jazz? Could rock withstand all of the many fusions it was being subjected to? Was it being overrun by technocrats?

Of all the groups that broke up, the most mourned, after The Beatles, was Simon and Garfunkel. *Bridge Over Troubled Water*, released on 26 January, became one of the most successful albums of all time, selling some 25 million copies. In the UK, it spent a total of 303 weeks on the chart including an incredible 40 weeks at number one, 23 of them in 1970. One of the attractions of the record is its array of sounds and styles and these are put to imaginative use by the production team of Simon, Garfunkel and Roy Halee. The impact of the title track, for example, lies in the gradual build-up from a quiet, gospel-flavoured opening to a searing climax with synthesiser and strings lending intensity to Garfunkel's impassioned vocals. Similarly, the arrangement in 'The Boxer' keeps close to the meaning of the song. Simon's acoustic guitar symbolises the obscurity from which the protagonist comes, and to which he returns; in between, there is a dramatic interlude where his miserable experiences in New York are given additional drama by harsh, synthesised percussive sounds.

Simon's song-writing too, is varied in its scope, from the world-weariness of 'Keep The Customer Satisfied' to the bittersweet 'Cecilia'; from the crude double-entendres of 'Baby Driver' to the whimsical homespun philosophy of his lyrics to 'El Cóndor Pasa'. Simon also wanted to include the politically-charged 'Cuba Sí, Nixon No', but this was vetoed by Garfunkel, an indication that they were no longer seeing eye-to-eye. In truth they were going through the process of break-up even as *Bridge Over Troubled Water* was being made and the theme of valediction runs right through the record. 'The Only Living Boy In New York' bemoans the absence of Garfunkel (referred to in the song as 'Tom', an allusion to their earlier existence as Tom and Jerry) while 'Why Don't You Write Me' suggests the same interpretation. Garfunkel had once been an architecture student, making 'So Long, Frank Lloyd Wright' a clear prophesy of the split – at the end of the song Halee is heard calling, 'So long already, Artie'. In this context, the inclusion of the live 'Bye Bye Love' was significant and laden with irony– the song had been the debut recording for their role models, The Everly Brothers, back in 1957. The last track is the brief, gentle 'Song For The Asking', an understated and poignant finale to the career of the most famous duo in pop music.

The demise of the Los Angeles band Spirit could hardly have presented a greater contrast – their final album, *Twelve Dreams Of Dr Sardonicus*, was their *worst* seller – at least at the time. Yet it was their most adventurous, incorporating some novel musical ideas and a wide range of subject-matter. It was almost as if they were presenting contemporary life as they saw it, but through a psychedelic prism. Thanks to Neil Young's producer, David Briggs, it was, however, shorn of any excess or self-indulgence. The most innovative songs were written by guitarist Randy California (whose father-in-law, Ed Cassidy, was the band's drummer): they include the remarkable 'Prelude: Nothin' To Hide' which delivers its ecological message through bizarre conceits such as 'nothin' to hide – we've got the same bride' and 'Nature's Way', possibly the only composition in rock music intended to make you feel good about death. 'Mr Skin', by singer Jay Ferguson, is on the equally unlikely theme of pornography and like California's 'Morning Will Come' juxtaposes a horn section with psychedelic guitar. Sadly, it was all too late – Ferguson and bassist Mark Andes were already plotting to form a new band and Spirit played their last show with the original personnel at the Fillmore East on New Year's Eve, 1970.

★ ★ ★ ★ ★

At their peak, The Beatles' music was broad enough in scope to encompass the extremes personified by Simon and Garfunkel and Spirit. Following their split in April 1970 there was speculation as to whether the band had been more, or less, than the sum of its parts. Lennon's prowess away from the group was to some degree already known from his three singles with The Plastic Ono Band: the anthem 'Give Peace A Chance'; 'Cold Turkey', with its hypnotic riff and harrowing lyrics; and 'Instant Karma', produced by Phil Spector and released in February 1970, which contained elements of both.

Yet nothing could have prepared listeners for *John Lennon/Plastic Ono Band*, recorded at Abbey Road in autumn 1970 and issued on 11 December. True, 'Instant Karma' had pioneered a harsh, stripped-down sound with minimal instrumentation and maximum reverb, and this also characterised the album, with Spector involved once again. The real shock, however, came with the lyrics, the direct consequence of a course of Dr Arthur Yanov's primal therapy which Lennon and Yoko Ono had attended in April. Here they learned how to release themselves from emotional repression by giving cathartic vent to their feelings of anger and resentment. Other pop composers had used a similar approach by creating imaginary characters like Pete Townshend's Tommy, but never had such a major figure expressed their innermost emotions in such a direct and candid fashion. In 1958 Lennon's mother Julia had been killed in a road accident near the home of her sister Mimi who, following concerns about Julia's chaotic lifestyle, had become his guardian. He had written her a love song, 'Julia', for the *White Album*; now all of the pain and fury comes flooding out in 'Mother' and 'My Mummy's Dead'. He deals severely with the myths surrounding the 1960s in 'I Found Out' and in 'God' excoriates religion and the deification of pop stars, including The Beatles: having survived the catharsis, reaffirms his faith in his own identity. 'Working Class Hero' carries the same message but it is delivered in a contrasting way: this time Lennon sounds weary and cynical and the subdued acoustic guitar accompaniment throws the stark, edgy sound of the rest of the record into sharp relief.

The companion album to *John Lennon/Plastic Ono Band* was *Yoko Ono/Plastic Ono Band*, released on the same day. With the exception of 'AOS', which was made with saxophonist Ornette Coleman's group during rehearsals for a show at the Albert Hall in February 1968, it was recorded in October 1970, probably at one of the sessions that produced the Lennon album. Although there is extensive use of sound effects, notably on the more abstract pieces like 'Paper Shoes' and 'Greenfield Morning I Pushed An Empty Baby Carriage All Over The City', the emphasis is on free improvisation, often with spine-tingling results. 'Why' is a shattering opener featuring smears of slide guitar from Lennon and thunderous bass from Klaus Voorman ; Ono applies a series of bloodcurdling warbles, squeals and shrieks to the title word before soaring into the stratosphere. On 'Why Not', the tempo slows and Ono takes the listener through another vocal *tour de force*, from a whisper to a scream: her attention to the detail of each utterance is almost pointillistic. 'Touch Me' is a slab of freeform rock with Lennon's scratching, scraping guitar preceding an interlude in which Ono bellows as if in great pain, showing that she, too, had been inspired by Yanov.

Taken together, these two albums amount to a milestone in both the development of these artists and in rock music in general, showing how far it had come in the seven short years since The Beatles made their first album, *Please Please Me*. They also provide proof, if any were needed, that Ringo Starr was one of the greatest of all rock drummers. Yet Starr's own album was at completely the opposite end of the spectrum. Entitled *A Sentimental Journey*, it was exactly that: a nostalgic tour through the Tin Pan Alley standards that had been his mother's favourite songs. By no means a gifted singer, Starr nevertheless coasts good-naturedly through the twelve tracks, much assisted by arrangers of the calibre of Quincy Jones, Chico O'Farrill and Elmer Bernstein and the accompaniment of the George Martin Orchestra.

A Sentimental Journey was released on 27 March 1970 and thus was the only Beatle solo album to have come out before the split. As we have seen, *McCartney* was only made available to the press on the day of the announcement and to the general public a week later. Much criticised at the time, the album also was widely misunderstood. Its home-made, rustic feel was a deliberate move away from the orchestrated polish of *Abbey Road* and a return to the sort of simplicity that the *Get Back/Let It Be* project had attempted, none too successfully, to achieve. The album sleeve is laden with images of McCartney and his family, reinforcing the impression that what this record was about was a retreat from all the trauma associated with The Beatles into the safety and security of home: the preponderance of instrumentals and half-finished tracks make it sound like some sort of spare-time activity carried out in the garden shed. However by paring back all adornment and playing all the instruments himself, McCartney allows us to hear his melodies in their purest form: 'Every Night', 'Junk' and 'Maybe I'm Amazed' rank with his very best compositions. The bluesy 'Oo You' and 'That Would Be Something' are also satisfying; 'Teddy Boy', though too short, is well-conceived; and the instrumental version of 'Junk', 'Singalong Junk', is sufficiently elegiac to suggest he did have some regrets at the disintegration of The Beatles. Perhaps the album's biggest fault is McCartney's persistent effort, through numerous breaks and solos, to demonstrate his ability as a drummer: sad to report, that turned out to be somewhat limited.

In many respects the records by Lennon, McCartney and Starr were predictable – each oriented towards tendencies they had been exhibiting with The Beatles. But George Harrison's triple-album set *All Things Must Pass,* issued at the end of November 1970 was a revelation. At the opposite extreme from McCartney's solitary endeavour, he made use of some of the biggest names in pop music history: Bob Dylan, Phil Spector and Eric Clapton all contributed in crucial ways. Yet Harrison was fully in charge of proceedings, to the extent that, as Spector has related in Martin Scorsese's film tribute, *Living In The Material World*, 'He wouldn't let anything go until it was right'. What really distinguished the album, however, was the quality of his compositions.

One reasonable explanation for Harrison's song-writing ability was that it was developed and refined through constant contact with Lennon and McCartney, either through osmosis or through observation of their methods. Evidence for this view is found in the fact that, culminating with *All Things Must Pass*, Harrison's songs improved incrementally up until

1970. From then on, that is, following the demise of The Beatles, they were never as good again. If this is correct, it would be extraordinary enough – if proximity to genius was all it took, why didn't Ringo Starr, or Brian Epstein, or roadie Mal Evans become great songwriters?

But supposing the opposite is true – that, even if he had never met Lennon and McCartney, Harrison would still have written songs of the quality of 'Taxman', 'Blue Jay Way', 'While My Guitar Gently Weeps', 'Something', 'Here Comes The Sun' and those recorded and released in 1970. That would be even scarier, and little short of miraculous – the odds against one band of four musicians containing three such superlative pop music composers are astronomical.

Whatever the case, *All Things Must Pass*, made after the split was announced, was an outpouring of all the talent that had been largely under wraps in The Beatles. Though brimming with positive energy, it also explores darker emotions with great sensitivity, and the strength of the material is much enhanced by quality of both the playing and the production. The set gets off to a downbeat start with 'I'd Have You Anytime', co-written with Dylan, but then follows a sequence of four tracks which would stand comparison with any Beatles release: the exultant 'My Sweet Lord' with its irresistible rolling momentum; the heavy yet melodic 'Wah-Wah'; 'Isn't It A Pity' – a stately, solemn, seven-minute epic; and the full-on elation of 'What Is Life'. Highlights then pop up with regularity: the surging 'Let It Down', the rich imagery and unorthodox melody of 'Beware Of Darkness' and, best of all, the title track which, like 'Isn't A Pity', was much rejected as a candidate for inclusion on Beatles albums, though now seemed like an epitaph on their career. Criticism that the third LP, essentially a jam session, is superfluous can be deflected by the knowledge that Harrison at this time was so prolific that a good deal of original material did not make it on to the finished product – better to regard it as more letting off steam after the tensions involved in the death throes of The Beatles.

Unfortunately the four ex-Beatles were never again able to reach the heights of their first solo albums, though McCartney came very close. Starr proved to be no front-man; Lennon, and, to some degree, Harrison, continued to make incisive statements about the world around them but by then they had been caught up, and emulated, by a new generation capable of producing a more potent mix of pop and politics.

CHAPTER 2:

Ball Of Confusion

What was to be a year of violence, insurrection and conflict began with the ending of a war. After two-and-a-half years of fighting and one million dead, the Republic of Biafra surrendered to the Nigerian army and, as a consequence, ceased to exist. Like many other African countries, Nigeria had been formed by the efforts of the colonisers – in this case, Britain – to weld heterogeneous geographical, ethnic and religious groupings into one political entity. This resulted in discord which, though suppressed during the colonial period, came to a head in the run-up to independence in 1960 and, especially, in its immediate aftermath. A military coup in 1966 seemed to quell the tensions between the three major regions but subsequent moves towards greater unification served to inflame them. After a period of coup and counter-coup, Lieutenant Colonel Emeka Ojukwu declared that the Eastern Region was seceding from the rest of Nigeria to form Biafra. However the new nation lacked the resources to repel the federal onslaught that followed. Thousands fled to refugee camps and once there faced disease and starvation; huge amounts of aid were pumped into Biafra to alleviate the crisis, though they only delayed the inevitable capitulation which came on 13 January 1970.

Despite the Nigerian government's strenuous attempts at reconciliation, the war left a horrendous legacy – even today the word 'Biafra' conjures up images of mass suffering and severely malnourished children. As ever in Africa, there were also questions about the backing given to the various powers by Western countries. There were rumours, for example, that France had supported the Biafran cause, partly because it tended to favour any secession from a former British federation but also due to its interest in the oil deposits to be found in the eastern regions. Britain certainly gave help to the federal forces, prompting John Lennon to return his MBE in protest on 25 November 1969.

Elsewhere in Africa, four days after the surrender of Biafra, Colonel Muammar Gaddafi took direct control of Libya. The country had been run by a civilian administration since the bloodless coup that had deposed King Idris I four months earlier, led by Gaddafi and his Free Unionist Officers. Yet there were tensions between ministers and the Revolutionary Command Council, and so Gaddafi – as, perhaps, he had intended all along – established an autocracy based on Arab unity, the rejection of the Western powers and the elevation of his own image to a cult of personality. As the years wore on, it was the latter that seemed the most important to him, although at the time his pan-Arab philosophy was echoed across North Africa and the Middle East, particularly in Syria where it was one of the tenets of the ruling Arab socialist Ba'ath Party. Indeed so firm were the Syrian government's principles that they intervened in the Jordanian civil war which began in September 1970.

Supporting the Palestine Liberation Organisation in its struggle against King Hussein was, however, too extreme a step for some Syrians and General Hafez Al-Assad led a successful coup, the 1970 Corrective Revolution, against the ruling faction. Political change was accompanied by religious change: Assad was an Arawite and represented all Syrian religious minorities in their struggle against the majority Sunni community. In time Assad was to create what amounted to a secular police state and employ increasingly violent methods to suppress opposition from the Sunnis and in particular the terrorist organisation, the Muslim Brotherhood, longstanding opponents of Assad and the Ba'ath Party. His son, Bashar Al-Assad, is, at the time of writing, the President of Syria and embroiled in a bloody civil war against the Free Syrian Army, a hotbed of Sunni Muslim extremism.

The spirit of rebellion that pervaded 1970 was not confined to the Arab world. As we saw in Chapter 1 a coup in Cambodia removed Prince

Sihanouk in March, thus setting off a sequence of events that led to the proclamation of a republic six months later. The consequences of an attempted coup in Japan, however, were rather more fleeting. The writer Yukio Mishima, of samurai ancestry and a committed devotee of traditional Japanese culture, was so incensed by what he saw as the lack of responsibility and order in contemporary Japan that, on 25 November, he led an attack on the Eastern Army Ground Defence Force at Ichigaya, capturing the commandant. Mishima wanted soldiers at the base to join him in restoring the authority of the Emperor; having failed, he committed hara-kiri, a hero's death and probably the motivation behind the whole enterprise in the first place.

In South America the relative stability of 1969 was beginning to dissolve. This was not unexpected since there had been political turbulence across the continent ever since the Second World War. Power lurched from democratically-elected governments to military dictatorships and back again, nowhere more dramatically than in Argentina. The post-War Peronist regime with its flamboyant brand of socialism was ousted by a coup led by General Pedro Eugenio Aramburu; his successor, Arturo Frondizi, was more liberal, provoking another military takeover in the Argentine Revolution of 1966. The new government, under Juan Carlos Onganía, immediately prohibited political parties and neutralised union and student organisations. Onganía was especially severe on young people and ordered police to invade the University of Buenos Aires on what became known as La Noche de los Bastones Largos (The Night of the Long Batons).

Such actions created outrage, especially among the exponents of *nueva canción*, the folk-based South American equivalent to the protest song movement in the USA. But governmental repression meant that, unlike their Northern counterparts, they often had to conceal their message within the imagery and subject-matter of traditional material. 'El Cóndor Vuelve' ('The Condor Returns') and 'Cancíon Con Todos' ('Song With Everyone') – each co-written by the Argentine poet Armando Tejada Gómez and sung by his wife, Mercedes Sosa – typify the genre at this time.

The latter was subsequently translated into 30 languages and was adopted as the anthem of Latin America. In May 1970 the backlash against the regime came to a head when the left-wing guerrilla group Montoneros kidnapped and executed General Aramburu. Onganía was felt to be ineffective in dealing with this, and earlier, acts of terrorism and was replaced the following month by Roberto Levingston.

Meanwhile, still more momentous events were looming in Chile. Here, the Christian Democrat Eduardo Frei had been elected President six years earlier in a surge of reforming zeal and with a large majority over the Communist-Socialist coalition led by Salvador Allende. Frei had been backed by the CIA, who dreaded the prospect of an Allende government, though once in power he introduced a programme which followed an orthodox left-wing agenda, including improvements in health and education as well as far-reaching urban and agrarian reforms. At the same time Frei wanted to encourage inward investment, especially from the USA, and some critics, including Allende, felt his relationship with big business was too close for the good of the Chilean workforce.

All of these developments set the country up for further change. Frei's measures, notably his support for local community groups, had the effect of politicising the poorest members of Chilean society, but the promised benefits were slow to arrive, creating both a sense of dissatisfaction and the belief that only a more left-wing government could finish the job he had begun. Accordingly, Allende formed a coalition, Popular Unity, comprising all of the parties of the left and far left, to fight the Presidential Election of September 1970. His opponents were the Christian Democrat candidate, Radomiro Tomic, and former President Jorge Alessandri, leader of the National Party. Though Allende commanded a good deal of support, it was mainly from the working classes; the rest of the electorate was split between those who were content with the Christian Democrats and those, mainly from the upper echelons of Chilean society, who felt they had gone too far. Alessandri represented the latter group and received 35.29% of the vote; Allende got a mere 1% more but it was sufficient to make him the front runner. Having signed the Statute of Constitutional Guarantees (effectively a promise that he would not wreck the Constitution), he was confirmed as President by the Chilean Congress. Allende thus became the first-ever Marxist Head of State to be democratically elected.

★ ★ ★ ★ ★

It was alleged that the KGB had helped fund Allende's campaign and, given that the CIA were doing all they could to destroy him, it would be surprising if they didn't. At the same time he received crucial support from key figures in the *nueva canción* movement, which had taken root in Chile some years earlier through the efforts of, in particular, Violeta Parra and her family. Parra, who committed suicide in 1967, personified the *nueva canción* blend of folk music and polemic. 'Porquè Los Pobres No Tienen'('Because The Poor Don't Have'), for example, excoriates the Catholic Church for its indifference to poverty while 'La Carta' ('The Letter') tells of a sister's grief on hearing her brother has been jailed for taking part in a strike. Parra helped revive the concept of the *peña*, a meeting place for artists and musicians and it was at one such venue in Santiago, owned by her son Ángel, that Victor Jara established himself as a leading light in *nueva canción*.

Like many South American singers, Jara was appalled by the death of the revolutionary Che Guevara in October 1967 and had anticipated it some months earlier with 'El Aparecido' ('The Ghost'); in the requiem 'Zamba Del Che' he uses the eponymous Argentine folk dance form to give drama and resonance to his emotions. Compositions such as 'Plegaria A Un Labrador' ('Prayer To A Worker') placed him squarely in the Popular Unity camp and when the 1970 election came round, he became volunteer for the Party and gave several free concerts. He also added his own words to Allende's rousing campaign song, 'Venceremos' ('We Shall Prevail'), written by another *nueva canción* artist, Sergio Ortega, with original lyrics by Claudio Iturra. Arranged as a military march, its simple structure, inspirational message and rousing chorus made it irresistible:

Peasants, soldiers, miners,

And the women of our country, as well,

Students, workers, white-collar and blue,

We shall do our duty.

We'll sow the land with glory.

Socialism will be our future.

All together, we shall make history

We shall prevail, we shall prevail

A thousand chains we'll have to break,

We shall prevail, we shall prevail

We know how to deal with misery.

Allende's presidency – and demise – was the subject of more songs by *nueva canción* composers such as Ángel Parra, Patricio Manns, Horacio Salinas, Luis Advis and the Cuban, Pablo Milanés. Sergio Ortega, this time with the group Quilapayùn, contributed another flag-waver, 'El Pueblo Unido Jamás Será Vendico'('A People United Will Never Be Defeated'), which eventually became an anthem of resistance against the Pinochet regime which seized power in September 1973 through a military coup supported by the CIA.

The CIA had been plotting to destabilise Allende from the very beginning. Even before he took the oath of office a plot was hatched to eliminate the Chief of the General Staff, René Schneider who, in a tradition unique to Chile, intended to resist any interference by the military in the electoral process. As Christopher Hitchens explains in *The Trial Of Henry Kissinger* (p. 85), such was the paranoia created by Allende's election that the plan was known about, and authorised, at the very top of the US government:

> The plan was to have him kidnapped by extremist officers, in such a
> way as to make it appear that leftist and pro-Allende elements were
> behind the plot. The resulting confusion, it was hoped, would panic
> the Chilean Congress into denying Allende the presidency. A sum of

$50,000 was offered ... for any officer, or officers, enterprising enough to take on this task.

Initially, CIA Director Richard Helms and his director of covert operations, Thomas Karamessines, were unable to identify anyone; they were, however, told by US Secretary of State Kissinger to 'press on in case'. In fact it was Kissinger himself who found the solution:

> On 15 October 1970, Kissinger was told of an extremist right-wing officer named General Roberto Viaux, who had ties to [neo-fascist group] Patria y Libertad and who was willing to accept the secret US commission to remove General Schneider ... Kissinger's Track Two group authorized the supply of machine guns as well as tear gas grenades to Viaux's associates. (*ibid.*,p. 86)

A week later, Schneider was killed by Viaux's gang, an act greeted with anger and disbelief: it was the first political assassination in Chile for 133 years. Any responsibility for his murder has been strenuously denied by the US administration, but Hitchens provides irrefutable proof of Kissinger's complicity; he also shows that President Nixon was aware of what was going on, even if he was not personally involved.

But it was by no means the only attempt to strangle Allende's presidency before it started: there were further attacks on individuals, on monuments and public buildings; a syndicate of conspirators made enormous withdrawals from the country's banks; and the written and broadcast media promulgated negative propaganda – all with the purpose of creating chaos and a sense of panic among the Chilean people. Allende, however, held his nerve and by the end of 1970 began his programme by nationalising the banks. He also successfully managed the tensions within the Left. In government he kept order by allocating equal status to each member of the coalition, while he dealt decisively with the internecine conflicts that still smouldered beneath. On 2 December, for example, the Communist Youth organisation clashed in Concepción with the

Movement of the Revolutionary Left (MIR), killing one of its members, Oscar Ríos. Allende intervened and from this unpromising situation brought the factions together to establish a mutually-agreed list of candidates for the forthcoming student elections.

The strength of Allende's beliefs was tested in a series of interviews with the French journalist Régis Debray, published as *Conversations With Allende*. Here a picture emerges of a sincere and principled individual, well versed in the history, not only of his own country, but of Latin America and the world beyond. He lacks almost entirely the empty rhetoric characteristic of politicians in such high office and is secure in his ideology, explaining its origin, and logic, in painstaking detail. What also comes across, however, is Allende's insecurity and his concern that, at any moment, the forces of the Right might exact their revenge on him. It took just under three years for that fear to be realised.

★ ★ ★ ★ ★

While the CIA were heavily involved in destabilising left-wing governments in South America, their sister organisation, the FBI, also had their hands full in 1970 dealing with what they saw as subversive elements in the USA itself. Alongside the usual suspects, chiefly Communist/socialist individuals and groups, these increasingly comprised civil rights leaders, activists and sympathisers. In theory, the Civil Rights Act of 1964 had done much to improve the lot of African-Americans in terms of education, housing and employment by outlawing racial discrimination and creating equality of opportunity. But the theory did not translate very quickly into reality and in some parts of the country the legislation was ignored altogether.

The assassination of Malcolm X in 1965 and Martin Luther King in 1968 had, as well as removing two titans of the movement, ended the polarisation of approach – segregation versus integration, violence versus non-violence, positive action versus passive resistance – that had characterised the struggle for civil rights during the mid-1960s. Yet even before King's death, there were moves towards a strategy which would bring all shades of opinion under a single unifying banner. As early as 1964 Stokely Carmichael was using the term 'Black Power' and in 1967 wrote, with Charles V Hamilton, a book of the same name; as well as its confrontational connotations, it included the concept of empowering *all* African-Americans to help themselves rather than rely on favours dispensed by whites.

Carmichael respected and understood the non-violent, passive doctrines of Martin Luther King but encouraged more proactive tactics. He attracted a good deal of kudos through his speeches which were logical in their argument and relaxed and witty in their delivery; his message, following so much turmoil and factionalism, was also irresistible – African-Americans should no longer be ashamed of being black, forget any geographical, economic or social distinctions between them, and unite to resist white oppression and carve out their own destiny. This, in essence, was Black Power. One of Carmichael's most potent strategies was to represent the atrocities perpetrated by whites as a premeditated policy. In a speech in San Francisco, for example, he declared that, 'The birth of this nation was conceived in the genocide of the Red Man.' He bracketed together as a conspiracy all of the assassinations of civil rights leaders – Medgar Evers, King, Robert Kennedy, Mark Clark and Fred Hampton – stating, 'When White America killed Dr King that night, she declared war on us.'

Clark and Hampton were killed by police officers during a raid on the latter's Chicago home on 4 December 1969. Both were prominent members of the Black Panther Party, founded in 1966 by Huey Newton and Bobby Seale. The initial purpose of the Party was to encourage self-defence against police brutality in Oakland, California, but it swiftly developed an ideology which incorporated Marxism and black nationalism. Carmichael was known as the 'Honorary Prime Minister' of the Black Panthers and it is easy to see why. They encouraged the sort of self-help he had been advocating through the provision of free medical care and legal services and free breakfasts for children, a measure that did as much as anything to attract the support of working-class families. And, as Michael Haralambos reported four years later,

> In the rural South, black co-operatives such as the Mississippi Poor People's Corporation and the Southwest Alabama Farmers Cooperative are springing up. In the North, Detroit's first black-operated bank, the First Independence National Bank, pledged to serve the black community, began in 1970. (*Right On: From Blues To Soul In Black America*, p. 143)

The Party also brought together the Northern and Southern elements of the civil rights movement, the advocates of violence and non-violence, and rejected the political system, and politicians, of the United States. Speaking of the 1968 Presidential Election, the Panthers' Minister of Information, Eldridge Cleaver, said,

> A line just has to be drawn ... a point where caution and cowardice begin. All three of these pigs that we have a choice of – Oink Nixon, Oink Humphrey, Oink Wallace – are not for us.

Similarly, in 1969, the Party's Chairman, Bobby Seale, declared its programme to be

> ... A very international-type programme for any human being who wants to survive. Socialism is the order of the day, not Nixon's black capitalism – that's out.

By this stage, however, Carmichael was in effect an exile. His marriage in 1968 to the South African singer Miriam Makeba had resulted in a backlash against her: recording contracts and tours were cancelled and a year later the couple emigrated to Guinea, where Carmichael died in 1998. However, his legacy has continued to resonate: as recently as 2010, the rapper Talib Kweli was questioned by the FBI for listening to his speeches.

★ ★ ★ ★ ★

Alongside the emergence of Carmichael and the Black Panthers came an increasingly militant attitude among African-American musicians. Traditionally they had tended to veil their response to hardship in allegory and allusion and confine any revolution to musical iconoclasm and the creation of new styles. True, jazz artists such as Charles Mingus and Oscar Brown Jr and blues singers like JB Lenoir had made more overt protests, but they were not sufficiently well-known to have much impact. It was only when, in 1964, figures of the status of Curtis Mayfield and Sam Cooke recorded their compositions 'Keep On Pushing' and 'A Change Is Gonna Come' that the spirit of the civil rights movement was reflected in the mainstream of African-American music.

Towards the end of the 1960s, songwriters increasingly began to pick up on the principles of Stokely Carmichael and the Black Panther Party. The DJ Nickie Lee, for example, released the gospel-flavoured 'And Black Is Beautiful' in 1968 while the following year saw The Staple Singers' 'When Will I Be Paid', an inventory of the monetary, moral and cultural debt owed to African-Americans; James Brown's 'I Don't Want Nobody To Give Me Nothing (Open Up The Door I'll Get It Myself)'; and the more orthodox call for solidarity, 'Message From A Black Man', recorded by Detroit groups The Temptations and The Spinners.

In 1970 African-American political pop and soul hit a new peak of intensity. To begin with, there were interesting meditations on the simple issue dividing the nation – skin colour. Swamp Dogg (Jerry Williams Jr) turned the whole idea on its head with 'I Was Born Blue' ('Why wasn't I born with orange skin and green hair, like the rest of the people in the world?'); Parliament's 'Oh Lord, Why Lord' mourns the equation of black with sin, but given the spoken interlude and over-the-top production incorporating Pachelbel's 'Canon In D', there is an element of parody not untypical of Parliament's leader, George Clinton. There was also the heartfelt ballad 'Cryin' In The Streets' by George Perkins and The Silver

Stars, a belated tribute to Martin Luther King, and Al Green's 'Gotta Find A New World', a plea for world peace released in the UK on 6 February 1970 as the B-side of the funky 'You Say it'.

Proof that social and political comment was really embedded within black pop music was provided by a series of releases on Motown. Up to that point the premier African-American label had tended to shy away from controversy: indeed it was owner Berry Gordy's deliberate policy to do so. Martha and The Vandellas' 1964 smash 'Dancing In The Street', with its apparent call to action, was therefore something of an aberration. By 1970, however, the voice and views of Motown's leading artists could no longer be kept silent. Edwin Starr, for instance, known mainly for the dancefloor fillers 'Stop Her On Sight (SOS)', 'Headline News' and '25 Miles', came up with the thunderous 'War' with its piledriving punchline 'What is the good of war – absolutely nothing'.

Even more remarkably, The Supremes, who ever since their emergence six years earlier had epitomised elegance, good taste and political vacuity, released the anti-war 'Stoned Love' which hit the US chart on 21 November 1970, and reached number seven; with Jean Terrell on lead vocal, it was to become the group's biggest hit after Diana Ross left the group. 'Stoned Love' was written by Kenny Thomas as 'Stone Love' (the final 'd' was added in error) and was another appeal for harmony across nations and an end to the Vietnam War. Frank Wilson's production pulls out all the stops in a manner reminiscent of the halcyon days of Holland, Dozier and Holland and the walloping accompaniment of session musicians The Funk Brothers completes the effect.

If The Supremes' entry into the political arena came as something of a shock, The Temptations, as we have seen, were already there. 1968's 'Cloud Nine' had been inspired by psychedelia, 'Message From A Black Man' by civil rights; now the two strands were combined in the album *Psychedelic Shack*, released in March 1970. The record is as much a creation of Norman Whitfield, who produced and co-wrote, with Barrett Strong, all of the material as it is of The Temptations. Gone is the conventional Motown sound and in its place is a maelstrom of wailing rock guitar, multitracking and electronic effects. The title track is a paean to LSD while the haunting 'Take A Stroll Through Your Mind' celebrates the self-discovery that comes from smoking marijuana. Motown considered 'War' too inflammatory for The Temptations to release as a single – Edwin Starr's career was clearly less of a priority! – but it is included here in a much inferior version, the impact of which is diluted by its excessive length. Much better is the driving 'Friendship Train', in which the familiar demand for peace in a world on the eve of destruction is underlined by a clever and varied arrangement incorporating exultant horns and locomotive noises.

The Temptations remained on message throughout 1970, following up *Psychedelic Shack* with two outstanding singles. 'Ball Of Confusion (That's What The World Is Today)' is an evocative and forceful piece with another imaginative production by Whitfield while the anthem-like 'Ungena Za Ulimwengu (Unite The World)' still has the power to stir the emotions 40 years later. Yet by the time it was released in autumn 1970, The Temptations' pre-eminence as the leading exponents of political soul was under threat: Curtis Mayfield was back.

In 1969, still with The Impressions, Mayfield had challenged racial stereotyping with the single 'Choice Of Colors', released on the Curtom label which he had co-founded with the group's manager, Eddie Thomas. In time, Curtom would become successful but there were no further hits for a year. Then, on 13 June 1970, 'Check Out Your Mind', the title track of Mayfield's final album with The Impressions, entered the US singles chart. Reflective, enigmatic, socially aware, it bore only a passing resemblance to The Temptations' 'Take A Stroll Through Your Mind' while its uncompromising lyrics and full-blooded orchestration gave a foretaste of his debut solo album, *Curtis*, which was released in September.

Curtis has been compared with Stevie Wonder's *Songs In The Key Of Life* in terms of its breadth of vision and variety of musical expression (each has been called 'the black *Sgt Pepper*'). And although both albums are far from perfect they do contain music of unsurpassed excellence. *Curtis* was recorded at the RCA Studios in Chicago and was written and produced by Mayfield, with the sparkling arrangements provided by Riley Hampton and Gary Slabo. The seven-minute opener, '(Don't Worry) If There's A Hell Below We're All Going To Go', paints a terrifying picture of an imminent apocalypse in which no-one will be spared – Mayfield's vision of the parlous state of race relations in inner-city America. It begins with a female voice citing the Book of Revelation over a background conversation and the sparse backing of bass and conga drums. Mayfield then shouts through an echo chamber

> Sisters, niggers, whities, jews, crackers!
> Don't worry, if there's hell below, we're all gonna go,

screams, and the band come surging in, a rich mixture of wah-wah guitar, horns, strings and percussion to underscore Mayfield's relentless tirade:

> Sisters, brothers and the whities
> Blacks and the crackers
> Police and their backers
> They're all political actors
>
> Hurry
> People running from their worries
> While the judge and the juries
> Dictate the law that's partly flaw
> Cat calling, love balling, fussing and cussing
> Top billing now is killing
> For peace no-one is willing
> Kind of make you get that feeling
>
> Everybody smoke
> Use the pill and the dope
> Educated fools
> From uneducated schools
> Pimping people is the rule

DIFFERENT TRACKS

Polluted water in the pool
And Nixon talking about don't worry
He says don't worry

But they don't know
There can be no show
And if there's a hell below
We're all gonna go

Everybody's praying
And everybody's saying
But when it comes time to do
Everybody's laying

Just talking about don't worry
They say don't worry

Sisters, brothers and the whities
Blacks and the crackers
Police and their backers
They're all political actors

Smoke, the pill and the dope
Educated fools
From uneducated schools
Pimping people is the rule
Polluted water in the pool

And everybody saying don't worry
They say don't worry

But they don't know
There can be no show

And if there's a hell below
We're all gonna go

Lord, what we gonna do
Tell me what we gonna do
If everything I say is true?
This ain't no way it ought to be
If only all the mass could see

But they keep talkin' 'bout don't worry
They say don't worry

This was revolutionary music in both senses: lyrics that exposed the rotting state of society and an unprecedented mix of sonic textures and effects.

And many of the tracks that followed were not far behind. 'The Other Side Of Town' describes the alienation and poverty of the ghetto, its bleak narrative cleverly juxtaposed with the lavish orchestration featuring a rippling harp introduction and cello, violin and harpsichord. 'We The People Who Are Darker Than Blue' is another meditation on colour while 'Miss Black America' is an expression of racial pride, a form of sequel to Nina Simone's 'To Be Young, Gifted And Black' from the previous year though with more sentimentality, a tendency in Mayfield's writing that, despite its superb arrangement, besmirches ' The Makings Of You'. 'Wild And Free' is bedevilled by cliché, 'Give It Up' by some unfortunate rhyming. 'Move On Up', however, is an indisputable classic with a motivational message that has endured through the decades, enlivened with a catchy riff and frenetic percussion. But for sheer consistency Mayfield was unable to match the year's output from a singer who, as it began, had been in the music business for over fifteen years.

★ ★ ★ ★ ★

At the beginning of 1970, the civil rights movement entered a new and more horrifying phase in which the stakes were raised, violence intensified and civil rights activists began to feel the full weight of the law pressing upon them. On 16 January, the Black Panther George Jackson, Fleeta Drumgo and John Clutchette, inmates of Soledad Prison, were charged with the murder of a guard, John V Mills – supposedly in retaliation for the killing three days earlier by another guard, Opie L Miller, of their fellow prisoner WL Nolen. By then Jackson had been in prison for nearly ten years, seven of them in solitary confinement, serving one year to life for stealing $70 from a gas station near Los Angeles. Jackson had protested his innocence but pleaded guilty to get a lighter sentence. In the event, he was never to leave prison for the rest of his life.

Nolen had radicalised Jackson while they were both in San Quentin Prison and together they founded the Black Guerrilla Family, dedicated to fighting racism and, ultimately, overthrowing the government. By the time of their transfer to Soledad in January 1969, Jackson was well-known as a fierce and implacable civil rights theoretician and writer and it was widely believed that Mills's murder had been pinned on him for this reason; the plight of the three men, dubbed the Soledad Brothers, thus became a *cause célèbre*. The Soledad Brothers Defense Committee was formed to raise funds and to draw attention to the case, attracting the support of high profile figures such as Jane Fonda, Marlon Brando, Jessica Mitford, Pete Seeger, Allen Ginsberg and the Communist lecturer, Angela Davis, who had been banned the previous year by California Governor Ronald Reagan from teaching in any of the state's universities.

On 7 August 1970, James McClain was being tried in the Marin County Courthouse for stabbing a guard at San Quentin, when George Jackson's seventeen-year-old brother, Jonathan, shouted, 'Everyone freeze', pulled out a gun and gave weapons to McClain and two San Quentin inmates called as witnesses, Ruchell Magee and William Christmas, whereupon the four of them took five hostages including the judge, Harold Haley, and demanded the release of the Soledad Brothers. They then escaped in a van, with the intention of taking over a local radio station to broadcast their demands, but were intercepted by police; Jackson, McClain, Christmas and Haley were all shot dead.

In the furore that followed it transpired that the gun brandished by Jackson had been registered to Angela Davis, who was then pursued and arrested in New York City. During her time in prison Davis went on hunger strike and was acquitted at her trial which took place in 1972. At the time of writing Magee is still in prison. On 8 October 1970 the Marin County Courthouse was bombed by another radical organisation, the Weathermen.

Meanwhile the FBI was becoming ever more assiduous in its efforts to destroy such groups and, in particular, the Black Panther Party. J Edgar Hoover had called the BPP's free breakfast initiative the 'most dangerous threat to the United States' and established the Counter Intelligence Program (COINTELPRO) to neutralise Black Power. One early manifestation of COINTELPRO was the trial of those radical party leaders accused of planning riots at the Democratic Convention of 1968. The FBI subsequently placed Angela Davis on their Most Wanted list, only the third woman to receive this categorisation.

The agency was also extremely active in the case of the New Haven Nine, a group of Black Panthers accused of killing Alex Rackley, a Panther whom they suspected of working for the FBI, in 1969. The trial began in May 1970 and became a focus for thousands of Black Panthers and protestors sympathetic to their cause, many of whom were accommodated in the nearby Yale University. Both the university president and chaplain spoke up in favour of the Panthers and again there was enormous media interest and celebrity involvement. Many of the Panthers had entered guilty pleas though one, Lonnie McLucas, had not and was sentenced to twelve to fifteen years. The founder of the BPP, Bobby Seale, who had been at Party headquarters while Rackley was being killed there, was also put on trial in October but acquitted. Some idea of the importance of the case can be gained from the fact that it took four months to select a jury for Seale's trial.

'And the band played on …' – such was the refrain of The Temptations'

'Ball Of Confusion (That's What The World Is Today)', neatly summing up the determination of African-American musicians to keep their resolve during the cataclysmic events that punctuated the year 1970. It also betrays a certain detachment from those events; certainly many black songwriters preferred indirect comment to overt declamatory fervour, or confined any revolution to the sights and sounds of their music. George Clinton did both.

In 1970, Clinton was maintaining two bands. Parliament had their roots in his late 1950s vocal group, The Parliaments; he now re-launched them with a new name and a new style – psychedelic soul. Parliament, however, were far from being routine practitioners of the genre. Their album *Osmium*, released in July, not only includes the aforementioned 'Oh Lord, Why Lord', with its ambiguous sentiments, but also the merciless parody of The Temptations, 'I Call My Baby Pussycat', in which Norman Whitfield's grandiose productions are mimicked to the last detail, including strings, rock guitar and bass voice interjections, while his portentous lyrics are replaced by banality.

There was a personnel overlap between Parliament and Clinton's other outfit, Funkadelic, though the latter took his methodology to greater extremes. Funkadelic, in fact, represented the latest stage in a cycle of black/white musical influence that had begun six years earlier when British rock musicians had looked to African-American urban blues players for their inspiration. The subsequent success in the US of bands like The Rolling Stones, Cream and Led Zeppelin had thus re-introduced the country to its own music and there was a further twist when Jimi Hendrix, an African-American who first made it in the UK, established himself as one of the world's leading rock stars.

Clinton picked up on the tangled web of transatlantic linkage, recognising the potential absurdity of blacks copying whites copying blacks – an element of satire is seldom far from his work. He was also alive to the hypocrisy of an industry in which the message of peace, love, good vibes and anti-materialism was underpinned by a money-making machine. Alongside the humour there is genuine reverence for Hendrix's musical and sartorial flamboyance and for the taut funk of James Brown but these are merely tributaries flowing into an idiosyncratic stream of sound, the like of which had never been heard before.

'Mommy, What's A Funkadelic?', the first track on their first album, *Funkadelic*, released in March 1970, contains many of these elements and so is tantamount to a prospectus for the new group. A riff reminiscent of Led Zeppelin's 'Whole Lotta Love' and vocal utterances resembling Hendrix's 'If Six Was Nine' are intertwined with a melange of striking psychedelic sound effects. The track ends with applause in the studio – almost as if the band were congratulating themselves on inventing something new. The next two tracks are re-makes of their first single releases. ' I'll Bet You', covered by The Jackson Five on their *ABC* album, features a funky drumming intro, African-style guitar, and a vocal arrangement alternating high and low registers, much in the manner of The Temptations. A pounding riff and psychedelic guitar solo complete the effect. 'Music For My Mother' starts with a reggae-tinged bass riff while clipped punctuation by guitar and drums builds the tension; the spoken narrative by Herb Sparkman anticipates Jim Morrison's dramatic vocal on 'The WASP (Texas Radio And The Big Beat)' by The Doors.

'I Got A Thang, You Got A Thang, Everybody's Got A Thang' is accurately, if comically, titled since it displays a bewildering variety of contributions – furious wah-wah guitar, gospel voices, a tight horn riff and a fast, straight-ahead rock section. 'Good Old Music' and 'Qualify And Satisfy' are more orthodox – the former amounting to little more than a jam session, the latter modelled on Bo Diddley's R&B classic, 'I'm A Man'. But 'What Is Soul' brings the album to a startling conclusion. Clinton begins the track with the declaration, 'Behold! I am Funkadelic – I am not of your world' and goes on to ask 'What is soul?' Among the answers are 'I don't know', 'a ham hock in your cornflakes' and 'the ring around your bathtub' – all of which reinforces the feeling that, probably stoned, the band are making it all up as they go along As such, it predicts the methodology of their next album, as does the final answer, 'Soul is you!'

For *Free Your Mind ... And Your Ass Will Follow*, issued in July 1970, was, according to Clinton, an attempt to 'see if we can cut a whole album while we're all tripping on acid' (sleeve note to CD reissue). In spite, or perhaps, because of this objective, the band's madcap wit is well in evidence. To begin with, there is the gatefold cover, the front of which illustrates the first part of the title with a photo of a woman reaching ecstatically for the skies, while the second part is reflected by the back cover picture of her naked bottom. Then there is the ironically-titled, deadpan 'Funky Dollar Bill', a sardonic comment on the destruction wrought by the pursuit of money, and the blues pastiche, 'Some More'. The record culminates with the bitterly satirical 'Eulogy And Light', written by Ernie Harris; a parody of the Lord's Prayer and the 23ʳᵈ Psalm, it savages the worship of both God and money:

> Our father which art on Wall Street
> Honoured be thy buck …
> Give us this pay, our daily bread
> Forgive us our goofs as we rob from each other
> He maketh me to sell dope to small children
> For thou art evil and we adore thee
> Thy destruction and thy power, they comfort me
> My Cadillac and my pinky ring, they restoreth me in thee
> Yeah, though I walk through the valley of the shadow of poverty, I must
>   feel their envy
> For I am loaded, high on all those other goodies
> That go along with the good God, big buck …
> Hysteria holds the room in sway I back away I run, I back away to hide
> From what? From fear? The truth, the light? Is truth the light?

As the track progresses, it moves from comedy to despair and for the final line the vocal is speeded up to chilling effect. The lyrics and structure of the piece are so well thought-out that it is hard to credit Clinton's assertion that this music was made totally under the influence of LSD. It is, on the other hand, very easy to believe that the rest of *Free Your Mind … And Your*

Ass Will Follow was made in those conditions. And, just as 'Funky Dollar Bill' and 'Eulogy And Light' are lyrically revolutionary, so is the balance of the album musically innovative. 'Friday Night, August 14th' and 'I Wanna Know If It's Good To You' take the Hendrix effect to new levels: the former has a riff and tempo that recall his 'Foxy Lady' but employ additional echo and vocal distortion, the latter is little short of a sonic holocaust with funky drumming, phasing and distorted guitar. 'Free Your Mind And Your Ass Will Follow', however, seems to come closest to the kind of spontaneous free-for-all conjured up by Clinton's statement. Running for over ten minutes, it opens with some arresting space-age effects, before settling into a pattern in which repetition of the chorus is interspersed with layers of electronic sound, psychedelic guitar and an insistent keyboard phrase. There could be no better way of reinforcing the sentiments conveyed in the track, and album, title.

With his unconventional methods and radical musical ideas, George Clinton took African-American music into a new phase although, as with many innovators, his work was not fully recognised at the time.

It was to be another six years before he made the US album charts and by then the sharp edges had been filed off his sound. But in 1970 he was one of a triumvirate that represented all that was creative in contemporary soul; another, as we have seen, was Curtis Mayfield; the third was the Godfather of Soul himself, James Brown.

★ ★ ★ ★ ★

Although he rarely made specific political statements, almost all of James Brown's music, from the late 1960s onwards, had a message. His was a creed of self-reliance, of get-up-and-go, not waiting for handouts from the authorities but of taking responsibility and carving out your own opportunities. In his youth he had been a petty criminal with little education, yet by 1971 he owned five radio stations and a chain of soul food restaurants, an indication not just of his fierce determination to succeed but of a strong sense of pride in his race and culture. This found musical expression in his 1968 single, 'Say It Loud – I'm Black And I'm Proud', a record that reflected the principles of the nascent Black Power movement and took African-American assertiveness up a notch from earlier civil rights anthems.

Nevertheless Brown also had respect for authority and the rule of law. In 1966 he had recorded 'Don't Be A Drop-Out' and in the immediate aftermath of Martin Luther King's assassination he appealed for calm, both in broadcasts on black radio stations in New York and at a concert at Boston Garden, an act for which he received personal praise from President Lyndon Johnson. By this time he had been a successful professional entertainer for over ten years and so he was known and trusted by the African-American community. This gave him sufficient sway both to quell the riots and to reach the hearts of millions with 'Say It Loud – I'm Black And I'm Proud', released four months after King's murder. It may have alienated the white audience – it was to be his final US Top Ten single – but it brought Brown closer than ever to the radical undercurrents in black America. And 1969's 'I Don't Want Nobody To Give Me Nothing (Open Up The Door I'll Get It Myself)' corresponded, as we have seen, to Black Panther ideology.

James Brown's output in 1970 merits, in terms of variety, quantity and quality, a whole book to itself. Although discographical information on the singer is often confusing, it is clear that during the course of the year he issued at least four albums and six singles, perfecting the genre he had created six years earlier, funk. The year began quietly with the release in January of *Ain't It Funky,* seven instrumentals made between 1966 and 1969. But on 9 March his band, some of whom had been with him since the mid-1960s, went on strike before a gig in Columbus, Ohio, whereupon Brown sacked them. There was immediate evidence of what a catastrophe this was likely to prove: guitarist Jimmy Nolen and saxophonists the Parker brothers had all made an input to the lively (and subsequently much-sampled) single 'Funky Drummer', issued the same month. Brown was, however, too experienced a campaigner to be caught out – he swiftly recruited a team of equally fine musicians including the brothers Phelps

'Catfish' Collins and William 'Bootsy' Collins, on guitar and bass respectively, the trumpeter Clayton 'Chicken' Gunnels and saxophonists Robert McCullough and Darryl 'Hasaan' Jamison.

Meanwhile, April saw the release of an album which featured Brown not with his own group, but with a 20-piece big band led by jazz drummer Louie Bellson. Its title, *Soul On Top,* seemed to be an assertion of the superiority of his music – and, indeed, himself: the cover photo by Dan Quest shows, in the background behind Brown, a log standing phallically between two trees – over other styles, including, presumably, the jazz he attempts on the record. In the liner note, Brown states, 'I've always been a jazz man' though it isn't clear whether that indicates personal taste or his perception of himself as a singer.

On the face of it, this was an unpromising combination – Brown: unvarnished, uninhibited, elemental; a jazz big band: smooth, sophisticated, technically adept. Yet when it gels, the outcome is electrifying. Admittedly this tends to be when Brown is on home ground. On 'It's A Man's Man's Man's World', for example, arranger Oliver Nelson sets up a thumping riff over which Brown extemporises at length (possibly too long) over saxophone obbligatos by Maceo Parker. The brooding 'Man In The Glass', written by Brown's production manager, Bud Hobgood, is even better: another dynamic Nelson arrangement stokes up the excitement while leaving room for horns, bass and drums to come to the fore and Brown's impassioned yet authoritative vocal meets the challenge with considerable verve.

But Brown shows he can excel outside his comfort zone. Well used to singing behind the beat, he adapts beautifully to the relaxed pace of the standard 'That's My Desire', improvising as a more authentic jazz singer might. He is equally at ease with the Bellson original 'I Need Your Key (To Turn Me On)' and, as might be expected, 'Every Day I Have The Blues'. Other tracks are less successful: ejaculations like 'Lookie here!' don't really suit Hank Williams's 'Your Cheating Heart' while, equally inappropriately, he funks up Kurt Weill and Maxwell Anderson's 'September Song' (some would substitute a 'c' for the 'n' in the verb). Some of these blemishes, however, could also be laid at arranger Oliver Nelson's door, and overall Brown emerges with great credit from what was a precarious enterprise.

Two outtakes from the *Soul On Top* sessions appear on the album *It's A New Day So Let A Man Come In,* which was released in June. One is an abbreviated version of 'It's A Man's Man's Man's World'; the other, 'Georgia On My Mind', is given the full Brown vocal treatment. In addition there are remakes of two other tracks from *Soul On Top* – a shorter version of 'The Man In The Glass' with guitar more prominent and 'If I Ruled The World', rendered yet more sentimental by the queasy organ accompaniment. The record also includes four tracks that had been hits over the previous year or so – all of them excellent. 'World' (Parts 1and 2) is a medium tempo piece with an interesting melody line and powerful vocals while 'Let A Man Come In And Do The Popcorn' is a freewheeling dance number with stream-of-consciousness lyrics. Showing that Brown was yet to catch up with female emancipation, 'It's A New Day' (Part 1 and 2) gives instructions to women on how to behave; despite the chauvinism it is a funk classic – tight but spacious with a rolling beat and irresistible groove. Not far behind is 'Give It Up Or Turnit A Loose', an object lesson in guitar-horn section interaction. The final track, 'I'm Not Demanding' (Part 1), could be dismissed as a string of clichés ('All I want for everybody is peace and understanding', etc) if it were not for Brown's obvious sincerity.

This hodgepodge of an album contained some superb music even if it was something of a filler in the Brown *oeuvre.* It was released too soon to feature his new band, the JBs, who had been in place since April. They were, however, in the middle of backing Brown on a series of magnificent singles. It was the first that made the greatest impact. 'Get Up, I Feel Like Being A Sex Machine' was recorded 25 April 1970 at Starday-King Studios, Nashville, with a band that included Bobby Byrd on organ and the Collins brothers (both of whom would join Funkadelic a year later). It is one of Brown's masterpieces, gliding from section to section, but racking up the tension as it does so. It begins with Brown bantering with the band, a dialogue that resurfaces at key strategic points during the track, and a jabbing five-note horn riff. Propulsion is drawn from the tightly-sprung rhythm in which guitar, bass, snare and hi-hat interlock in shifting, repetitive riffs, with occasional piano interludes cooling the temperature. Brown's vocal is more a series of exhortations – 'Get up' (answered by Byrd with 'Get on up'), 'Get it together', 'Take it to the bridge' – than conventional singing, and it is one such, 'Can we hear it and quit?', that signals the return of the horn riff and the abrupt, dramatic conclusion. The piece is built with very simple materials yet their integration and juxtaposition creates an inexorable momentum. Ostensibly spontaneous, it is music of great discipline with not a note wasted, the African-American counterpart to the musical minimalists operating in contemporary classical music. In short, this is the apotheosis of funk.

It was succeeded by three more classics of the same calibre: the relentless 'Soul Power', 'Super Bad' in which melody and percussion become pretty much the same thing and, to round off the year, the ferocious 'Get Up, Get Into It, Get Involved', another rallying-cry from Brown. The JBs appeared, too, on Brown's double album *Sex Machine: Recorded Live At Home In Augusta, Georgia With His Bad Self.*

On 10 May 1970, three months before *Sex Machine* was issued, there had been riots in Augusta, stemming from the death in police custody of a sixteen-year-old African-American, Gary Oatman. A student from Paine College had burned the Georgia flag and Governor Lester Maddox had added, almost literally, fuel to the flames by branding the demonstrations a Communist conspiracy. As the riots spread there was widespread looting and a thousand National Guardsmen arrived with machine guns, barricades and roadblocks. Just as he done two years earlier, Brown took to the airwaves to try to stop the violence, which eventually died down after two weeks. And so, when his new album was being planned he was determined to emphasise his close connection with the city – hence its cumbersome sub-title. In fact the majority of the tracks were not live at all, but studio recordings doctored to sound like they were, and the live material that *was* included came not from Augusta but from concerts in Miami the previous year.

In addition, possibly as a consequence of this mishmash, Brown constantly recycles his stock of words, phrases and other utterances – including name-checks and quotes from his other compositions – while his repertoire is filled with familiar items. (In 1970, 'It's A Man's Man's Man's World' and 'Give It Up Or Turnit A Loose' were on three of his albums, 'The Man In The Glass', and 'If I Ruled The World' were on two each.) However, all of this is not untypical of Brown and, remarkably, has virtually no negative impact on the quality of the music.

The first two tracks on the first album are especially good: 'Get Up, I Feel Like Being A Sex Machine' is superbly executed with Brown's grunts and squeals intensifying the already heavy sexuality of the piece. 'Brother Rapp' Part 1 and Part 2 exemplifies the Brown tactic of reversing instrumental roles – bass leads the way with horns employed as a percussion instrument, resulting in an uncompromising, unstoppable groove. 'Licking Stick', despite its brevity, takes off like a rocket and the euphoric version of 'There Was A Time' has Brown name-checking Augusta and uttering 'Freedom!' Not all the music is great – the perfunctory instrumental 'Spinning Wheel' is anticlimactic, and 'If I Ruled The World' features a hideous, caterwauling coda – but, despite the fakery, we get a real sense of Brown's explosive on-stage appearances, from the extended, at times frantic, instrumental workout of 'Mother Popcorn (You Got To Have A Mother For Me)' to the hard-hitting 'I Don't Want Nobody To Give Me Nothing (Open Up The Door I'll Get It Myself)' with its passionate plea for equal opportunities.

Like Curtis Mayfield and George Clinton, James Brown was making music in 1970 that was revolutionary in both its sound and its message, reflecting the conviction of millions of African-Americans that the time for change had finally come. However this was no blunt instrument: all three artists saw the bigger picture. Mayfield's critique of race relations found fault on both sides; Clinton satirised superficialities and easy solutions; Brown advocated self-help. This gave their records a profundity seldom found in this year of violent protest.

★ ★ ★ ★ ★

The white rock music of the 1960s had also been revolutionary – sometimes lyrically, sometimes instrumentally, sometimes both – but not always with overt political intentions. True, the artists concerned may have held such convictions and their music would often find a place in the soundtrack to political events and demonstrations, fuelling thoughts of revolution without actually preaching it. Such an artist was Captain Beefheart (who was also an artist in a more specific sense, being a recognised painter and sculptor). Given that his music was such an uncommercial proposition – essentially Delta blues filtered through the spiky, irregular rhythms of avant-garde jazz – Beefheart acquired a large following in the 1960s, possibly because of its shock-value. His importance to the story of 1970 lies in the fact that the album he made that year symbolises the end of an era when experimentation, idiosyncrasy and sheer chaos were essential elements in the rock music scene. After *Lick My Decals Off, Baby* neither Beefheart nor any of his compatriots would venture into such dangerous waters again.

Made in May, released in December, *Decals* may not have reached the dizzy heights of his 1969 absurdist classic, *Trout Mask Replica,* though there is still plenty of oddly-flavoured but agreeable meat to chew on. Rather like James Brown (and here the parallel ends) Beefheart makes music that seems wild but in reality is rigidly disciplined. The stop-start structure of the title track on its own provides sufficient evidence of that. In effect this is an anti-love song, perhaps a metaphor for the end of the decade when flower power has given way to street fighting ('Rather than I want to hold your hand, I want to swallow you whole'). Similarly, 'Space-Age Couple' seems to bemoan progress and the disappearance of the natural world.

'Bellerin' Plain', and 'Flash Gordon's Ape' are impenetrable, though one must assume that the free-form soprano saxophone piece 'Japan Is A Dishpan' refers both to the circular shape of the pan and the disk in the middle of that country's flag. In fact, half the fun lies in guessing what the compositions are about, the other half in enjoying Beefheart's sense of humour – notably in the blues parody 'I Wanna Find A Woman That'll

Hold My Big Toe Till I Have To Go', the celebratory 'I Love You, You Big Dummy' with its strangulated harmonica, and the juxtaposition of 'dinosaur's shoes' and 'Dinah Shore's shoes' in 'The Smithsonian Institute Blues'. Although the album marks the end of Beefheart's halcyon days, at least one track looks forward; the contrast between Beefheart's gruff croaking and the soft tones of the marimba on 'Woe-Is-Uh-Me-Bop' anticipates the textures used by Tom Waits in the *Rain Dogs* period of the mid-1980s.

Forbidding though Beefheart's music was at times, even he stopped short of deliberately alienating his fans. Yet that, apparently, was Tim Buckley's intention with *Lorca*, released in May 1970. Certainly the record lacks many of the orthodox components of the standard rock album. There is no kit drummer, but a conga-player, Carter CC Collins, which immediately releases the rhythm section from the regular, four-square, 4/4 time signature that dominated popular music (Beefheart, too, was a rare exception). There are also no electric guitar solos in the conventional sense and no histrionic vocals. Instead, the five tracks meander mournfully along with lengthy improvised intervals and frequently unintelligible vocals. The nine-minute title-track, for instance, includes rubato guitar, repetitive chanting, fragments of poetry and a long electric piano solo. The slow 'Anonymous Proposition' features just electric guitar and bass and finds Buckley experimenting with the timbres of his voice while on 'Driftin'' he soars up and down the registers over a sombre guitar riff. 'I Had A Talk With My Woman' is a bit brighter, though the brisk tempo of the closing 'Nobody Walkin'' belies its depressing sentiments ('Ain't gonna be nobody to keep you warm'); much of the time, however, Buckley shifts from wordless murmuring to incomprehensibility.

With *Lorca* Buckley broke away decisively from the mainstream and created a harrowing but memorable record that he never fully followed up; five years later, he died of a drug overdose, aged 28. Had he lived a little longer, he would have seen his attitude, if not his music, adopted by some of the leading punk performers. In 1970, however, he was a lone voice among singer-songwriters, a long distance away from the fashion for well-crafted, confessional love songs. Neither was his predilection for experimentation replicated, at least in the USA. As we shall see, innovations in rock were more likely to occur thousands of miles away, across the Atlantic Ocean.

CHAPTER 3:

Save The Country

The problem with the 1960s was that they raised expectations, especially among the young. As the decade drew to a close it became increasingly obvious that the world was not going to change for the better; in fact on some fronts it was getting worse. That is not to say that the ideals nurtured during, for example, 1967's Summer of Love, withered away prematurely: quite the opposite. Huge numbers of young people carried them forward into their personal, professional and political lives. In time, too, there were victories to savour, one of them major: the Vietnam War finally came to an end in 1975.

But in 1970 there was frustration, at times anger, at the inflexibility and intransigence of those in authority – governments, police, universities – which seemed, in some cases, to be hardening into counterrevolution. Such feelings were, furthermore, endemic to a huge mass of young people. Although, as we saw in Chapter 1, there was some ill feeling at the Isle Wight between those who had paid and those who wanted to turn it into a free festival, the 500,000 who attended were pretty much of one mind politically (and for that matter in the catholicity of their taste). Them and Us meant the Establishment versus The Young.

Such was the distrust of the older generation that even good news was greeted with indifference or ignored altogether. On 16 April, strategic arms limitation talks (SALT) between the USA and the USSR began in Vienna; five days later President Nixon announced a US troop reduction of 150,000 in Vietnam over the coming year. But a further nine days after that, the sceptics were vindicated: American troops were in Cambodia.

For those who had been protesting the war in South-East Asia, this was the final straw. Contrary to Nixon's statement of just a few days before, this looked very much like escalation, bringing further instability to an already precarious regime and dragging thousands of innocent civilians into a conflict they had nothing to do with. Unbeknownst to the public, Nixon had already authorised the bombing of Cambodia over a year before, with the intention of destroying Communist forces using it as a base. Nixon had not sought congressional approval then, and nor did he do so now, reinforcing the growing impression that he was prosecuting the war for personal rather than political reasons and, worse, that he was beginning to lose control of the whole situation. Stanley Karnow (*op. cit.,* p. 610) relates,

> Nixon went into a rampage even before the full storm of domestic opposition had burst, almost as if he relished the coming onslaught. At the Pentagon on the morning after the invasion, he interrupted a briefing and embarrassed the officers present by exhorting them in foul language to "blow the hell out" of the Communist sanctuaries in Cambodia. Out in the corridor, he also uncorked a diatribe against antiwar students, whose fresh round of demonstrations had not yet even occurred. Not knowing that his remarks were being taped, he branded the youths as "bums blowing up campuses".

Such outbursts had the effect of identifying Nixon so closely with the escalation of the war that for many people, especially the student population, he came to personify it: the fear was that with Nixon in power it would never end. Secretly, however, peace talks with the North Vietnamese had begun in Paris on 21 February 1970, with Secretary of State Henry Kissinger representing the US. The incursion into Cambodia and the reaction it provoked put Kissinger at a disadvantage, adding further pressure to get the war over with as soon as possible. The North Vietnamese, on the other hand, were in no hurry and believed they could extract more concessions from the Americans the longer the war went on.

The South Vietnamese were kept out of the talks (just as the Cambodian government were not informed of Nixon's decision to invade their country), possibly because they were likely to fight any compromise that affected them negatively, though their absence hardly made the negotiations progress any more quickly.

By October 1970 the talks were at a stalemate. The North Vietnamese position was that they would not withdraw troops from South Vietnam under any circumstances. This put paid to the US proposal that both sides should relocate to where they were when the war began. Fearing heavy losses in the impending congressional midterm elections unless a breakthrough was found, Nixon and Kissinger came up with their 'standstill cease-fire' initiative, to end the hostilities at the very spot they were taking place. Although this approach found favour with Nixon's domestic opponents, it soon petered out, largely because the President, in order to calm the South Vietnamese, soon began to refer to 'mutual withdrawal' again, the very policy the North had resisted. As far as the midterms were concerned it was no better than a damage-limitation exercise: the Republicans still lost twelve seats to the Democrats in the House of Representatives; future President Jimmy Carter became Governor of Georgia, replacing the segregationist Lester Maddox.

Meanwhile the antiwar protests were becoming more widespread and more strident. Typical, at least at the outset, was the demonstration at Kent State University, Ohio. On Friday 1 May, students gathered on campus to voice their displeasure at the expansion of the war into Cambodia: there was the by-now frequent spectacle of draft-card burning though this time a copy of the US Constitution was added to the fire. Unrest continued into the evening, degenerating into bottle-throwing and vandalism whereupon all the bars in the town were closed by order of the mayor. By this time the whole of the local police force were involved and tear-gas was used to disperse the crowd. In a rapidly descending spiral of events, the National Guard were called in the following day and Ohio Governor Jim Rhodes became ever more vehement in his denunciation of the demonstrators.

On Monday 4 May, the university authorities announced they were banning an on-campus protest planned for midday, but the students went ahead nevertheless and rang the giant Victory Bell to summon the demonstrators. The National Guard intervened and had largely succeeded in scattering the crowd before coming upon a small group moving slowly towards them. At that point they opened fire and over the next few minutes wounded nine students and killed four: Allison Krause, Jeffrey Miller, Sandra Scheuer and William Knox Schroeder. The latter two were not participating in the demonstration but walking between classes when they were shot dead.

The killings at Kent State were greeted with outrage, not only in the student population but across the wider community, and came to symbolise the brutal intolerance of authority. Within days, there were mass protests – 150,000 in San Francisco and 100,000 in Washington. Nixon, fearful that the four students would become martyrs, was defensive in his response:

> I would certainly regret that any use of the word "bums" was interpreted to apply to those who dissent. All the members of this press corps know that I have for years defended the right of dissent. I have always opposed the use of violence. Now on university campuses the rule of reason is supposed to prevail over the use of force and when students on university campuses burn buildings, when they engage in violence, when they break up furniture, when they terrorise their fellow students and terrorise the faculty, then I think "bums" is perhaps too kind a word to apply to that kind of person.

By now, however, it was clear that the vast majority of those who were participating in the student demonstrations were not 'that kind of person', not Communist agitators nor anarchists, but ordinary young Americans sick and tired of the war. Four million of them, studying at more than 450 higher education establishments, now went on strike, and resolved to do so on the fifteenth of each month until the war was over.

At the same time, it is undeniable that the level of violence had risen since the more peaceful protests of the 1960s. Some of this can be laid at the door of the authorities, whose reaction to opposition could often be disproportionately aggressive. Yet some demonstrators were also too ready to resort to hostile behaviour, whether provoked or not: why was this?

Certainly events in South-East Asia were becoming intolerable, and there was a personal as well as a moral dimension to the horror. Between 1967 and 1969 over 40,000 Americans died in Vietnam, over two-thirds of the total who would perish in the entire 20-year war (source: US National Archives). It follows that huge numbers of young people were friends or siblings of those killed and it is not difficult to see a link between this carnage and the ferocity shown by at least some of the protestors. International events elsewhere were a further source of aggravation: excluding Vietnam, no fewer than eleven wars were in train at the beginning of 1970.

Moreover violence was becoming part of everyday culture. Films, for example, had been increasingly explicit since the mid-1960s and 1969 had seen possibly the most violent picture in the history of the cinema to date, *The Wild Bunch*, directed by Sam Peckinpah; there were also violent climaxes to the biggest and third-biggest box office successes of the year, *Butch Cassidy And The Sundance Kid* and *Easy Rider*. And in the real world, gruesome role models were to be found in recent cases where young people had perpetrated horrific acts of violence, such as the Manson Murders and Altamont.

All of these factors added to the increasing belligerence of the 1970 student demonstrations. Yet of equal importance was the background of the protestors. In the main they were white and middle-class and therefore accustomed to getting their own way. The huge death-count and now the escalation of the war into Cambodia were as far from what they wanted as it was possible to be. It also goes some way to explaining the severity of the response from those in power: civil disobedience from the usual suspects – the poor, African-Americans – was only to be expected, but when your friend's, neighbour's , or even your own, son or daughter was involved, then it was really time to worry. As Karnow (*ibid.*, p. 610) relates,

In many instances, top administration figures were stunned by the anguish of their children. A poignant scene occurred at the home of one senior official who had strenuously worked against the Cambodian offensive from behind the scenes. His two sons, unaware of their father's exertions, denounced him over dinner – and walked out of the house.

Increased militancy among young whites was also part of the understandable need to take things to a higher level than their immediate forebears, in the same way that music was getting louder, stage-acts were becoming more extreme and festivals were growing in scope and size. The dichotomy between passive and active forms of protest was, however, not necessarily generational. Jenny Slaughter, founder in 1970 of the important Manchester co-operative On The Eighth Day, says that at that stage the difference in approaches were more a question of individual life experiences than age-group, although it would not be long before divisions occurred between the 'hippie-dippies and the politicos'. Writing in 1970, Germaine Greer attributed the mobilisation of the young to the deficiencies of the old:

> Generation X, the generation gap, the Mods, the Rockers, the Hippies, the Yippies, the Skinheads, the Maoists, the young Fascists of Europe, rebels without a cause, whatever patronizing names their parent generation can find for them, the young are accusing their elders of spurious assumption of authority to conceal their own confusion. Vandalism, steel-capped boots, drugs, football rioting, these are chaos and the attempts of instituted authority to deal with them are more chaotic still ... The only way the state-father can deal with its uncontrollable children is to bash them and shoot them in the streets or send them to war, the ultimate chaos. (*The Female Eunuch*, p. 237-8)

Of course opposition to the war did not come only from young whites. On 29 August 1970, the National Chicano Moratorium March against the

Vietnam War took place in East Los Angeles. During the event, an officer from the Los Angeles County Sheriff's Office killed the Mexican-American journalist, Rubén Salazar, an act that came to epitomise the oppression of the Chicano community by the authorities.

Martin Luther King had also spoken out against the war, the first prominent figure to do so, according to Angela Davis. King equated militarism with racism, and many African-Americans felt unhappy about fighting for their country while they were still suffering from discrimination and abuse. Resisting the draft in 1966, Muhammad Ali is alleged to have said, 'No Viet Cong ever called me a nigger'. Perhaps the fact that they were fighting injustice on so many fronts has tended to obscure the input made by African-Americans to the antiwar effort.

Just eleven days after Kent State, an equally horrific incident occurred at Jackson State College, Mississippi. Around 100 African-American students gathered on campus to protest the incursion into Cambodia. As the demonstration intensified, the police and the Mississippi Highway Patrol arrived on the scene and, just as at Kent State, had just begun to disperse the crowd when they opened fire. Twelve students were wounded and two were killed, Phillip Lafayette Gibbs and James Earl Green.

On 13 June, Nixon established the President's Commission on Campus Unrest, chaired by William Scranton, to investigate Kent State, Jackson State and other conflagrations in American colleges. Its report, published in September, concluded that there had been no justification for the killing of the six students. But it was too late to stem the tide: that same month, Vietnam Veterans Against The War, whose membership had almost trebled since Kent State, marched to Valley Forge, Pennsylvania, site of the winter camp of the American Continental Army during the Revolutionary War. At the ensuing rally the speakers included Donald Sutherland, Jane Fonda and future Presidential candidate and Secretary of State, John Kerry; the demonstrators sang The Plastic Ono Band's 'Give Peace A Chance', now the undisputed anthem of the antiwar movement.

★ ★ ★ ★ ★

The composer of 'Give Peace A Chance', John Lennon, was one of the very few songwriters to foresee the violence that was now becoming synonymous with student demonstrations. 'Revolution 1', included on the 1968 double album, *The Beatles*, had found him ambivalent on the subject, counting himself both 'in' and 'out' when it came to talk about destruction. 'Revolution 9', the recording of which commenced on the same day, 30 May 1968, was equally equivocal. A collage of sound representing an actual revolution, it portrays the confusion and chaos that would ensue but without any suggestion that it was to be avoided on this basis. However by 10 July, the date on which he recorded 'Revolution' (released as the B-side of the single 'Hey Jude') he was certain that he wanted to be counted out of any violent conflict. Just under a year later he wrote 'Give Peace A Chance'. Yet as we have seen, Lennon's solo album of 1970, *John Lennon/Plastic Ono Band,* was an exclusively inward-looking affair, a brutal and uncompromising exposure of his own psyche and not at all concerned with the wider world. In the last few months of The Beatles' existence, his fellow band-members were just as self-absorbed, finding solace in their own recordings as the group slowly disintegrated.

Crosby, Stills, Nash and Young were, on a number of levels, the logical successors to The Beatles' throne. Four identifiable individuals who also operated effectively as a band, they worked in a variety of styles from romantic ballads to full-on jam sessions with long guitar solos. They also resembled The Beatles in terms of age and, somewhat, in experience; Graham Nash was a former member of The Hollies, a Manchester group who owed their existence to Mersey Beat, and David Crosby had founded The Byrds, who were marketed as America's answer to The Beatles and even went as far as using the same Gretsch and Rickenbacker guitars and Ludwig drums as their British role models.

When, in 1969, the Canadian guitarist and singer-songwriter Neil Young joined the already established trio of Crosby, Stills and Nash, he brought a harder edge to the group whose eponymous debut album released that May was a beautifully crafted record if lacking in bite or, for that matter, political consciousness. On CSNY's *Déjà Vu,* issued on 11

March 1970, there is evidence of both. True, there are tracks that would not have been out of place on *Crosby, Stills And Nash*, in particular, the paeans to cosy domesticity 'Our House' and 'Teach Your Children', both by Nash (who at this point seemed to be growing old before his time); Young's nostalgic 'Helpless'; and '4+20', a somewhat self-pitying autobiographical ballad by Stills.

Each of these tracks evinces the sentimentality that in this period often went hand-in-hand with narcissism and self-analysis. Scaled up, it also surfaced in contemporary message songs with their banal lyrics and anthem-like choruses. *Déjà Vu* is under the constant threat of these pitfalls, though the skill of the writing – and the excellence of the singing and musicianship – more often than not pulls it clear. 'Carry On' and 'Everybody I Love You', for example, both have anthemic tendencies but are redeemed by the pragmatism of the lyrics; at the other end of the spectrum, yet no less attractive, is the dreamlike title track. Young's 'Country Girl' is a well conceived and constructed love song, while Crosby's 'Almost Cut My Hair' is a symbol of personal and political defiance. The cover version of Joni Mitchell's 'Woodstock' is, however, routine in comparison with the keening anxiety and chilly atmosphere that pervaded the original. Whatever its faults, *Déjà Vu* was at the cutting edge of mainstream rock music in early 1970: Gary Burden's sleeve design with its gothic lettering and grainy monochrome photograph of the band as nineteenth century backwoodsmen was also in tune both with the album title and with the yearning for a mythical past that was so modish in 1970 and about which much more will be said in Chapter 5.

Déjà Vu was a massive success, the first of CSNY's three consecutive US number one albums; in the UK, where *Crosby, Stills And Nash* had not even charted, it reached number five. As such it paved the way for albums by each of the principals. Young's *After The Goldrush*, released in August, was actually his third solo record and is considered by many critics to be one of his best. Certainly it crystallises the qualities that made him such an asset to CSNY and which have characterised his career ever since. The bittersweet ballads 'Only Love Can Break Your Heart' and 'Don't Let It

Bring You Down' explore the dividing line between sorrow and joy and there is a double edge, too, in the title track, which sets the gloom of the present against an optimistic future. Here, as in *Déjà Vu*, there are also trips into the past: 'Cripple Creek Ferry' recalls the golden age of the American riverboat while, underpinned by a relentless rocking rhythm, 'Southern Man' is a horrific portrayal of the slavery era doubling as an allegory of contemporary racism.

At the time, *After The Goldrush* looked hard to top, but *Stephen Stills*, issued in November 1970, was of equal calibre. Dedicated to Jimi Hendrix, who had died two months previously, it is the only album to feature both Hendrix and Eric Clapton, the twin guitar deities of the 1960s. The former makes a typically storming contribution to 'Old Times Good Times', a much more convincing piece of Stills nostalgia than '4+20'. 'Go Back Home' is simply one of the finest guitar showcases of the period. Stills builds up the brooding atmosphere with extensive and incisive use of the wah-wah pedal before Clapton enters magisterially for a dazzling display of virtuosity: it is unlikely that he, nor indeed any other rock guitarist, ever came up with such a ringing, authoritative opening to a solo as he executes here.

Other highlights include the grandiose, hedonistic 'Love The One You're With' and the pulsating 'Cherokee', with Booker T Jones on organ and a saxophone solo by Sidney George. Stills looked more like an all-American boy than a hippie, though he was as politically committed as any of his peers: with Buffalo Springfield he created 'For What It's Worth', a biting commentary on the Sunset Strip Riots of the late 1960s and for CSNY's live performances he converted his wistful '49 Reasons' into a romping, stomping anti-establishment rant. For *Stephen Stills* he came up with 'We Are Not Helpless', seen by some as an answer-song to Young's 'Helpless' but in reality a clarion-call to a generation at risk of letting peace and love degenerate into violence and hatred. Musically, too, the piece is inspirational; driven along by Ringo Starr's crisp, propulsive drumming, it swiftly builds from a quiet opening to a rousing gospel chorus with pounding piano from Stills and a vigorous vocal ensemble including

Crosby, Nash, Booker T, Mama Cass Elliot, Rita Coolidge and John Sebastian.

Different in mood, yet equally affecting, was Stills's requiem for the Vietnam war dead, 'Find The Cost Of Freedom', the B-side of a CSNY single which, released in June 1970, represented one of the best political rock couplings to date. For the A-side was 'Ohio', written by Neil Young and recorded just seventeen days after Kent State. Set to a lugubrious, grinding rhythm and delivered by Young with his characteristic mix of melancholy and malice, the song lacerates the forces of authority behind the shootings. Towards the end of track Crosby, almost as if he cannot contain his rage, can be heard interjecting 'Four, why? Why did they die?' and 'How many more?', a chilling finale to a record which in barely three minutes summarised the feelings of millions.

Crosby continued the assault into his own solo album, *If I Could Only Remember My Name*, recorded in late 1970 and early 1971. The accusatory 'What Are Their Names' is rendered by an all-star vocal chorus to rival 'We Are Not Helpless': Crosby, Nash, Joni Mitchell, David Freiberg, two members of Jefferson Airplane (Grace Slick and Paul Kantner) and two from The Grateful Dead (Jerry Garcia and Phil Lesh). But the highlight of this excellent record is the eight-minute 'Cowboy Movie', Crosby's allegorical Wild West dream/fantasy starring himself, the other members of CSNY and Rita Coolidge in the roles of Fat Albert, The Duke, Young Billy, Eli and the Indian Girl. The playing is as dramatic as the narrative with shimmering guitar work from Garcia and Crosby underpinned by Lesh's penetrating bass. The album comes to en eerie conclusion with Crosby's echoing, wordless *a cappella* vocal 'I'd Swear There Was Somebody Here', a vision of his recently-deceased girlfriend, Christine Hinton.

Finally, just over a year after *Déjà Vu*, came Nash's *Songs For Beginners*. 'Chicago/We Can Change The World' alludes to the trial of the Chicago Eight (for alleged offences committed at the Democratic Party Convention of 1968), one of whom, the Black Panther founder Bobby Seale, was bound and gagged in the courtroom during the proceedings. 'Military Madness', which includes a remarkable wah-wah guitar solo by Dave Mason, is a condemnation not just of Vietnam but of all wars. Most of the songs on the rest of the album deal with Nash's breakup with Joni Mitchell. To devote so much space to something so personal may seem excessive yet by this time, May 1971, no self-respecting singer-songwriter could do otherwise.

★ ★ ★ ★ ★

In the United States there had been no tradition of violent protest, at least in the 20th century and certainly not by young people. Europe, however, was a different story. There was a range of anarchist groups in Spain, for example, whose history stretched back to the Civil War, while in France the Situationist International had existed long before it inspired the student disturbances at the Nanterre and Sorbonne Universities. The UK was more like America, though by 1968, protests were becoming more active: the demonstration outside the US Embassy on 17 March that year attracted a crowd of 10,000 and ended with 200 arrests and 86 injured. Before the follow-up demonstration on 27 October, one of the organisers, Tariq Ali, was approached by a group called the Angry Brigade with a view to bombing the embassy. They were refused and less than two years later embarked on a two-year campaign of terrorism, not aimed at the Vietnam War any more but against representatives of the British Establishment.

The Angry Brigade included, at various times, Stuart Christie, Christopher Bott, Jake Prescott, John Barker, Hilary Creek, Anna Mendelson, Jim Greenfield, and Anna Mason, founder of the gay rights group, Stonewall. Bott and Barker were influenced by the situationists and Christie had links with Spanish anarchists such as the First of May Group, who carried out a series of bombings in London, mainly of buildings associated with Spain, from 1968 onwards.

On 18 August 1970, the Angry Brigade bombed the home of the Commissioner of the Metropolitan Police, Sir John Waldron; on 8 September, that of the Attorney General, Sir Peter Rawlinson. At first it was thought that, despite the specifically British nature of these targets, these attacks were the work of the First of May Group. But on 4 December the Angry Brigade issued a communiqué via the *International Times* claiming responsibility for these and other attacks, including the machine-gunning of the Spanish Embassy and the bombing on 20 November of a BBC van stationed at the Miss World beauty contest in London (later the scene, also, of a women's liberation demonstration).

What the Angry Brigade had concluded was that big demonstrations such as those in Grosvenor Square were ineffective in getting their grievances publicised; the October event had shown that the police were now so accustomed to containing large numbers of people that the shock value of earlier protests had been lost. They continued their campaign into the following year, when the targets included the Secretary of State for Employment and Productivity, Robert Carr, the Secretary of State for Trade and Industry, John Davies, the Metropolitan Police, the Territorial Army and the Biba boutique in Kensington. By the autumn, however, its leading members were in custody and the Angry Brigade began to fizzle out. Despite its brief existence it was important on three levels. Firstly, its concerns were exclusively domestic, lacking entirely the international/separatist agenda that lay behind most acts of terrorism in this period; secondly, and as a consequence, its legacy was enshrined in a series of initiatives which took on the British Establishment: self-help programmes, a claimants union and a newspaper, *Strike*. But perhaps most significant of all, the Angry Brigade symbolised the craving among many young people for direct action, the rejection of talking and writing and peaceful protests in favour of violent attacks on high-profile individuals and institutions.

Such actions had been the province of the long-established terrorist groups who, in many cases, reached a peak of activity in 1970. In Guatemala, for example, the Rebel Armed Forces (FAR) guerrilla group, formed in 1961, kidnapped the German ambassador, Karl von Spreti, on 31 March and later murdered him when the government refused to negotiate with them. Exactly four months later, the Uruguayan Tupamaros guerrillas attempted three kidnappings on the same day. US Foreign

Service Officer Michael Gordon Jones eluded them, though the FBI agent and government adviser Dan Mitrione was seized and later executed, while the Brazilian consul Aloysio Mares Dias Gomide was ransomed on 21 February 1971 for $250,000, paid by his wife. On 7 August the Tupamaros seized American agriculture expert Claude Fly, but released him nine days after Gomide.

As we saw in Chapter 1, this was a period of unremitting action for the Front de libération du Québec (FLQ), originally formed in 1963. In the election to the National Assembly of Quebec held on 29 April 1970, the new Parti Québécois, led by former Liberal cabinet minister René Lévesque, won seven seats with its secessionist agenda, yet far from pacifying the FLQ, this only seemed to encourage them. On 5 October they kidnapped the British Trade Commissioner, James Cross; five days later they murdered the Québec Labour Minister, Pierre Laporte. On 15 October some 3,000 students attended a rally in support of the FLQ. In response, Canadian Prime Minister Pierre Trudeau invoked the War Measures Act, which suspended civil liberties and within the next two months Cross was released and his kidnappers given safe passage to Cuba.

But whereas the Canadian October Crisis effectively put paid to the FLQ, the Basque Separatist organisation ETA was still going strong at the end of the year. In December, they kidnapped the German consul in San Sebastián, Eugen Beilh, in an effort to bring about the release of comrades incarcerated for the murder of the city's chief of secret police, Melitón Manzanas, in 1968. Also in December the Brazilian guerrilla group Vanguarda Popular Revolucionária (VPR) kidnapped Swiss Ambassador Giovanni Bucher for similar reasons, killing his chief of security Hélio Carvalho de Araújo in the process; seven months earlier, the VPR assassinated a military police officer Alberto Mendes Júnior.

Elsewhere during 1970, Archbishop Makarios and Pope Paul VI both survived assassination attempts, as did King Hussein of Jordan, who was involved in a bitter struggle with the Palestine Liberation Organisation, led by Yasser Arafat. On 6 September the Popular Front for the Liberation of Palestine (PFLP) hijacked four aeroplanes with the intention of freeing

Palestinian prisoners held by Israel. Two of the planes landed at Dawson's Field, a remote airstrip in Jordan; a third, a Boeing 747 too big to land there, was diverted to Cairo. On the fourth, the hijackers, Patrick Argüello and Leila Khaled, were overpowered and the plane landed at Heathrow. Argüello had been shot during the melee and died of his wounds, but Khaled was imprisoned, whereupon a fifth plane was hijacked in order to pressurise the British government to free her: this, too, was taken to Dawson's Field.

Meanwhile King Hussein reacted to the hijackings and to the deliberate and provocative use of Dawson's Field by declaring martial law in Jordan, and thus in effect ignited a civil war (Black September) with the PLO. By the end of the month he had triumphed and on 1 October, much to the chagrin of the USA in particular, Khaled was released by the British government, as were all of the other captured terrorists. Around 5000 people were killed in the civil war; just one, Argüello, died in the Dawson's Field hijackings.

★ ★ ★ ★ ★

The conflicts in South-East Asia and the Middle East had sucked Western European countries into them and it seemed whichever stance they took, young people would contest it. At the same time, there was friction between governments and their citizens on a range of internal issues. Some nations, such as France and Italy, were getting used to civil disobedience and violent incidents. The French President, Charles de Gaulle, had almost been driven from office by the student protests of 1968; although he survived, and in fact improved his majority in the Assembly, young people remained at odds with their government and with their nation. When de Gaulle's successor, Georges Pompidou, visited San Francisco as part of an official visit to the US in February 1970, he was met by 10,000 demonstrators, an eventuality for which President Nixon apologised two days later. The mood was summed up by the singer-songwriter Léo Ferré with his 'Paris, Je Ne T'aime Plus' ('Paris, I Don't Love You Any More'), ostensibly a love song but with heavy political overtones.

In Italy, the Milan bank bombing of 1969 was followed in July 1970 by a still more violent act of terrorism, probably by the same unidentified group: a train was derailed near Rome, killing six people and injuring a hundred. The same month there was a revolt in Reggio at the government's decision to make the smaller town of Cantazaro the regional capital of Calabria. Beginning with a train bombing and several days of street violence, the disturbances persisted until February 1971, fuelled by the neo-fascist Movimento Sociale Italiano, and resulted in some ten deaths and several hundred injured.

Prior to 1970, both the UK and the Netherlands had also had their moments but not on this scale. True, the 1968 demonstration in Grosvenor Square had turned nasty, yet there were no fatalities or serious injuries; even the Angry Brigade's activities caused damage only to property. And Amsterdam had become a mecca for hippies, attracted by the liberal soft drugs laws and the relaxed ambience of the city. However all this changed on 25 August 1970 when, in response to the large number of hippies sleeping on the national war memorial and the surrounding area, the mayor called in the police to disperse them, sparking off a riot and still more violent suppression, this time by the marines.

The publication of Albert Speer's autobiography, *Inside The Third Reich*, served as a reminder of Germany's Nazi past – not that any were needed, at least in the eyes of the country's young people. Born just after the Second World War when the country was newly partitioned, they had grown up without getting the answers they wanted (or indeed any answers at all) when they quizzed their parents about their roles during the war, and specifically about their support for Nazism. They were conscious, too, that many former Nazis were still in positions of power and influence. As Amon Düül II guitarist John Weinzierl relates in the BBC television documentary, *Krautrock*,

> After the War you wouldn't just erase all people, especially judges, teachers – [even] if they were Nazis, they had to take them, 'cause you can't just kick them out and have no teachers at all. It was all still

there but it wasn't as loud anymore. In those days there were bloody Nazis around all over the place ... there was rebellion against them. All Munich was on the street. We didn't have guns or the tools to chase them away but we could make music and we could draw audiences, and we could draw people with the same understanding, the same desire.

Amon Düül II were the product of a political art commune in Munich, itself called Amon Düül and, as their name suggests, were the second band formed there; some members of the commune, such as Weinzierl and drummer Peter Leopold, played with both groups. Amon Düül attracted radical thinkers and activists, including Red Army Faction founders Gudrun Ensslin, Andreas Baader and Ulrike Meinhof, who wanted faster, more decisive action than the commune seemed prepared to offer. Weinzerl recalls,

> One day Andreas and Ulrike started: "They're not really listening to us ... We actually have to make something drastic like burn something down or blast something."

The RAF's thirst for dramatic action had its roots in the events of 2 June 1967, when the Shah of Persia, Reza Pahlavi, came to West Berlin. Meinhof, then a journalist, had written an open letter to the Empress of Iran, citing the contrast between the luxury enjoyed by the royal family and the poverty of their subjects, and her views were echoed by the hundreds of students who turned up to protest the visit. On his arrival at the Schöneberg City Hall, the Shah's supporters (many of whom were members of the Iranian secret service) turned on the demonstrators and, without any intervention from the police, belaboured them with wooden placards. Soon the demonstration turned into a full-scale riot with the police taking the side of the Persians. The protestors attempted to defend themselves but this only increased the violence, culminating in the shooting by Detective Sergeant Karl-Heinz Kurras of Benno Ohnesorg, a 26-year-old pacifist attending his first demonstration. As Stefan Aust writes in his definitive study of the RAF, *The Baader-Meinhof Complex*,

> Beaten, desperate and filled with hatred, many of the demonstrators met that night at the Berlin SDS [Socialist German Students Union] centre on the Kurfürstendamm. There was much agitated discussion on the form reaction to Benno Ohnesorg's death should take. A slim young woman with long blonde hair was weeping uncontrollably, crying, "This fascist state means to kill us all. Violence is the only way to answer violence. This is the Auschwitz generation, and there's no arguing with them!" Gudrun Ensslin had said exactly what many of them were thinking and feeling. Next day she was one of a group of eight students staging a protest on the Kurfürstendamm, although there was a ban on demonstrations.

This little protest gained huge TV coverage and the demonstrators subsequently met at the flat of Ensslin and her partner, the publisher Bernward Vesper (son of the Nazi writer, Will Vesper). Also present, newly released from jail, was Andreas Baader.

Exactly nine months after the demonstration against the Shah, Baader and Ensslin made good on the promise made at Amon Düül by firebombing the Kaufhaus Schneider department store in Frankfurt. As the devices did not go off until well after the store was closed, no-one was hurt, and Baader, Ensslin and their two accomplices were apprehended the following day. Nine days later, the radical student leader Rudi Dutschke was shot by a right-wing extremist, Josef Bachmann. Dutschke survived, though the incident nevertheless inflamed the student community and the blame was placed at the door of the Axel Springer Press, publishers of the rabidly anti-Communist *Bild Zeitung,* the most popular newspaper in West Germany. Hundreds of demonstrators headed for Springer's printing works, where despite violent clashes, delivery trucks got through. Among the protestors was Ulrike Meinhof.

In October 1968, the trial of Ensslin and Baader began. The

firebombing of the store had been intended to shock the public out of its apathy – a tactic not unlike those used by the SI and, ultimately, by the Angry Brigade. Ensslin and Baader were convicted of arson and were sentenced to three years, but were released fourteen months later, while their appeal was being processed. In November 1969, the appeal was rejected though by this time they had gone underground, resurfacing in Paris where they stayed at the apartment of Régis Debray, later moving on to Italy to plan their activities for the year 1970 with Horst Mahler, a left-wing lawyer who had played a prominent part in the anti-Springer demonstration. On their return to Berlin, however, Baader was arrested after being picked up for speeding.

On 14 May 1970, Baader was escorted from Tegel Prison, Berlin, to the German Central Institute for Social Issues, in order to meet Ulrike Meinhof and, apparently, discuss with her a proposed book about disaffected young people. In fact her visit masked an attempt to free Baader. Just after they began their conversation, the building was stormed by four accomplices, including Ensslin, and one of the Institute staff was shot. Baader leapt through a window, followed by Meinhof, and the whole gang escaped in two cars. It was at that moment that the Red Army Faction, popularly known as the Baader-Meinhof group, was born.

In order to pursue their agenda, the RAF needed weapons and while a Palestinian supplier had already been found a condition of the deal was that the group receive military training from Fatah, the largest grouping within the PLO. And so on 8 June 1970 they departed for Jordan from Schönefeld Airport, East Berlin. But first they capitalised on their new-found notoriety by recording a statement by Meinhof in which she justified the breakout and the shooting of the Institute employee, Georg Linke. At this stage Meinhof appeared to speak on behalf of the RAF though her articulate, intellectual approach was the antithesis of Baader's craving for direct action: he was sick of discussions that led nowhere. Thereafter her authority began to wane in favour of his equally uncompromising partner, Ensslin.

Fatah were ideally placed to provide the RAF with the training they required; in 1969 alone they had carried out 2,400 attacks on Israeli targets. But from the beginning there was friction between the two parties. Baader, in particular, reacted badly to instruction and wanted to do things his way, and the spartan conditions led to vociferous complaints. The Germans also had a habit of firing their guns indiscriminately just for the fun of it and so their ammunition was rationed. The upshot was a 'strike' by the RAF during which the women sunbathed in the nude to provoke the Algerian camp commandant; in the end the training was abandoned.

Back in Berlin, the RAF began to build the infrastructure they would need for their campaign: documentation, identity papers, cars and hideouts were all procured over the succeeding months. But not without a cost: such were the number of arrests that the RAF held a crisis meeting on 26 December 1970. The eight present included Baader, Meinhof and Ensslin as well as Holger Meins and Jan-Carl Raspe, both of whom were to play a huge role in the RAF during the years to come. Meinhof argued for better planning and organisation and an evaluation process when something went wrong, but she was shouted down by Baader whose drive for action without analysis eventually held sway. Stefan Aust sums up the position at the end of 1970 as follows:

> This was the end of the training phase of urban guerrilla warfare. No one could guess that the RAF would keep the country on edge for decades. The underground battle was developing its own dynamic. It was never the group as a whole that determined the course of events, it was Baader and Ensslin … Illegality became an end in itself, the means of holding the group together. (*ibid.* p. 99)

At first sight, it may seem odd that the RAF emerged just at the time when, thanks to Chancellor Willy Brandt, relations were warming between West Germany and the Eastern European countries with whom it had been at odds for a quarter of a century. On 19 March 1970 he visited the East German Prime Minister, Willi Stoph, at Erfurt, the first time the leaders of West and East Germany had met since 1949. Stoph reciprocated on 21

May by coming to the West German city of Kassel, although the occasion was nearly ruined when what sounded like a gunshot rang out: fortunately, it was nothing worse than a car backfiring. On 12 August, Brandt signed a pact of friendship with the Soviet Union and on 18 November he concluded a peace treaty with Poland confirming the existing border between the two countries, and in a spontaneous gesture he fell to his knees at the memorial to the Warsaw Ghetto Uprising of 1943.

Yet while Brandt was looking to the future, the RAF were focussed on the past, or at least how it had shaped the present. They believed that what they perceived as the violence of the state – repression of student protest, support for the Vietnam War, tolerance of Nazism and ex-Nazis, encouragement of right-wing regimes – must be met by a violent response, in effect, terrorism. Martina Gedeck, who played Ulrike Meinhof in the film version of *The Baader-Meinhof Complex,* says that the RAF were

> acting on behalf of their parents' generation, like it was some sort of revenge war game, or they were paying off some kind of debt, but they were also acting it out for themselves. (Documentary *On Uli Edel*)

Despite their violent tactics, they struck a chord with the German public. Stefan Aust reports the findings of the Allensbacher Institute of Public Opinion survey *The Baader-Meinhof group: criminals or heroes?* in which one in ten North Germans said they would shelter fugitive underground fighters overnight, and one in four respondents under 30 felt 'a certain sympathy' for the RAF. Despite a campaign of terror which led to 34 deaths, this support held up, peaking when any perceived injustice was perpetrated against one of their number.

However, it is hard to avoid the feeling that, whatever the merits of their original stance against the forces of authority, the RAF became trapped in a vicious circle of violence that got increasingly out of hand. Once they were committed to the agenda, they could not withdraw from it. In doing so, they forfeited the moral high ground: as the 1970s unfolded, their activities became ever more extreme.

At the beginning they seemed to delight in the havoc they wrought, especially Baader. There are perhaps some parallels with the Manson Family who had gloried in the gruesome murders they committed in 1969. The motivations of the two groups were not dissimilar, even if they came from diametrically opposed ends of the ideological spectrum. Manson was a racist, who wanted to provoke a war (which he called 'Helter Skelter') between black and white: his intention was that the murders be pinned on the African-American community. Like Baader he attracted young women to his cause with a combination of charisma and intimidation. The violence employed by the RAF, however, at least had its source in sound principles, whereas Manson's philosophy– if one can call it that – was feeble and amoral. In contrast the RAF might be said to have taken morals to excess. As Stefan Aust stated in the documentary film *History In The Making*:

> People with an inflated moralistic sense of their mission completely lose sight of the fact that their own actions are blatantly immoral … the worst acts of violence through history have always taken place under the guise of morality.

Of course RAF sympathisers would argue, with some justification, that what they did was no worse than the atrocities committed by their opponents; but it was certainly no better. Furthermore the air of self-righteousness they exuded in earlier times became what appeared to be an addiction to their own notoriety. Perhaps it came with the realisation that they were now operating to different standards and rules: in effect they were living in a new world.

★ ★ ★ ★ ★

Rooted in the same commune culture that produced the Baader-Meinhof gang, Amon Düül II also inhabited that new world, rejecting the prevalent rock orthodoxy sourced in American blues, rhythm and blues and rock and roll. To some degree their music reflected an environment in which everyone was encouraged to play an instrument whether they knew how to or not. It was also far removed from the inanity of contemporary German pop. According to John Weinzerl, 'We had to come up with something new ... space was one solution'; guitarist and fellow founder-member Chris Karrer links the music with the politics: Amon Düül II had 'revolutionary ideology and visions'.

The band recorded their second album, *Yeti*, at Trixi Studios, Munich, at the beginning of 1970. Produced by the band with their manager, Olaf Kübler, it is a sprawling, open-ended epic which balances composition and improvisation, past and present: though looking back to psychedelia, it also prefigures punk. There is also a healthy dose of anarchy. It opens with the suite 'Soap Shop Rock' which consists of four pieces: the hard-driving 'Burning Sister' is a vision of hell, with incisive guitar and whining vocals that surely must have influenced Tom Verlaine of the new wave band Television; 'Halluzination Guillotine' is slower if equally nightmarish. 'Gulp: A Sonata' lasts just 46 seconds but the six-minute 'Flesh-Coloured Anti-Aircraft Alarm' is a dramatic, free-flowing piece featuring guitar and violin. The side ends with the acoustic, Eastern-flavoured 'She Came Through The Chimney'. Side Two explores yet more textures. 'Pale Gallery' is bleak and abstract, 'Cerberus' amounts to a crazed folk-dance, and 'Eye Shaking King' is dominated by electronic effects. 'The Return Of Rübezahl', takes up the Eastern feel, this time with electric instruments, while 'Archangel's Thunderbird', sung/wailed by Renate Knaup, has surreal, apocalyptic lyrics and ferocious accompaniment.

The album's centrepiece is the eighteen-minute 'Yeti (Improvisation)' which takes up the whole of Side Three. After a quiet start, electronic noises, bass, guitar and drums all come to the fore in turn; the piece then accelerates to a raga-like extemporisation before slowing to a melodic wah-wah guitar riff and soaring violin. On 'Yeti Talk To Yogi (Improvisation)' drums, bass and vocals are subjected to electronic effects before the whole track heads off in the direction of white noise. The closing 'Sandoz In The Rain (Improvisation)' is an intricate, shifting piece which features two guests from Amon Düül I, Rainer Bauer and Ulrich Leopold, as well as flautist Thomas Keyserling who had played on *Electronic Meditation*, the debut album by Berlin-based Tangerine Dream. Recorded in 1969, it was the first in over 200 record releases by a band whose impact on electronic dance music was on a par with that of Düsseldorfers Kraftwerk, who recorded their own eponymous debut album in 1970; at that stage, however, they sounded more like Jethro Tull on speed.

For Amon Düül II and Tangerine Dream the great advantage of electronic music was that, in least in rock music terms, there was little or no previous history, so it could be created without deference, or reference, to any of the icons from America or Britain – it really was a new musical world. As the composer Klaus Schulze, a fleeting member of Tangerine Dream, related in the documentary *Krautrock*: 'The War had one positive point – there was nothing else to lose'; for Wolfgang Seidel of Ton Steine Scherben it represented 'a sort of promise that there is a way out of the surrounding society'. So electronic music was both personally and politically significant for young Germans at the turn of the 1970s.

Paradoxically, however, the most revolutionary sounds emanated from a band who, as far as one can tell, were carrying out their experiments for purely musical reasons. Can (or The Can, as they were known in their early days) were formed in Cologne in 1968 by Irmin Schmidt, Holger Czukay and David C Johnson, all of whom had studied with the eminent contemporary composer, Karlheinz Stockhausen. Czukay wanted to be a composer, too, but was failing his exams, so in a typical illogical-yet-logical gesture Stockhausen took him under his wing, and Czukay thus had access to the obsolete recording equipment donated to Stockhausen by a local radio station. Schmidt felt they could create an unprecedented blend of avant garde classical music, jazz and rock, though Johnson didn't share his vision, and left the group, which by now also included one of Czukay's students, guitarist Michael Karoli (sometimes spelled Caroli), the jazz drummer Jaki Liebezeit and the American vocalist Malcolm Mooney. It was this line-up that recorded the first Can album, *Monster Movie*, in 1969.

The title may not have been deliberately solicitous, but offers from film-makers poured in, so much so that the follow-up album could be called, with complete veracity, *Soundtracks*. Released in September 1970, it contains music from no fewer than five films; however it is no exaggeration to say that the music has outlasted them all. Two pieces were recorded before Mooney left the group, the bluesy chant, 'Soul Desert' (from *Mädchen Mit Gewalt*, released in the US as *The Brutes*), and 'She Brings The Rain', a low-key jazz piece, featuring guitar, violin and walking bass, which has appeared in a total of four films to date.

However the real quality lies in the compositions recorded after the recruitment of Japanese vocalist Damo Suzuki in May 1970. Suzuki was busking in a Munich street when he was invited by Czukay and Liebezeit to perform with the band the same night at the Blow Up club. A few weeks later he was singing on 'Don't Turn The Light On, Leave Me Alone', used in the film *Cream*. His mumblings enhance the brooding atmosphere of a piece which integrates percussion, bass, acoustic guitar and flute into a single, relentless flow. 'Mother Sky', from *Deep End*, is a high-energy workout showcasing Karoli's sinuous playing: in 2005 Q magazine named it as one of the top 50 guitar tracks of all time. Also worthy of note are Suzuki's gentle vocals, Czukay's probing bass and the way in which Liebezeit leads the piece from extreme intensity to a cool finale. The balance of the album comes from the western *Deadlock*. The title music is slow and stately with yearning guitar and thumping drums while the track entitled 'Deadlock' provides variations on the same theme. 'Tango Whiskyman' is an early manifestation of Liebezeit's signature drum technique: playing freely around the tom-toms and side drum (with the snare turned off) he sets up a hypnotic groove effect redolent of African percussion. As Schmidt had foreseen, this was music which combined an array of styles and traditions so seamlessly that they forfeited separate identities to become part of something entirely new.

Meanwhile in the UK it was becoming increasingly difficult to find such creativity. Whereas Amon Düül II, Tangerine Dream and Can were able to ignore the blues-rock tradition, British bands were frequently shackled by it. This did not make for poor musicianship – on the contrary, standards of playing were higher than ever – but the formula of guitar-hero plus histrionic vocalist and heavy backing band was beginning to wear thin. From this straitjacketed position, few were able to comment on what was going on in the world around them, though one band who did were The Groundhogs.

Thank Christ For The Bomb, released in June 1970, came as a surprise for a number of reasons. The Groundhogs had been operating for years as the quintessential British blues band, traversing the college circuit and occasionally sharing the bill on blues package tours with the likes of John Lee Hooker. Their guitarist, Tony McPhee, was known for his technical ability and had recorded an excellent acoustic version of Rosco Gordon's 'No More Doggin'' a couple of years before. However everything he, and they, did was ultimately derivative. *Thank Christ For The Bomb*, composed in its entirety by McPhee, launched them into unchartered waters. To begin with, the cover design, by artist Alan Tanner, was striking. By portraying the band in World War I uniforms, he reinforced the message contained inside: that war is eternal – and dehumanising. 'Soldier', for example, describes how the enemy are no longer seen as men but 'enemies of the King' while the title track is a sardonic comment on the way nuclear weapons are invoked as means of preserving peace. Yet more prevalent is the theme of alienation and its antidote, drop-out. McPhee describes how the experience of a 'Strange Town', where difference is not tolerated, leads to the rejection of 'Status People', and a carefree existence as an 'Eccentric Man'. In 'Garden' he even manages to weave in an environmental theme:

> But I'm not going to cut a single blade of grass, my garden will look just
>   like the distant past,
> Before the days of agricultural land, before the time when pebbles turned
>   to sand.
> When I leave this house I'm going to stay, I'm forsaking my comforts to
>   live another way,
> Get my clothes from heaps, my food from bins, my water from ponds and
>   have tramps for all my friends.

As for the music, this too is an evolution from blues-rock, if a limited one. Simple, incisive riffs ('Garden' has the best), sledgehammer drums, throbbing bass and squally guitar comprise the staple menu, so subtle it ain't. In any case The Groundhogs, a guitar trio, were unable, and possibly incapable, of producing the variety and virtuosity of bands such as King Crimson, The Nice and Pink Floyd, who were using multiple keyboards, horn sections and, occasionally, full scale symphony orchestras. However its subject-matter, arrangements, production values (the fashionable De Lane Lea Studios were chosen with this in mind) and packaging place it firmly in prog territory.

Thank Christ For The Bomb represents, albeit inadvertently, exactly where British rock had reached in 1970: rooted in blues, with a heavy element of prog; social comment alongside more personal songs of innocence and experience. As the year progressed, however, that balance began to shift, not just in the UK but across the rock songwriting world. Global concerns gave way to individual agendas, macro became micro and selfless switched to selfish. Let's see exactly what happened and why.

CHAPTER 4:

I Me Mine

The UK General Election of 1970 was the first in which eighteen-year-olds were allowed to vote. The Representation of the People Act 1969 had been brought in by the then Labour government, perhaps in the hope that younger people would gravitate towards its policies. However if that was the intention, it backfired, since in 1970 the Conservatives achieved an overall majority of 30 seats. The electorate, owing to the extension of suffrage, had grown by over a million, though the turnout actually fell, by 3%. Labour received 12.2 million votes, exactly the same as in their winning campaign of 1964, and that should, therefore, have given them a similar result. They came to grief, however, in the marginal seats, thwarted by a last-minute surge in Tory support. As we saw in Chapter 1, there were various reasons for this, but among the most important was the continued influence, despite his expulsion from the Shadow Cabinet, of Enoch Powell.

Periodically over the last 50 years, Britain has been engulfed in a wave of anti-immigration paranoia. In 2013 the focus was on illegal immigrants and asylum seekers, and the Conservative-Liberal Democrat coalition reacted by sending a fleet of vans through London calling on such people to return to their native countries. Back in 1970 the same message was addressed to immigrants from the Caribbean, India and Pakistan though this time it was transmitted from outside government. The stance of Powell and his supporters was far from official policy yet they held an enormous amount of sway both within the Conservative Party and in the country as a whole. At the Tory conference of October 1969, for example, the Party's line on immigration was passed by only 395, a slim majority given that 4,000 delegates were eligible to vote. Not long afterwards, there was a series of challenges to left-wing Conservative MPs by constituency members representing the Powellite faction. As Robin Oakley and Peter Rose recall in *The Political Year 1970*,

> The case which captured the headlines was that of Surbiton's MP, Mr Nigel Fisher, whose opponents were derided by the Prime Minister [Harold Wilson] as "skinheads". Centring their opposition on Mr Fisher's views on race, immigration and Rhodesia, a group of five rebels built up support for a campaign to unseat him and demanded a referendum of the local Conservative Association as to whether they were satisfied that Mr Fisher adequately represented their views. (p. 142-3)

In the end opposition to Fisher petered out, but the incident, seized on by Labour as a Tory swing to the Right, became known, inevitably, as the Skinheads Affair.

1970 was the mid-point of the first, and by far the most significant, manifestation of the skinhead youth sub-cult. It is not known whether they turned out in force at the General Election, though it is certain that many skinheads were fervent supporters of Enoch Powell and his anti-immigration message. Indeed, even Powell was too moderate for some, who drifted towards the right-wing extremist National Front party, formed just a couple of years before.

Yet further investigation of the skinheads reveals that they were more heterogeneous politically than might be imagined. The common bond was not so much party politics as a sense of loyalty to their class, their city and their country. Admittedly, these were often exhibited in football hooliganism and racial violence, just about the skinheads' only outlets: invariably poorly educated and in low-skilled jobs, they tended to lack alternative vehicles for self-expression.

Skinheads had their origin in the mod sub-cult of the early 1960s, itself a product of UK working-class, inner-city culture. Around 1965, the mods began to orientate to one of two camps. The first took the all-consuming sartorial obsession in a more flamboyant direction, symbolised by leading mod band The Kinks, who began to wear frilly shirts and waisted jackets – the sort of styles, in fact, that shortly afterwards became associated with Carnaby Street, a scene which was eventually satirised by The Kinks themselves in 'Dedicated Follower Of Fashion' (1966). This sort of dandyism was too close to the pretentious, artsy world of the middle classes for many mods whose response was to retrench into an inward-looking attitude that reflected, and in time celebrated, their working-class environment. Again, the preoccupation with clothing was pushed to its extreme, but this time in the very opposite direction: minimalism. Cropped hair, T-shirts/no shirts, turned up jeans and industrial boots were all practical essentials for the manual worker and thus became the basic skinhead uniform.

Yet the working garb was no mere fashion accessory. The skinheads had an all-embracing, organic relationship with their culture. As Nick Knight has written,

> Attitudes to parents, school and the police were not specifically skinhead, but like that of other working class youths. Being a skin did not normally imply a break with your family. Mothers welcomed the short hair because it presented less problems than long hair. Fathers liked the style because it was neat and workmanlike. Unlike the families of middle class dropouts, skinhead families were generally supportive, helping with money and acting as some sort of barrier against school and the police. A skin would normally live at home.
> (*Skinhead*, p. 21)

Of course the racism displayed by the skinheads was also a function of the same culture, or at least a minority aspect of it (regrettably, the stain of racism runs through the entire British class system). That the skinheads' musical taste was centred on Caribbean styles may therefore seem paradoxical. Part of this was no doubt rooted in the working-class ability to get along with one's neighbours in spite of ethnic and cultural differences. But adopting ska, rocksteady and ultimately reggae also helped to distance them from hippies, students and the middle classes generally. For these styles were derided in such quarters as repetitive and simplistic, particularly by an ignorant and ill-informed British music press (which later, just as it had done with blues, was to perform a spectacular U-turn). Above all, reggae was the ultimate music of the dispossessed, made by and for people with nothing to their name and with little prospect of gaining very much.

In the discography appended to *Skinhead*, Harry Hawke makes his selection of the best and most popular records among skinheads in 1970. Many of them reflect what was happening at the cutting edge of Jamaican music, in particular the rise of the deejay. Ever since the ska period of the early 1960s deejays at dances had, while the records were playing, added their own comments, statements, ejaculations and catch phrases which, in time, were incorporated into the piece itself during recording. One of the first deejays to issue singles on this basis was King Stitt, and it is his lively 'Herbsman' (made with Andy Capp) that makes the top of Hawke's list. As Stitt recalled for *Reggae: The Rough Guide,*

> Down at the studio, Dynamic, they was playing, redoing, "Beardman Ska", and at that time you had an engineer by the name of Lynford Anderson – they call him Andy Capp. The tune was playing, now, and one of my friends in the studio made a big spliff. And I took the spliff from him, and light it, and I just say, "Smoking is a habit." And Andy Capp say, "Drag it! Crab it!" That was how "Herbman Shuffle" was born. (p. 115)

U-Roy was one of the first deejays to make a success of the new methodology; his 'Rule The Nation' is number seven on Hawke's chart.

> I do the first two tune for him [producer Duke Reid] – "Wake The Town" and "Rule The Nation" ... we never thought people would

ever make money out of this deejay business, talking over records …
The two tunes come out and play on the radio a lot, until they reach
number one and two. That was a big surprise. I was never checking
for that. (*ibid*., p. 117)

'Rule The Nation' has more than a hint of dub, which as tempos began to
decelerate, became more prominent in reggae, whereupon the skinheads
began to lose interest: dub was too slow for their liking and, even worse, too
arty. But in 1970 it was an exciting new sound and part of the mix of the
traditional and the innovatory that characterises Hawke's list. Thus alongside
the orthodox rocksteady balladry of John Holt ('Love I Can Feel') and Alton
Ellis ('Remember That Sunday') we find the soul-influenced Maytals with
'Monkey Man'; the formidable coupling of The Upsetters' instrumental
'Vampire' and 'Check Him Out' by The Bleechers; Count Sticky and The
Upsetters' powerful 'Dry Acid'; and the gentle 'Duppy Conqueror' by The
Wailers – the latter four records all produced by Lee 'Scratch' Perry.

During the first half of 1970 The Wailers worked with Leslie Kong at
Dynamic Sounds in Kingston and the outcome was extremely satisfactory.
In June, for example, they recorded 'Back Out', 'Soul Shake Down Party'
and 'Do It Twice', all Bob Marley compositions and cleanly produced by
Kong, capturing their rhythmically tight yet rolling ensemble sound. Lee
Perry, however, gave them additional dimensions. 'Soul Rebel' gains depth
from the echo on the vocals and 'Sun Is Shining' is memorable for the
presence of the melodica, an early appearance on record for this wind-
operated keyboard instrument that became such a feature of Jamaican
music in the early 1970s. On the other hand, 'Don't Rock The Boat' is
sparse, almost minimalist, with bass guitar prominent; 'Small Axe' quietly
introduces horns and piano and 'Mr Brown' features some creepy sonic
effects. Admittedly these songs, again all written by Marley, tend to be more
profound than those made with Kong – 'Small Axe', for instance, is a clever
attack on the dominating forces of the island's recording industry – but
Perry's ingenuity lifts them to a new level, so much so that in August the
band asked him if he would make a whole album with them.

The result was *Soul Rebels*, the first Wailers album to be released outside Jamaica. Like the other Perry-produced tracks, it was recorded at Randy's Studio 17 in Kingston: sessions continued until November and the record was released the following month. Whether due to Perry's influence or not, the band at this time displays a remarkable rhythmic feel, holding slow tempos hypnotically and stretching the beat to create extra tension. Perry emphasises these features further with a spartan production that lets the music do the talking. Much of this is American-flavoured. 'My Cup' is a remake of James Brown's 'I Guess I'll Have To Cry, Cry, Cry'; 'Soul Almighty', though it verges on rock, has echoes of 'Land Of 1000 Dances'; 'It's Alright' recalls Otis Redding's 'Respect'; and 'Rebel's Hop' is a medley of what was happening in contemporary soul music with elements by Curtis Mayfield, Barrett Strong and Norman Whitfield. In contrast, 'Try Me' amounts to a resume of recent Jamaican styles, with strains of ska, rocksteady and reggae. But while all these tracks in their various ways filter existing or past idioms, two tracks are clear pointers to the future. Marley's 'Corner Stone' uses striking imagery to comment on love and on life, while Peter Tosh's '400 Years' is a powerful condemnation of oppression, ignorance and racism which set the tone for vast swathes of reggae in the 1970s. With such compositions Marley and Tosh began to demonstrate a view of the world that was moving away from songs about self. Most contemporary singer/songwriters were, however, heading in exactly the opposite direction.

★ ★ ★ ★ ★

In 1970 young people's disaffection with the forces of authority had reached such a pitch that there were two basic alternatives: retreat or stay and fight. Chapters 2 and 3 demonstrated how the latter option played out in the USA, UK and across Europe. Those who took the former course went down one of two paths (although some traversed both). One was to escape into a fantasy world in which reality could be put on hold or ignored altogether; this route will be discussed at length in Chapter 5. The other was to become ever-more inward looking and preoccupied with the personal rather than the social or political.

In 1964 Bob Dylan had turned his back on protest singing, in favour of what were, in the main, love songs or at least compositions that focussed on individual concerns and circumstances. His new music proved even more popular than the old and established a template which was followed by a new generation of singer-songwriters. Escalating events in Vietnam galvanised many of these into anti-war rhetoric but by the end of the decade most were on the verge of making their own transition into relationship-based material, or had done so already.

We have already seen how David Crosby, Stephen Stills, Graham Nash and Neil Young offered a mixed thematic diet both separately and collectively. Of the songs on their album *Déjà Vu* the ratio of political to personal was 2:9, the two being Crosby's 'Almost Cut My Hair' and 'Woodstock' by Joni Mitchell, the Canadian singer-songwriter with whom the band were closely associated. On Mitchell's own 1970 album, *Ladies Of The Canyon,* the ratio was very similar, 2:10. Again, one of the two is 'Woodstock' though unlike the rather perfunctory CSNY version, this is a rendition of enormous distinction, one of Mitchell's best-ever recordings and among the finest tracks of the year.

For a song celebrating such a momentous occasion the mood is surprisingly sombre: the pace is funereal, her self-accompaniment on electric piano stark and unsettling – all of which reflects what was, in Mitchell's eyes, an awe-inspiring event, transcending a mere rock festival to become an occasion of historical significance. As she sings, 'Maybe it's just the time of year but maybe it's the time of man.' The narrative is a compelling vision of what the new world could, indeed, must be: a return to the genuine nature of mankind ('we are stardust, we are golden'), free of war and the horrors of progess ('we've got to get ourselves back to the garden'). The piece concludes with an eerie wordless chant and the poignant piano melody with which it began, confirmation that Mitchell was not seeking cosy commercialism here – how easy it would have been to omit this section – but attempting a statement of some gravitas. This spine-chilling climax is the proof that she has succeeded.

With the listener's emotions still running high, Mitchell delivers the knockout punch with the next, and final, track, 'The Circle Game', a touching and at times heart-rending account of the cycle of the seasons, and of life. Earlier in the record there is also much to admire: the cheery portrait of small-town America, 'Morning Morgantown'; 'For Free', which contrasts her wealth and fame with the street musician who has neither; and 'Big Yellow Taxi', one of the earliest environmentalist rock songs only spoilt by the forced laughter at the end. The title track is also an impressive achievement, a portrayal of three notable women which has strong feminist overtones. Singer-songwriters of this period are often maligned for their confessional inclinations and, in particular, their veiled references to other celebrities with whom they were having – or, more usually, had recently had – a relationship. Here there is 'The Conversation' (subject unspecified) and 'Willy', Mitchell's paean to Graham Nash. Though beautifully written, both sail close to sentimentality and to modern ears can be hard to take. Yet they are just part of the varied canvas Mitchell presents on *Ladies Of The Canyon*, the first in a series – also comprising *Blue*, *For The Roses* and *Court And Spark* – as good as any sequence of four albums by any major rock artist. Yet while her songs about relationships reached new levels of expressiveness, those about anything else began to disappear.

Like the CSNY and Mitchell albums, Melanie's *Candles In The Rain* presented an assortment of topics but, if anything, was wider in its scope. Certainly she remained committed politically – she was the only artist to defy the injunction which in effect cancelled the Powder Ridge festival in Middlefield, Connecticut, scheduled to take place between 31 July and 2 August 1970. The bill was to have included some of the biggest names in rock, many of whom – Sly and The Family Stone, John Sebastian, Joe Cocker, Mountain, Ten Years After and Richie Havens – had appeared at Woodstock. Despite the ban 30,000 fans turned up at the site, as did Melanie who performed for free on a makeshift stage with power supplied by a Mister Softee ice-cream van.

Melanie herself had played Woodstock and, inspired by the matches lit by the crowd during her set there, wrote 'Candles In The Rain' and 'Lay Down' which appear as a mini-suite at the start of *Candles In The Rain.* An a cappella chant and brief sung verse establish a spiritual mood which continues into full-blown gospel, powered by The Edwin Hawkins Singers and pierced by Melanie's ecstatic exhortations. Her voice is naive, almost childlike (though tinged with melancholy) and a major part of her appeal lies in the way in which that apparent lack of sophistication allows her to get straight to the heart of her material. So the same figure who adapts the children's poem 'Forgiven' by AA Milne as 'Alexander Beetle' can also query urbanisation in 'Citiest People', sound genuinely homesick on James Taylor's 'Carolina In My Mind' and find tender new dimensions in 'Ruby Tuesday', regretful where The Rolling Stones' original exuded condescension and cynicism. On 'What Have They Done To My Song Ma', she even contrives to shroud a song about repression in a cloak of self-mockery.

For reasons that seem hard to explain (possibly anti-East Coast prejudice), New Yorker Laura Nyro received a hostile reception from the crowd at the seminal Monterey Pop Festival of 1967. Yet her political credentials were sound; in response to the assassination of Robert Kennedy, she wrote 'Save The Country', a US Top 30 hit for the 5th Dimension in June 1970. *Christmas And The Beads Of Sweat,* which came out six months later, completed a trilogy of albums considered to be her definitive work. But although it derives elements from its predecessors, *Eli And The Thirteenth Confession* and *New York Tendaberry,* it has an atmosphere all of its own and, like the Mitchell and Melanie albums, maintains a balance – in Nyro's case, between the subjective and the objective, the observed and the experienced, the personal and the political. Thus 'Brown Earth' and 'Blackpatch' are sharply drawn depictions of street life and 'Been On A Train' is a bleak dirge denouncing hard drugs. 'Map To The Treasure' is a love song, while Gerry Goffin and Carole King's 'Up On The Roof' gives literal and metaphorical perspective. There is textural variety, too: the outstanding 'Upstairs By A Chinese Lamp' features Joe Farrell on flute and

Alice Coltrane on harp, and Duane Allman contributes rocking guitar to 'Beads Of Sweat'. But it is the singer's own dramatic piano-playing that provides the most fitting accompaniment to her highly wrought, impassioned songs, nowhere more effectively than on the closing, climactic 'Christmas In My Soul': it is here that Nyro reaffirms that political rock was not quite dead in 1970:

> I love my country
> As it dies
> In war and peace
> Before my eyes
> Black Panther brothers
> Bound in jail
> Chicago Seven
> And the justice scale
> Homeless Indian
> Of Manhattan Isle
> All God's sons have gone to trial
> And all God's love is out of style
> On Christmas

★ ★ ★ ★ ★

As the singer-songwriters looked ever inward, so they began to explore issues, and express feelings, of a deeper, darker character. Much of this was to do with the anguish stemming from the break-up of a relationship, though not exclusively so; some of the scenarios painted were often well out of range of orthodox pop or rock material. Bereavement, mental illness and child abuse were, for example, all the subject of songs in 1970 – themes that would have been unthinkable just a year or two earlier.

In the case of Nico's album *Desertshore*, the gloomy nature of the lyrics is matched by the doom-laden instrumentation; her own swirling harmonium and producer John Cale's trenchant viola help create the gothic, almost supernatural atmosphere that pervades the record. 'Janitor Of Lunacy' is a requiem for Nico's former boyfriend, Brian Jones of The Rolling Stones, who had drowned in a swimming pool the previous July; 'Abschied' ('Farewell') and 'Mütterlein' ('Matriarch') are for her deceased mother. The words to 'The Falconer' are more positive though the medieval imagery and lugubrious pace drag it down and 'Le Petit Chavalier', though rendered by a child, contains the sinister promise 'J'irai te visiter' ('I am going to visit you'). Finally, there are masochistic undertones in both 'Afraid' and 'All That Is My Own': the former counsels complete subjugation to another's will, while the latter paints a terrifying picture, sharpened by sonic effects, of a relationship in which her whole personality has been moulded by her partner and yet, 'Your ways have led me to bleed'.

Desertshore, for all its emotional power and artistic unity, failed to trouble the chart compilers on either side of the Atlantic. Not so James Taylor's *Sweet Baby James*, an album in which the ambience could scarcely have been more dissimilar but which also dealt with some disturbing issues. In reaching number three (US) and number seven (UK) on the album charts, it established Taylor as an international star and led to a coveted appearance on the cover of *Time* magazine. It was in fact, Taylor's second album. The first, *James Taylor*, had been released on The Beatles' Apple label two years earlier. He had come to London in part to put his past behind him: as a teenager he had been diagnosed with depression and spent nine months at the McLean psychiatric hospital in Belmont, Massachusetts; shortly afterwards he became hooked on heroin while playing in The Flying Machine, a band he formed in New York with guitarist Danny Kortchmar.

Through Kortchmar, whose band The King Bees had once supported Peter and Gordon, Taylor was able to give tapes of his music to Peter Asher, then Head of A&R at Apple. Both Asher and Paul McCartney were impressed with what they heard but Taylor lapsed back into heroin use and was unable to promote the album adequately. Following his return to the US he succeeded in kicking his habit and, with Asher producing, recorded

Sweet Baby James. Kortchmar was recruited into a backing group that included top studio musicians such as bassist Leland Sklar and drummer Russ Kunkel as well as Carole King who with her husband, Gerry Goffin, comprised one of the great pop songwriting teams of the 1960s. King was shortly to re-launch her career in spectacular fashion though on this occasion was content merely to play piano.

Sweet Baby James is notable for the clean simplicity of the production and of the music, a gentle fusion of folk, blues and country. Taylor's warm voice creates a feel of intimacy and approachability which is enhanced by his portrayal on the sleeve as a handsome, clean-shaven young man in a denim shirt – yes, with long hair, but not too long. All of this made the album stand out like a beacon from the noisy furore characteristic of so much contemporary rock and soul: released in February 1970, it created a blueprint for singer-songwriters to follow both for the rest of the year and beyond. Much of the appeal lay, too, in the autobiographical nature of the content, with all of its highs and, especially, lows.

For instance, 'Fire And Rain', a number three hit single in America, conveys the generality of his experience in getting past his mental health and drug-use issues as well as alluding to some poignant specifics. The 'Suzanne' referred to is his friend Suzanne Schnerr who committed suicide while Taylor was in London: he was not told of her death until later ('just yesterday morning') for fear of distracting him from making his debut album. It also mentions The Flying Machine which like his 'sweet dreams' was 'left in pieces on the ground' by his heroin addiction. 'Country Road' is about the highway adjacent to the McLean hospital while the title track, ostensibly a lullaby for his nephew, refers to the turnpike from Stockbridge to Boston, Stockbridge being the location of the Austen Riggs Center to which Taylor committed himself on his return from the UK.

The combination of such subject-matter and Taylor's relaxed, mild-mannered delivery means that the album is frequently on an emotional knife edge: even superficially happy songs like 'Sunny Skies' and 'Blossom' are invested with melancholy and his delightful version of the Stephen Foster standard 'Oh Susannah' brings a touching new dimension.

Occasionally, however, optimism wins out, as in the gospel number 'Lo And Behold' and the affectionate blues pastiches 'Steamroller' and 'Oh Baby, Don't You Loose Your Lip On Me'. In contrast, 'Anywhere Like Heaven' overlays a love song with social comment by contrasting the rural idyll with the oppressed, uptight inhabitants of the city. Perhaps the greatest achievement of all is the closing 'Suite For 20G', its title an allusion to the $20,000 he would receive from Warner Brothers on delivery of the completed album. With no songs available to wrap it up, Taylor combined three previously unfinished compositions to make a suite which, as it turns out, is an artistic triumph: punctuated by guitar and piano solos, it glides seamlessly between themes, sections and moods, ending with an exultant slab of R&B.

On the face of it, Dory Previn's *On My Way To Where*, released in July 1970, evinces a similar balance to *Sweet Baby James*, that is, autobiographical songs of various types and moods.

Previn, however, operates at a more intense level. In Taylor's work there are references aplenty to places, events and people involved in his traumas but very little description of what being an addict or suffering from depression is actually like. Previn, on the other hand, introduces us to a cast of characters, including herself, who only too graphically reflect the reality of both suffering and inflicting unhappiness.

In 1969 Previn had split with her husband, the composer and conductor André Previn, following his affair with and impregnation of Mia Farrow (their divorce became final the same month *On My Way To Where* came out). 'Beware Of Young Girls' relates how Farrow inveigled herself into the Previns' home, befriending them, flattering them and then going off with André. 'Scared To Be Alone' contains no specific references to the break-up though the implications are clear; 'He Lives Alone' sees loneliness from another angle. There are songs, too, about what it means to be rejected: 'I Ain't His Child' and 'Michael Michael', the All American Boy whose mother wanted a girl and who now pushes drugs. Michael's female counterpart is the protagonist of 'Esther's First Communion', a humorous tale of a good girl gone bad, and the comedy continues into

'Twenty-Mile Zone' which has Previn picked up by the police for screaming in her car. More subtle is 'The Veterans Big Parade', a celebration of war heroes in which 'all the widows proudly smiled, except for one with an infant child'.

But it is the last track on each side that administers the emotional coup de grace. 'With My Daddy In The Attic' takes on the previously taboo issue of child abuse, its narrative made all the more harrowing by the touches of detail – 'the mattress ticking showing and the tattered pillow slip', 'he'll play his clarinet when I despair' – and the tense, insistent musical backdrop. 'Mister Whisper' is an account of creeping insanity: the visions, the voices and the imaginary friend are conveyed by an unnerving passage in which Previn's spoken voice is electronically processed, dismembered and merged with her singing; then comes the denouement, the sudden realisation that 'I paid my airplane fare, I was on my way to … where?' These two songs took Previn into compositional territory occupied by very few singer-songwriters in 1970. Yet unlike artists such as Nico and John Lennon, both of whom went to similar extremes, Previn attempted to lift the mood with the occasional use of humour.

* * * * *

Proof that humour could be used more extensively without compromising seriousness of purpose or emotional intensity was provided by Loudon Wainwright III whose eponymous album was one of the best debut releases of the year. Unlike *On My Way To Where*, in which Previn was backed by the cream of Los Angeles session musicians, here we have Wainwright with only his acoustic guitar to accompany his unique nasal drawl, capable of expressing wonder, pathos and desperation – sometimes in the course of the same song. In the autobiographical 'School Days', for example, he lists his teenage fantasies with a mixture of awe and horror; there is also nostalgia in the refrain 'in Delaware, when I was younger'. 'Hospital Lady' is a portrait of an elderly patient, approaching death, who was 'once a young girl, don't forget that'; the clarity of Wainwright's observation is much enhanced by his use of colours – pink, red, blue and green – to describe the scene, though the song turns rather sour as he moves from affection to brutal reality. Heavy irony pervades his depictions of Pittsburgh ('Ode To A Pittsburgh') and New York ('Uptown'), but in 'I Don't Care', in which he admonishes the lover for whom he is affecting no longer to have feelings to 'go to San Francisco, we all know what happens there', the joke is on the speaker, not the city. 'Movies Are A Mother To Me' gives a clue to an important aspect of Wainwright's *modus operandi*: 'Central Square Song' is a cinematic portrayal of two blissful drunken lovers, with intervals of wordless chanting supplying the soundtrack, and 'Bruno's Place' is populated by larger-than-life characters who would be quite at home in a sitcom. The latter also lampoons the then fashionable you-are-what-you-eat philosophy with the despairing cry 'I don't eat meat, it's bad for my feet'. Elsewhere, Wainwright is severe on more commonly held beliefs. 'Glad To See You Got Religion' is acerbically dismissive, 'Four Is A Magic Number' mocks superstition, and 'Black Uncle Remus' satirises the perennial stereotypes of the African-American.

Wainwright's unconventional subject-matter, distinctive voice and biting wit immediately earned him accolades from the critics though not, alas, from the record-buying public – a fate suffered, too, at least at this stage – by the most original songwriter to emerge since Bob Dylan, Randy Newman. A multitude of stars had covered songs from his 1968 debut *Randy Newman*, especially the bleak 'I Think It's Going To Rain Today' but the album itself was a commercial flop. Hopes that things might improve were raised by *Nilsson Sings Newman* – a collection of his compositions sung by Harry Nilsson and released in February 1970. Five months earlier Nilsson had reached number six on the US chart with 'Everybody's Talkin'' from the hit film *Midnight Cowboy* and was seen as one of the up-and-coming talents on the US pop scene. But even his name failed to elevate Newman to a level beyond the cult success he was already enjoying; indeed the record was less then helpful to Nilsson's own career, according to undercover research carried out by Newman himself:

"I went into a shop to see how the album was selling in LA," Newman explained to Keith Altham of the New Musical Express. "This assistant comes up and asks if he can help. 'Sure,' I say. 'Do you have any Nilsson albums?' He goes through 'em all one by one, saying how well they are selling and how he can recommend this one and that one. Then he comes to Nilsson Sings Newman and says, 'And this is the one that nearly finished him off'". (Kevin Courrier, *Randy Newman's American Dreams*, p. 122)

It is certain that Newman would have delighted in that story: sardonic, self-deprecating and swift to see the funny side of things, he specialised in songs that deflated bombast and took the side of defenceless and the dispossessed. Nilsson captures something of the essence of them on *Nilsson Sings Newman*. For example, 'Cowboy', a song about the decline and death of the old ways of life, is given an austere setting which begins with Nilsson's solo voice accompanied only by a howling wind. 'So Long Dad' describes a son's brief visit to his lonely father, his hearty platitudes barely masking a desire to get away as soon as possible; 'Living Without You' is about dealing with the tedium of everyday life after a break-up. Nilsson respects the meaning of both compositions while imposing his own vocal style and arrangement. The more orthodox love song 'Caroline' was specially written by Newman for the album and so it is not surprising that it works best of all – in fact it was considered commercial enough to be released as a single, though it failed to chart.

Other tracks are less successful. 'Love Story' begins as a vision of the ideal relationship, marriage and family, but the happiness turns to horror as it becomes clear that the protagonist is taking the tale to its logical conclusion – retirement, infirmity and death. Nilsson's version lacks Newman's edge and is generally too straight. The line referring to the son he expects to have, 'Someday he'll be president if things loosen up', needs the more ironic touch the composer gives it. Two years later Newman would record a delightful version of 'Dayton Ohio 1903', applying just the right amount of sentiment to stay on the acceptable side of nostalgia – here there is too much romanticism in Nilsson's voice, let alone the intrusion of Glenn Miller's 'Moonlight Serenade' which entirely dissipates the mood. In short, Newman's deadpan delivery, nuanced when necessary to comic or tragic effect, suited his compositions best.

Newman's *12 Songs* was released two months later and, in contrast, is a 100% success. The opening 'Have You Seen My Baby?', set to a full-blooded New Orleans rock and roll arrangement, tells of a woman on the loose; the next track, 'Let's Burn Down The Cornfield', could hardly present more of a contrast – slow and sinister, it features the sinuous slide guitar of Ry Cooder. 'Suzanne' is the first of five love songs – of a sort. The scenario is a real or imagined stalking of a prostitute, with the crawling tempo, barroom piano and ghostly organ reflecting the theme of obsession. 'Lover's Prayer' is a comic plea for a no-nonsense woman – not a kid, nor a raconteur, nor anyone unhinged, romantic or intellectual. With 'Rosemary' Newman comes as close to convention as anywhere on the album; 'Lucinda', however, is a dark and disquieting story of a dead body on the beach. In 'If You Need Oil' a lonely gas station attendant is the desperate protagonist.

Though not announced as such, tracks seven, eight and nine amount to a sort of suite satirising stereotyping and prejudice. Fun-loving, carefree African-Americans populate 'Underneath The Harlem Moon' while the more overtly sarcastic 'Yellow Man' assaults racism full on. In 1852 Stephen Foster wrote 'My Old Kentucky Home', a somewhat ingenuous account of life on a Southern plantation; here Newman responds with 'Old Kentucky Home', in which the bright tempo and jovial delivery belie the disturbing goings-on. Hideous Sister Sue is only let out at night and

Brother Gene is big and mean
And he don't have much to say
He had a little woman who he whupped each day
But now she's gone away
He got drunk last night
Kicked mama down the stair

But I'm alright so I don't care

Oh the sun shines bright on my old Kentucky home

'Uncle Bob's Midnight Blues', another piece with a rural feel, describes the ravings of a drunk.

Perhaps the best-known song on the album is 'Mama Told Me Not To Come', originally written for Eric Burdon but a huge international hit for Three Dog Night in the summer of 1970. Even at this distance, after hearing it by all three artists on multiple occasions, it is difficult not to chuckle at the indignation of the wide-eyed innocent experiencing the joys of his first wild party.

'Mama Told Me Not To Come' was the first track on *Randy Newman Live*, recorded between 17 and 19 September at the Bitter End East, New York City. Many of the songs date from an earlier period and/or have been discussed above though mention should be made of another unusual love song, 'Tickle Me', covered by Alan Price but not recorded elsewhere by Newman, and 'Last Night I Had A Dream' (more like a nightmare) and the merciless satire on the narcissism of the superstar, 'Lonely At The Top', both of which were to appear on his magnificent *Sail Away* album of 1972.

To round off a memorable year, Newman made an important contribution to the soundtrack of the film *Performance*, directed by Nicolas Roeg and starring James Fox and Mick Jagger. The musicians involved comprised many who also worked on *12 Songs*, including Ry Cooder and drummer Gene Parsons, and Jack Nitzsche, co-producer of 'Let's Burn Down The Cornfield', composed most of the music and arranged and produced it all. Newman sang and co-wrote, with Russ Titelman, the first track on the soundtrack album, 'Gone Dead Train', an up-tempo yet nihilistic piece; he also conducted the orchestra throughout the recordings. In a poll of 150 film experts, conducted in 2011 for the magazine *Time Out*, *Performance* was ranked the seventh best British film of all time.

Originality of conception, subject-matter and delivery were not the exclusive property of Wainwright and Newman. Tom Rapp, for instance, exhibited those same qualities on the album *The Use Of Ashes*. It was released in August as the third album by Pearls Before Swine, the band founded by Rapp five years earlier, but by then only he and his wife Elisabeth remained; so here they are backed by a coterie of top Nashville session musicians – an interesting development in itself, when most singer-songwriters seemed to be gravitating to Los Angeles. The record is dedicated to Elisabeth's native country, the Netherlands, where Rapp composed most of the songs. Though not a concept album as such, motifs of isolation, transience and insecurity run right through the record, but they are realised in a variety of ways. 'Song About A Rose', as the title suggests, uses natural imagery; 'When The War Began' bemoans the destruction of a couple's brief happiness; and 'Rocket Man' (on which the Elton John hit was based), written on the day of the US moon landing, depicts the physical and emotional alienation of a boy from his father. Not many songwriters were dealing with historical events at that time although 'Riegal', about the sinking of a wartime prison ship, is as much to do with how such tragedies are easily forgotten as it is about the incident itself. However the album's masterpiece is its opening track, 'The Jeweller'. There is more than a hint of metaphysical poetry in Rapp's portrayal of a craftsman whose spirituality overlaps with his profession and the memorable refrain 'He knows the use of ashes, he worships God with ashes' is reinforced with an arrangement which sweeps from gentle folk-rock to lavish orchestration.

Records like *The Use Of Ashes* gave further breadth to a genre that already encompassed a huge range of performers. At one extreme was the ultra-soft romantic rock of David Gates whose band Bread topped the US chart in August with 'Make It With You': at the other, serial killer Charles Manson's album *Lie: The Love And Terror Cult*, issued in March and containing his one memorable song, 'Look At Your Game, Girl'. Though there were occasional exceptions – Nico, Joni Mitchell, Neil Young – these were predominantly American artists forging a style of music which combined the narrative tradition reinvigorated by Bob Dylan with songs in which the main focus was themselves. At the same time, a sub-style had formed, headed by Randy Newman and Loudon Wainwright III, in which the writers saw the world as through a camera lens or assumed so many other identities that it was hard to know what their real persona was. As we have seen, however, this approach was doomed to commercial oblivion. What people wanted were the intimate details of the artists' real lives and the singer-songwriter boom of 1970 meant they were not disappointed.

★ ★ ★ ★ ★

Ever since the emergence of The Beatles and the other bands that followed them, the UK had taken America's place as the world's leading pop music nation. The 1960s British 'Invasion' of the US had come in two waves; the first was in 1964 in the wake of The Beatles' first tour of America, the second towards the end of the decade with prog/blues bands such as Cream, Led Zeppelin, Deep Purple and Jethro Tull. In 1970 Americans were yearning for a superstar to rival such acts, though this was not to come until five years later with the rise to glory of first Bruce Springsteen and then Michael Jackson.

Yet this is not to say American music was without influence: ironically, it was some of the big names of the British Invasion who were its closest adherents. Van Morrison, for example, whose band Them had reached the US singles charts twice in 1965 had, three years later, recorded his seminal *Astral Weeks* with top jazz musicians Richard Davis and Connie Kay. But whereas the selling point of that album had been its loose, open-ended structures, *Moondance,* released in February 1970, was crisp, tight and precise. Once more Morrison gravitated to American idioms for the soul ballad 'Crazy Love', the bluesy 'These Dreams Of You' and the country-tinged 'Come Running'. The title track was tantamount to jazz, with its cool swing, walking bass and piano and tenor saxophone solos. At the same time Morrison was receptive to more contemporary music, especially that of The Band, whose version of Dylan's 'I Shall Be Released' apparently informed 'Brand New Day'; the melody, imagery and arrangement of 'And It Stoned Me' are also redolent of tracks on their *Music From Big Pink*.

Another fan of The Band was Eric Clapton: their down-home, ego-free music had such a profound impact on him that he decided to disband Cream, whose methodology was the exact opposite. When he resurfaced, it was with the white Southern soul duo, Delaney and Bonnie Bramlett. For the millions who worshipped Clapton for his virtuoso guitar marathons, it was something of a shock to hear him restricted to brief, pithy solos, and while many stuck with him nevertheless, others transferred their loyalties to Led Zeppelin, a group very much in the same vein as Cream. In December 1969 Clapton toured the UK with Delaney and Bonnie and Friends (including, at various times, George Harrison and Traffic's Dave Mason); the following month they were at the Village Recorders, West Los Angeles, making Clapton's eponymous debut album.

For many years *Eric Clapton* was a bargain-bin regular, spurned no doubt by those same fans who had deserted him following Cream's demise. All of Cream's albums prior to their split had made the UK Top Ten and their final release, the double *Wheels Of Fire*, was a US number one for four weeks. His solo album, however, made only seventeen and thirteen respectively. It is immediately clear that this is new Clapton music: the cover photo, for example, could hardly be further from his Cream image. Not, as before, clean-shaven with an Afro and psychedelic clothes, but bearded, with straight hair and wearing a suit; more significantly (and perhaps provocatively), he has by his side not the famous black Gibson Les Paul but a brown sunburst Fender Stratocaster. The new guitar was, in fact, far more suitable: its clean yet mellifluous sound complements both the material and Clapton's voice which, though not strong, holds up commendably. The backing band are consistently excellent and even if the album is in some respects as much the work of Delaney Bramlett (he produced and arranged it and wrote eight of the eleven tracks) as it is of Clapton, the overall outcome is far from unpleasant. 'Lonesome And A Long Way From Home' and 'Told You For The Last Time' are quintessential blue-eyed soul, neatly and imaginatively arranged and Clapton gets the chance to show his familiar cascading guitar style on the sizzling instrumental 'Slunky', the rocking 'Blues Power' and 'Bad Boy' where he duets with Stephen Stills. Less distinguished are 'Lovin' You

Lovin' Me' with its excruciating lyrics and puerile la-la-la chorus and 'After Midnight' which, due to its too-fast tempo, lacks the sensuality of JJ Cale's original.

The acoustic ballad 'Easy Now'; 'Let It Rain', featuring a lengthy, blistering guitar solo; and 'Don't Know Why' – possibly the best-quality song on the album – were all about George Harrison's wife, Patti, who was at that stage the object of Clapton's infatuation. With his next release, the double set *Layla And Other Assorted Love Songs*, infatuation became obsession. The whole project began as a jokey attempt at anonymity: Clapton called his group Derek and The Dominos and when recording began it was pretty much a jam session, during which he swapped solos with guest guitarist Duane Allman. In the event these workouts turned into outstanding tracks, in particular 'Key To The Highway', 'Nobody Knows You When You're Down And Out' and 'Have You Ever Loved A Woman'. All three were blues standards, though given Clapton's mental state the latter title was loaded with implication.

The specially written originals allude to Patti Harrison more overtly, for example, the self-explanatory 'I Am Yours' and 'Why Does Love Got To Be So Sad?' or 'I Looked Away' with its reference to 'loving another man's woman'. But the title track is the ultimate expression of Clapton's unrequited love. He had been given a copy of Nizami Ganjavi's 'The Story of Layla and Majnun', a classic of Persian literature in which a young man goes insane when he is prevented from marrying the object of his desire. Moved by the tale and its relevance to his own situation, Clapton wrote 'Layla', which swiftly became one of the classic rock songs of the era (the Dominos' drummer, Jim Gordon, composed the second, instrumental, section of the piece, playing the piano part himself). Since his debut album, Clapton had become a more confident singer and his voice had acquired an anguish which he puts to full use here though it is his compelling seven-note guitar introduction that has given the track its immortality. Of course, when the album was released in December 1970, very few knew of the story behind it; the fact that it was still quite clearly a milestone in the music is perhaps the greatest praise it can be given.

Clapton had used the stimulation he derived from The Band to recharge his creative batteries; for other British artists it was more of a mixed blessing. At the beginning of 1970 Elton John was making some headway as a solo performer with the songs he had written with wordsmith Bernie Taupin. Rather worryingly, he had assumed an American accent, but he was a good piano player with a strong stage-act. His second album, *Elton John*, released in April, contained some excellent material such as the touching 'Border Song' and the ebullient 'Take Me To The Pilot'. However, 'Your Song', the object of great praise both then and since, had its lyrical infelicities: there can be few more bathetic lines than 'If I were a sculptor, but then again, no'. Like Eric Clapton and Van Morrison, Taupin had huge admiration for The Band, so much so that John's next album, *Tumbleweed Connection,* which came out in October, took their partiality for America's past as its governing principle. The record is essentially a homage to the Old West, with songs about guns, shooting, fighting and death but the problem is that, coming from two Englishmen, it has an ersatz quality. Certainly the right place names, imagery and vocabulary are all there but they are applied rather gratuitously, so that several songs amount to little more than a series of clichés. And again, some of the lines are clumsily written – take, for instance, 'Thanks a lot, it's been great talking to you' from 'Talking Old Soldiers'. Despite all of that, there are some good moments. 'Ballad Of A Well-Known Gun', one of the tracks most reminiscent of The Band, is energetic and catchy; 'Country Comfort' exudes bonhomie; and 'Burn Down The Mission', with its uninhibited gospel piano and rich orchestration, brings the record to a rousing finale. There is also, too, an attractive element of self-mockery: the cover design features a sepia photograph of John on a deserted, run-down railroad station, clearly evocative of Americana – yet the products featured on the advertising signboards are all British.

★ ★ ★ ★ ★

In the early summer of 1969, UK folk singers John Martyn and Beverley

Kutner were to be found in Woodstock, New York, headquarters of America's rock music elite – Jimi Hendrix, Bob Dylan, and The Band whose house, Big Pink, was in nearby West Saugerties. The couple had met in January and shortly afterwards, encouraged by producer Joe Boyd, began to work together. The time in Woodstock helped them develop their ideas and within weeks they were with Boyd in A & R Studios, New York City, recording ten of their songs; among the backing musicians were The Band's producer, John Simon, and their drummer, Levon Helm. In February 1970, the results were released as the album *Stormbringer!*. By then, they were John and Beverley Martyn.

'Traffic Light Lady', written by John back in Britain, bears the imprint of their native folk scene, in particular the guitarist and singer, Bert Jansch. However the title track, again by John, epitomises their current direction of travel – its folksy melody segues into a more reflective, pop-oriented sound with strings and a long piano solo; Beverley's 'Can't Get The One I Want' is on similar lines. Helm appears on the medium-paced folk-rock pieces 'Sweet Honesty' and 'John The Baptist', yet the influence of The Band is more apparent in 'Go Out And Get It', the melody of which resembles Elton John's 'Country Comfort', a coincidence no doubt but indicative of the kind of the sound he was aiming at. 'Woodstock' celebrates their new environment; it is not, of course, the song inspired by the festival (though the Martyns' fellow British folk-rockers Matthews Southern Comfort *did* cover Joni Mitchell's composition, reaching number one on the UK singles chart in October). With 'Would You Believe Me?' we get a glimpse of the future. It is a slow, almost mournful piece in which the duo's gentle vocals float over a hard-hitting rhythm section, though its most original feature is the use, for the first time on record, of John's Echoplex tape delay unit, a sound which came to characterise his music for the next few years.

In spite of their productive sojourn in America, John and Beverley Martyn retained their quintessential British style on their next album *The Road To Ruin* (it was also to be their last, lending an unforeseen irony to the title). While acoustic folk is still part of the picture ('Tree Green'), the instrumental palette is more varied, incorporating elements of jazz ('Primrose Hill'), funk ('Sorry To Be So Long'), soul ('Say What You Can') and gospel ('The Road To Ruin'). There is originality, too, in the songs themselves: the jointly-written 'Auntie Aviator', for instance, contrasts the enterprise of the intrepid relative with the inertia of the protagonist: 'I was a dreamer but all I did was sit and stare'; in 'Parcels', the exchange of packages denotes a switch from sadness to madness.

In fact, the duo's style was starting to resemble that of their friend, Nick Drake, whom they had met on their return from the USA. According to Chris Nickson,

> Drake soon became a fixture at John and Beverley's Hampstead flat. Journalist Brian Cullman noted that "whenever there was any kind of social gathering ... Nick was always there, but was always in the background". (www.propergandaonline.com/in-depth-john-martyn)

Later Martyn would write 'Solid Air', possibly his best-known composition, as a tribute to Drake, who committed suicide in 1974 at the age of only 26. Grossly undervalued in his lifetime – none of his three albums made the charts – he has been deified ever since, an eventuality that would doubtless have perplexed such a shy, sensitive and introspective man. *Bryter Later*, issued on 1 November 1970, was his second album and in some respects his most accessible. In parallel with the Martyns, Drake was starting to make use of new sounds and also employed some of the same musicians – saxophonists Ray Warleigh and Lyn Dobson, for example, appear on both *The Road To Ruin* and *Bryter Later.* But his writing was in a class of its own in terms of imagination, imagery and impact.

It is often said of Drake that he operates as a detached commentator on the people and events in his songs. It is, nevertheless, impossible not to be drawn right into the narrative of compositions like *Bryter Later*'s 'At The Chime Of The City Clock', where the precise descriptive detail – of sounds, colours, the weather – has such significant bearing on its meaning, in this case how, in a city, people conceal their emotions from others. Here, as elsewhere, a further layer of expressiveness comes from Robert Kirby's evocative orchestration. One of the prevalent themes in Drake's work is the fine line between joy and sorrow. His voice will sound insouciant one minute, haunted the next, and he builds structures into his music to reinforce the point. In 'Hazy Jane II', for example, Kirby's brass arrangement establishes an upbeat mood, though this is quickly moderated by the pessimism of the lyrics. However he excels, too, at the straightforward love song, and the poetic and poignant stanza that opens, and closes, 'Northern Sky' has seldom been surpassed, by Drake or any of his peers:

> I never felt magic crazy as this
> I never saw moons, knew the meaning of the sea
> I never held emotion in the palm of my hand
> Or felt sweet breezes in the top of a tree
> But now you're here
> Bright in my northern sky

Like the other singer-songwriters discussed in this chapter, Drake's focus was on what he himself experienced, observed and felt. There is no sense of the wider world, only *his* world. But that was sufficient to sustain a level of creativity that showed little sign of declining, even on his final, harrowing album *Pink Moon*. It also represented for many, and certainly for Drake, too, an escape both from the harsh realities of everyday life and the horrors being enacted around the globe. In 1970, as we shall see very shortly, many others were following the same path.

CHAPTER 5:

Gotta Find A New World

In 1970 rock music had reached a crisis. The deaths of Jimi Hendrix and Janis Joplin; the break-up of The Beatles; the separation of Simon from Garfunkel; the apparent decline of Bob Dylan, The Rolling Stones and The Who – all this left the field wide open. It was an exhilarating prospect, yet daunting, too, with no obvious Messiah waiting in the wings. Various candidates were advanced though none could claim to encompass the entire range of what was understood as rock at the time: the problem was that slowly but surely the music was beginning to fragment. Initially this was of enormous benefit, since it led to an unparalleled richness of diet for rock fans, most of whom were more than ready to accept the spectrum of what was on offer. Indeed, the search for new sounds and the resultant eclecticism of taste were characteristic of both musicians and listeners during this period. But how long could this continue without the structure of the music caving in?

That is a question to be confronted in Chapter 8; for now the issue lies in the reasons for the disintegration and its immediate consequences. So far we have charted the enormous effect that global events had on music of various kinds during 1970. In some cases, artists responded by confronting the issues. Nevertheless, the impulse to disengage was, on the whole, much stronger. We have already seen how several singer-songwriters traded the political for the personal. Another option was to escape reality by going back in time. There was something comforting, for example, in losing oneself in a musical style from a bygone era. The rock and roll revival represented such a refuge, both for new fans and dyed-in-the-wool enthusiasts. Most of the music's originators, too, were still young enough to deliver the goods: by 1970 Elvis Presley had moved on to new pastures, but Little Richard, Chuck Berry and Jerry Lee Lewis had all made comebacks while Fats Domino – after a string of Beatles covers comprising 'Lady Madonna', 'Lovely Rita' and 'Everybody's Got Something To Hide Except Me And My Monkey' – was back on home turf with the spirited 'New Orleans Ain't The Same'.

Quite when the resurgence began is hard to pinpoint, though the seeds may have been planted two years earlier on the album *The Beatles*, where the last line of Paul McCartney's 'Rocky Raccoon' refers to 'Rocky's revival', thus suggesting an allegorical interpretation of the whole song. It was certainly given impetus by Sha Na Na's performance at Woodstock and, just four weeks later, at the Toronto Rock And Roll Revival festival which featured Berry, Richard, Lewis and Bo Diddley alongside more contemporary acts. The event also included an unannounced appearance by The Plastic Ono Band whose set, including Carl Perkins's 'Blue Suede Shoes', was released in December as *Live Peace In Toronto 1969*; it was, however, the first album in most people's collection to bear the date 1970 on the sleeve. It entered the US album chart on 24 January and made number ten, despite a second side consisting of two disquieting and utterly uncommercial Yoko Ono compositions, 'Don't Worry Kyoko (Mummy's Only Looking For Her Hand In The Snow)' and 'John John (Let's Hope For Peace)'.

From then on, no self-respecting festival was complete without a rock and roll singer or, at the very least, a rock and roll medley by a present-day band like Ten Years After, who had started the trend at Woodstock during their marathon version of 'I'm Going Home' and repeated the feat at the Isle of Wight the following year. Mainstream pop caught on, too: The Dave Clark Five had UK hits in 1970 with 'Good Old Rock 'N' Roll' and its inevitable sequel, 'More Good Old Rock 'N' Roll'; Dave Edmunds' Rockpile topped the chart for six weeks with 'I Hear You Knocking' in which Edmunds calls out various names including Chuck Berry, Fats Domino and its composer, New Orleans R&B singer Smiley Lewis.

Ultimately the revival became something of a boom, spawning concert packages, radio shows and re-issue labels. Interest in rock and roll also brought with it a reminder that rock music had a distinguished past. Up to now there had been few serious studies of the music but Tony Palmer's *Born Under A Bad Sign*, published on 1 January 1970, heralded a proliferation of critical histories, scholarly surveys and detailed biographies.

Equally, blues music was continuing to hold its popularity. For the greater part of the 1960s it, too, constituted an escape route, not so much from everyday life – that was its stock-in-trade – but from commercial pop. Artists like The Rolling Stones, John Mayall and Cream had championed blues, first as fans and then as exponents, and thus created a surge of interest in an idiom that epitomised authenticity and the desire to make music for reasons of expression rather than financial gain. Support for blues was especially strong in Europe and there were frequent visits from the African-American giants of the genre, often as part of touring troupes such as the American Folk Blues Festival, organised by the German impresarios Horst Lippmann and Fritz Rau.

The 1970 Festival was the last in an eight-year sequence and although the bill was not quite as strong as in previous years, its appeal, judging by the live recording made on 16 November at the Jahrhunderthalle, Frankfurt, was undiminished. Sonny Terry and Brownie McGhee had been perennial visitors to Europe and so their repertoire – up-tempo showcases for the former's breathy, percussive harmonica and medium paced vehicles for the latter's resonant voice and neat guitar – was familiar, perhaps too familiar. Yet this does not worry the German audience who gamely attempt to clap along, even when on the wrong beat, as in 'Walk On'. The Chicago Blues All-Stars, featuring Walter 'Shakey' Horton on harmonica and guitarist Lee Jackson, are competent if unexciting, though their pianist, the Chess Records session man Lafayette Leake, does an excellent job on the technically demanding 'After Hours'.

Champion Jack Dupree, by then resident in Europe, gives a characteristically powerful performance though both of his tracks are flawed by circumstances beyond his control: 'Going To Louisiana' is marred by a clumsy bass solo by Willie Dixon and more boisterous clapping along ruins the meditative feel of 'Blues Before Sunrise'. The best contribution comes from the oldest man on the tour, Bukka White, whose 61st birthday fell four days before the concert. 'World Boogie' and 'Old Lady' romp along in style but the standout track is his intense, moving rendition of 'Maggie Lee'.

In the same month in which these recordings were made, the first-ever blues festival produced by African-Americans *for* African-Americans was staged in Washington, DC. As a manifestation of the Black Panther self-help philosophy, this was an event of some significance, but of only passing interest to the blues fans whose emotional commitment to the music was invested in its past rather than its future. Through studying the work of the old masters – most of whom were long dead – it was possible to become instantly sealed off in a bubble where all the music was perfect and none of its practitioners could lapse into bad taste and/or commercialism.

★ ★ ★ ★ ★

In the meantime some of the big names in rock were gravitating towards the past for different, though related, reasons. Commencing with 'Proud Mary' in 1968, Creedence Clearwater Revival had started the trend though their focus tended to be as much geographical as historical. Bob Dylan's songs had often explored myth and legend and he had also pursued Biblical themes on *John Wesley Harding*. By common consent his two 1970 albums, *Self Portrait* and *New Morning,* are among his weakest and signalled a creative drought that was to last for five years. One of the very few outstanding tracks on either is *Self Portrait*'s 'Days Of '49', a rollicking tale of the California Gold Rush. It is likely that Dylan knew of the song from Logan English's *The Days Of '49: Songs Of The Gold Rush*, a collection of prospecting songs dating back to the mid-nineteenth century. Sourced from the archive of the Smithsonian Center for Folklife and Cultural Heritage, the album was released in 1957. So why record this particular song now?

The answer is to be found not in Dylan's music but in that of his former backing group, The Band, whose star, in marked contrast to their old employer, was beginning to rise. *Music From Big Pink*, as we saw in Chapter 4, was hugely influential among musicians, though it only just scraped into the US Top 30 and did not make the UK chart at all. But the follow-up, released in January 1970 and entitled simply *The Band*, got to number nine in America and 25 in Britain. To a greater extent than its predecessor, it plunged the listener back into a bygone era. The back cover photograph shows the group wearing nineteenth-century outfits and lined up in a log cabin with piano, acoustic guitar, double bass and an antiquated-looking drum kit. In the course of the album we also hear violin and mandolin, both anachronisms in 1970, and organ – not the behemoth of contemporary rock but the breezy, wheezy old-fashioned fairground instrument.

Having set the musical context, The Band supply the songs to match. All written/co-written by their guitarist, Jaime Robbie Robertson, they are predominantly stories of the old country and almost all make reference to specific places and events, populated by characters with names like Virgil, Jemima, Bessie and Ragtime Willie. Robertson's vision of the past is affectionate, though not uncritical. 'Up On Cripple Creek' and 'Rockin' Chair' both extol the virtues of home-sweet-home, and 'Rag Mama Rag' and 'Jemima Surrender' feature a hapless country bumpkin incapable of controlling his girlfriend – all four songs are gently satirical in the manner of Randy Newman at his most benign. There is unequivocal sympathy, on the other hand, for 'The Unfaithful Servant' dismissed from a Southern mansion and the hardworking farmer, dreaming of a better future in 'King Harvest'.

'The Night They Drove Old Dixie Down' is tantamount to a history lesson on the American Civil War. The story is told by Virgil Kane who 'served on the Danville train', that is, the train between Danville and Richmond, Virginia – the 'Richmond that fell' on 3 April 1865. The 'Stoneman's cavalry' who 'came and tore up the tracks again' refers to Unionist General George Stoneman's 1865 Raid which traversed

Tennessee, Virginia and North Carolina between 20 March and 12 April, destroying towns and railroad tracks, including that at Danville. Back in Tennessee, Virgil's wife calls him to come and watch the defeated Commander of the Confederate Army of Northern Virginia, Robert E Lee, riding by. The precision of the detail (somewhat blunted by Joan Baez, whose version of the song substituted 'so much cavalry' for 'Stoneman's cavalry') is combined with an emotive refrain to make the song an outstanding example of how to apply rock music to history – and vice versa.

Unfortunately very few songwriters accepted the challenge and The Band themselves, perhaps fearful they might be trapped in an artistic dead-end, went more mainstream for their next album, *Stage Fright*, which came out in August. Indeed, possibly because it was rather less fixated on American history than its predecessor, it delivered their best chart result so far in both the US and UK, reaching number five and fifteen respectively. Like *The Band* it blends down-home solidity in the playing with sensitivity in the singing and songwriting, and some songs – 'The WS Walcott Medicine Show', 'Daniel And The Sacred Harp' – dig once again into rural folklore. The whole effect, however, is much closer to the norms of contemporary rock with guitar and drums especially prominent. Even a potential period piece like 'Just Another Whistle Stop' alludes to police sirens. But there is no denying the quality of the music: 'Strawberry Wine', for example, is a dynamic opener in which the sounds of accordion and cymbals mesh to give a striking textural blend, and the title track tells the absorbing tale of the man who wants to start his life all over again. 'Time To Kill' is a catchy medium-pacer, released as a single two months later with 'The Shape I'm In' as the B-side: this ostensibly jolly song is in fact a window into the disturbed mental state of the group's pianist, Richard Manuel, with the churning organ and harsh guitar reinforcing the impression that things are not quite right.

Ry Cooder had his own take on American history: rather than write about it, he simply revived its songs. His debut album, *Ry Cooder,* which came out in December, featured material from a bewildering variety of sources, but all of them within the American tradition, an approach prefigured by the front cover picture of Cooder alongside a 1937-model trailer. Three of the eleven selections are contemporary pieces yet they all reflect this context: Tommy Tucker's 'Alimony' features gospel-flavoured backing vocals; his own instrumental, 'Available Space' is a slide guitar duet; and Randy Newman's 'Old Kentucky Home', as we saw in Chapter 4, is a take on a Stephen Foster song from the 1850s.

Of the other eight tracks, five are by African-Americans born in the nineteenth century. 'France Chance' is a reworking of 'Love Me Baby Blues' by Mississippi Joe Callicott (and is perhaps a tribute: Callicott had died the previous year) and 'Police Dog Blues' and 'Goin' To Brownsville' are by Blind Blake and Sleepy John Estes respectively. Leadbelly's 'Pigmeat' features a clever horn arrangement with a two-beat rhythm reminiscent of early jazz. Blind Willie Johnson's original recording of 'Dark Was The Night – Cold Was The Ground' is one of the great masterpieces of American music in which the ultra-slow slide guitar and wordless funereal chanting create a unique atmosphere – majestic and chilling at the same time; Cooder's version is beautifully played and he has repeatedly returned to this sound ever since, notably for his music for the 1984 film, *Paris, Texas*. The rest of the record consists of Woody Guthrie's 'Do Re Mi', Blind Alfred Reed's 'How Can A Poor Man Stand Such Times And Live?' and 'One Meat Ball', written in 1944 by Louis Singer and Hy Zaret but based on Harvard Professor George Martin Lane's comic song of 1855, 'The Lone Fish Ball' – here the humour is restored by an incongruously melodramatic orchestration by Kirby Johnson.

The music may be archaic, but the settings are lively and refreshing, the production (by Van Dyke Parks and Lenny Waronker, Randy Newman's producer) imaginative, and the musicianship – headed by Cooder on guitar, bass and mandolin – immaculate. Unfortunately the attention to detail does not extend to the back cover where the names of no fewer than three backing musicians are misspelled. Among them is Richie Hayward, drummer with the Los Angeles band Little Feat, whose own eponymous debut album, recorded in late summer 1970, featured Cooder and came out the month after his.

Stylistically, there are similarities between the two records including, for example, a medley of two numbers by the blues giant Howlin' Wolf, yet thematically Little Feat's approach is at variance with both Cooder and with The Band, in that they mythologise the present rather than the past. So here are tales of the road, of rigs, truck stops and hamburger joints and plaintive contemporary ballads such as 'Takin' My Time', 'I've Been The One' and 'Willin''. The latter was first recorded by Johnny Darrell, also in 1970, with a full country and western arrangement but here it is rendered by its composer, Lowell George, in his characteristically parched vocal style, accompanied only by his own acoustic guitar and Cooder on electric slide.

This is music about the country as opposed to country music, though that, too, attracted numerous rock bands in 1970 especially those from America's West Coast. There was, however, a profound difference between these musicians and the authentic country practitioners. The latter sang about their own day-to-day lives and those of poor white communities across the USA, while for the former, it was music of romance and myth with connections to the Old West and legends of gunslingers, outlaws and cowboys. Among the first musicians to fuse country with rock was Gram Parsons, first in 1967 with his own group The International Submarine Band and then as a member of The Byrds, whose *Sweetheart Of The Rodeo* from the following year was the first major milestone in the new genre. Parsons left The Byrds shortly afterwards but the country element remained, though now jostling for position with the band's former psychedelic style – a dichotomy reflected in the title of their 1969 album, *Dr Byrds And Mr Hyde*.

The double LP set *Untitled*, released on 14 September 1970, took the process a step further by encompassing the entire range of Byrds music – past, present and future. Versions of their old hits 'Mr Tambourine Man', 'So You Want To Be A Rock 'N' Roll Star' and 'Mr Spaceman' appear on the live album, as does a thrilling sixteen-minute jam on 'Eight Miles High'. There are covers of such diverse material as Bob Dylan's 'Positively 4th Street', 'Take A Whiff On Me' by Leadbelly and Little Feat's 'Truck Stop Girl' as well as some excellent new songs. 'Yesterday's Train' is orthodox country-rock but 'Hungry Planet', 'You All Look Alike' and 'Well Come Back Home', all written or co-written by bassist Skip Battin, venture into new thematic and sonic territory. On the first, the ecological message is conveyed by a hypnotic rhythm and the beguiling combination of twelve-string guitar and moog synthesiser; the second voices the standard hippie critique of straight society; the third – at over seven minutes, the longest studio recording the band ever made – sends a greeting to the soldiers returning from Vietnam and concludes with a Buddhist mantra.

Roger McGuinn, the only surviving original Byrd, had been collaborating with Broadway theatre director Jacques Levy on a country-rock stage show, based on Henrik Ibsen's *Peer Gynt* and anagrammatically titled *Gene Tryp*. Though the project came to nothing, four of the songs were included on *Untitled*. Two – 'All The Things' and 'Just A Season' – are rueful reflections on the past; the ferocious 'Lover Of The Bayou' (included on the live album) is about a wheeler-dealer who worked for both sides in the American Civil War. But the track for which the collaboration, and in fact the whole album, is best remembered is 'Chestnut Mare', the half-sung, half-spoken tale of the pursuit of the eponymous horse. Issued as a single, it made number nineteen in the UK, The Byrds' highest chart position for six years, while the album got to number eleven, their second best placing ever; yet in the US it only made number 40, perhaps squeezed by the release only a few weeks earlier of a greatest hits package.

Meanwhile, Gram Parsons had formed another band, The Flying Burrito Brothers, whose second album, *Burrito Deluxe*, was released in April 1970. By now the line-up included two founder-members of The Byrds, bassist Chris Hillman and drummer Michael Clarke, pedal steel guitarist Sneaky Pete Kleinow and Bernie Leadon on guitar and dobro. Hillman also doubles on mandolin, and with a backing band that includes fiddle, accordion, tuba and fluegelhorn one might expect a record laced with both authentic sounds and unusual textures. In the event, despite their individual excellence, the guest musicians are under-used. The originals, all bar one written by Parsons with Hillman and/or Leadon, are pretty much straight rockers; the best are the celebratory 'Lazy Day', 'Man In The Fog' and 'Older Guys'. Dylan's 'If You Gotta Go' is also taken fast, probably too fast; in contrast, 'Wild Horses', one of the more maudlin Jagger-Richards compositions, drags along drearily. The older songs – 'Image Of Me' by Nashville songwriter Harlan Howard and the country gospel staple 'Farther Along' – receive respectful but unimaginative treatment. In the end, therefore, despite the high-class musicianship, this is an album of country *and* rock, rather than country-rock.

It was somewhat perplexing that Parsons should have failed to consummate an idiom he had invented while, also in 1970, a rock band who had never before touched country music achieved the perfect synthesis. The Grateful Dead's *Workingman's Dead* was voted the best album of the year by the readers of *Rolling Stone* magazine, thus, self-evidently, putting it ahead of any other records discussed in this book. Certainly it is near flawless in conception and execution. The Dead had been pioneers of acid-rock and at one point they were believed to be the loudest band in the world; they also used two drummers. Yet for all that, their music had a feeling of buoyancy and space, nowhere more evident than on the epic 'Dark Star', the highlight of the double album *Live/Dead*, released the previous year. So they had little trouble in adapting to country music – at its best, uncomplicated and uncluttered – without sacrificing their individuality.

The title of *Workingman's Dead* sums up its intent – Grateful Dead music for working people, that is, country music fans – and is reinforced by a cover photograph in which the band, two in ten-gallon hats, are standing on what first appears to be a Wild West street; but in the distance are three factory chimneys, thus bringing any romantic notions back to everyday reality. There is, however, a further, more subtle layer of meaning, evinced by the opening track, 'Uncle John's Band'. As Matthew Greenwald has written,

"The first days are the hardest days," sing the Grateful Dead in the opening line to "Uncle John's Band," the first song on the

Workingman's Dead album. It's for good reason, too, as this song and album clearly announced a new beginning to the band's history. After the over-amped psychedelia of 1966-1969, as well as the horror of the Altamont festival, the Dead now mutate into an almost folksy, singer/songwriter vein, and in this song, they are essentially asking their audience to go with them. (*allmusic.com*)

The lilting tempo, quiet percussion and sweet harmonies (the band had been spending time with CSNY) make the journey an inviting one. On 'High Time', a gentle swaying waltz, the country flavour becomes stronger: we hear Jerry Garcia's pedal steel guitar for the first time and the natural whine in his voice suddenly seems more pronounced. There is more pedal steel on 'Dire Wolf', and 'Cumberland Blues' features his nimble, bluegrass-style guitar picking and an (uncredited) banjo-player. 'Easy Wind' and 'New Speedway' are more bluesy, perhaps a concession that not all workingmen are white, though 'Casey Jones' is a return to country music folklore, the tale of the train driver who goes too fast. The Dead comically attribute his recklessness to drug abuse – 'high on cocaine', he is told to 'watch your speed' – and the piece is set to an ironically chugging tempo. The weakest track is 'Black Peter', a not untypical slower Dead piece of the period in which Garcia's vocals lack the authority to carry the languid, meandering verse, and the chorus looks like it will never arrive.

Similar traits bedevil 'Candyman' and 'Box Of Rain', the two longest tracks on *American Beauty*, the follow-up to *Workingman's Dead*. Although it was released six months later, on 1 November 1970, the CSNY influence still lingers. Both 'Sugar Magnolia' and 'Till The Morning Comes' borrow the closing theme of 'Suite: Judy Blue Eyes' from the *Crosby, Stills And Nash* album and there is more close harmony singing: this time, however, the quality falls well short of their mentors. On the positive side, 'Friend Of The Devil' is a lively original, its folksy cadences and subject-matter reinforced by Garcia's acoustic guitar and guest musician Dave Grisman's mandolin. Grisman also features on 'Ripple', a slice of unadulterated country with an anthem-like melody. Yet the wisdom of allowing organist

Ron McKernan to sing is questioned by 'Operator' while 'Attics Of My Life' displays the kind of pretentious imagery satirised the previous year by The Bonzo Dog Doo Dah Band with 'The Canyons Of Your Mind'. The tune to 'Truckin'' has echoes of 'The Ballad Of John And Yoko' by The Beatles, also from 1969, and the theme is similar, too, though in the Dead's case the period reviewed in the song is their entire career, not just the last few months. Like 'Uncle John's Band' it seems to draw a line under an era with the immortal line 'What a long strange trip it's been'.

The Band, Ry Cooder, Little Feat, The Byrds, The Flying Burrito Brothers and The Grateful Dead all, in their various ways, found outlets in the music of the past, in the instrumentation and lyrical vernacular of rural America, largely country music but also folk and blues – in short, what was to become known as roots music. The cycle was repeated in the 1980s when, taking refuge from synth-pop, New Romanticism and rap, many musicians, writers and record-buyers turned to the global sounds offered under the heading of World Music. This led to a revival of interest in American musical traditions – what today we describe as Americana.

Yet in 1970 not everyone wanted to go back in time as a means of escape; some wanted to create their own, imagined universe. Though this approach tended to be characteristic of British rock, some American bands flirted with it, too, none more eminent than The Beach Boys. Their album *Sunflower*, issued on 31 August, was the celebration of an idyll in which the simple things in life – family, love, music, nature, even water – were to be cherished and protected. Yes, there was a traditional aspect to this – the band were, for example, shown on the record sleeve wearing period costumes – but it was very much about the here-and-now: in that same picture, they are accompanied by their children, in modern dress.

The circumstances in which the album was created reinforce the impression of fortified domesticity. Produced by the whole band, it was made at their own Brother Records studio one year after they had been dropped by Capitol, the company who had released fourteen of their fifteen albums to date. That alone seems to bind the band into a display of unity not always evident previously. Yet if the messages were simple, the ways of conveying them were less so. 'All I Wanna Do' and 'Add Some Music To Your Day', for instance, could hardly be more straightforward lyrically but are bathed in lavish and complex vocal effects. The latter includes a dreamlike interlude to distance it yet further from external reality, typical of its creator, Brian Wilson, who also indulges his imagination on 'Cool, Cool Water' with the sounds of thunder, surf noise and eerie disembodied vocal harmonies.

As befits this family project, however, other members of the band get their share of the limelight. Dennis Wilson, for example, contributes 'Slip On Through', which juxtaposes anxiety with optimism, the pounding 'Got To Know The Woman' and the tender love song, 'Forever', the sentiments of which are picked by brother Carl on the following track, 'Our Sweet Love' – 'our sweet love could last forever' – a clumsy reiteration, perhaps, but in line with the theme of all-pervasive love that surfaces earlier in 'This Whole World'. It is also symptomatic that Leadbelly's 'Cottonfields', which had appeared on The Beach Boys' previous album, *20/20*, was included on *Sunflower* (albeit only for the European release) in rearranged form, the steel guitar of Red Rhodes bringing a distinctly nostalgic atmosphere. The only songs to break the mood of unwavering serenity are, interestingly, by the non-family member, Bruce Johnston. Both are arranged by Michel Colombier: 'Deirdre' amounts to an orthodox pop song with a trombone solo but 'Tears In The Morning' is a waltz with an unusual structure employing effects both predictable – 'you moved to Europe', enter accordion – and unexpected, as in the unnerving piano finale.

Sunflower was well received by the critics though not by the public. It failed to get into the US album chart and barely made the UK Top 30 (*20/20* had got to number three). Those who liked The Beach Boys for their catchy tunes could, instead, take advantage of greatest hits compilations. For those who responded to the adventure and experimentalism of *Pet Sounds* and *Smiley Smile,* its message was too conservative and conventional. And anyway, there were far more exciting things going on, not just in music but in society more widely.

★ ★ ★ ★ ★

At 11 am on Saturday 5 September 1970, a new shop opened in Manchester's New Brown Street. Except that it wasn't a shop – at least in any normal sense of the word. Despite its location in the northwest equivalent of Carnaby Street, it stocked no mass-produced merchandise: all of the items on offer, largely clothes and pottery, were individually made and were as likely to be bartered for other goods as sold for cash. Customers might be offered some vegetarian food, for free, or somewhere just to chill out; those who shared the ideals of the enterprise might end up working there. But no-one who went into On The Eighth Day would ever forget it.

Founded by hippies Jenny Slaughter and her future husband Mike, solicitor Brian Livingstone and businessmen Phil Aaronson and Ray Kay, the Eighth Day, as it soon came to be known, was not the first venture of its kind in the world, nor even in the UK. Yet it is questionable whether many similar concerns have made more of an impact or in fact are still thriving in 2014. Furthermore, for the young people of Manchester it *was* something new – not just the products but the lifestyle that went with them. This included providing practical help and support to those in material, spiritual or social need. According to one estimate, the number of people who have benefited from their contact with the Eighth Day runs into the high hundreds and many still adhere to the beliefs they first espoused there.

From the very beginning it ran as a workers' co-operative, a familiar enough concept now, yet in 1970, thanks to legislation introduced five years earlier, to operate on such lines meant registering as an industrial provident society – not a concept that many hippies were acquainted with nor, come to that, most members of the general public, then or since. Before long the Eighth Day became the hub of Manchester's alternative society: from dealing in clothes and pottery, it progressed to selling vegetarian food products – brown flour, muesli, brown rice – not widely available at the time, and eventually opened a wholefood café. It also sold records and underground newspapers. However financial gain was never an objective. Jenny recalls,

> It was so idealistic to start with. We weren't there to make money, we were there to demonstrate a new way of life. One Saturday we brought all the takings to our house and told [our partner] Ray, "Look, it's not about the money – the money's not important". Ray replied, "If the money's not important, then put the takings on the fire!"

Needless to say the cash stayed intact though Jenny and Mike made sure that any profits went straight back into the business. They also made sure that all members of the co-operative were well looked after. Some were so committed to the principles the Eighth Day stood for that they were willing to work for next to nothing; others who had nowhere to live were put up in the couple's home. One such was Nicky Crewe who discovered the organisation as a sixteen-year-old and later became its treasurer. She is thus in a unique position to observe how the Eighth Day operated. Manchester was a fashionable city in 1970: George Best had his own boutique, 'dolly birds' populated the streets and there were lots of expensive nightclubs. Yet, Nicky says,

> It wasn't about being trendy. It was about being alternative. You looked for somewhere you could buy the clothes, and then to follow that lifestyle you needed the food. And we always had music playing – you didn't hear underground music much on the radio back then, so it was like following a trail. That this was retail was incidental.

In short all of the activities at the Eighth Day were interdependent. They also performed a social service by giving shelter to young drug users in need of a place to hang out until the Lifeline Trust began operations in the city the following year. Most of all, it was synonymous with vegetarianism which in 1970, was not at all widespread, even in the USA. Most sources agree that interest only began to grow with the publication the following year of

Frances Moore Lappé's *Diet For A Small Planet*. Jenny Slaughter, however, was already a committed vegetarian and brought her beliefs to the Eighth Day when she introduced food to its shelves, a move that turned out to be far more significant than she could have expected. Over 40 years later and still a co-operative, the Eighth Day is regarded as the major vegetarian healthfood shop and café in the city: at the time of writing, the BBC had just completed filming there for a documentary on vegetarianism.

The alternative lifestyle promoted by the Eighth Day encompassed food, crafts, clothing, drugs, music and the environment as well as spiritual, social, political and community issues; though – at least at the outset – not feminism. In time that, too, would be an important part of the picture and active encouragement given to individuals and to women's groups. But In 1970 what became known as women's liberation was underdeveloped; in the alternative society at that time, women were not necessarily seen as inferior to men, just destined for different roles. As Jenny puts it,

> The whole movement came with gender equality and free love. There was also the earth mother image of the hippie movement which was very much long hair, plaits, long dresses, cooking and kids. I have to say it was more about sexual liberation than domestic liberation.

The British underground press were scarcely more progressive in their opinions. The leading publications – *International Times* (*IT*), *Oz* and *Black Dwarf* – were, in general, unremittingly chauvinistic. *IT*, for example, though it did run a feature on the feminist writer Jane Arden in Issue 66 (October 1969), constantly portrayed women as sex objects, creating characters like the 'IT girl' and 'Trudy' whose main activity was to remove their clothes. *Black Dwarf* gave serious coverage to women's liberation and even employed a feminist, Sheila Rowbotham, on its staff. Yet its stories were frequently couched in sexist terminology and illustrations, prompting Rowbotham to resign towards the end of 1969. Nevertheless, any chauvinism in this publication was dwarfed, so to speak, by *Oz*, in which the depiction of women verged on pornography.

That the editor of *Oz*, Richard Neville, employed fellow Australian Germaine Greer is no mitigation – in fact, it seems in retrospect to be a provocative move. For what Neville seemed to be doing was stoking up the debate on women's liberation – displaying images of men's emasculation on the one hand (Issue 26, February 1970) and giving Greer the right to respond on the other. He was safe in the knowledge, however, that Greer was no typical feminist: in the same issue she writes,

> Many militant women show too plainly by their inefficiency, their obesity and their belligerence that they have not succeeded in finding any measure of liberation in their own company.

This suggests that, strange as it may seem, Neville and Greer shared a common enemy – the middle-class, left-wing activists who seemed to be dominating the movement. Certainly they comprised a high percentage of the first-ever British National Women's Liberation Conference, which took place at Ruskin College, Oxford, in the same month. But working-class women were also represented as, indeed, were men, although the latter were banned from attending workshops. Jonathon Green describes the impact of the event as follows:

> The Conference was a major turning-point: where before there had been tens of women's groups, now there were scores, springing up across the country ... A national co-ordinating committee, a loose network of women, was set up, and put forward four demands: free 24-hour nurseries; equal pay now; equal education and job opportunities; and free contraception and abortion on demand ... And, in the way of the counter-culture, it was immediately understood that while conscious-raising might help internally, the movement as a whole needed something a little more dramatic to get that all-important attention: the media. (*All Dressed Up*, p. 406)

Progress was painfully slow on all of the objectives put forward by the committee – true, there was now an Equal Pay Act, introduced in early 1970 by the Labour Government in response to the strike by women sewing machinists at Ford two years earlier, though that was not due to come into effect until 1975. However the oxygen of publicity was pumped into the movement in November when, as we saw in Chapter 3, there was a demonstration at the Miss World beauty pageant: 30 brave feminists got to their feet shouting, waving football rattles and pelting the MC, Bob Hope, with flour and abuse.

Such antics were inspired by their US counterparts, who had recently staged a similar protest at the Miss America event. In fact things generally seemed to be moving faster across the Atlantic: 1970 saw the first women, Anna Mae Hays and Elizabeth P Hoisington, to be appointed as generals in the US Army and, at the other end of the spectrum, the first Virginia Slims women's tennis tournament took place on 23 September in Houston, Texas, thus prompting the formation by Billie-Jean King of the Women's Tennis Association. To celebrate the 50th anniversary of female suffrage, the Women's Strike for Equality took place on 26 August, its objectives similar to the British National Women's Liberation Conference which American activists had helped to organise.

In truth, the US women's movement had been growing ever since the publication of Betty Friedan's seminal work, *The Feminine Mystique*, in 1963. One key strategy was consciousness-raising – that is, the process of awakening in a woman the understanding that she, and millions of others like her, was the victim of patriarchy, predestined to play the predictable and permanent part of wife, mother and home-maker. That these roles were rooted in history, literature and psychology was comprehensively demonstrated by Kate Millett, whose *Sexual Politics* was published in 1970.

Millett uses the term politics to refer to 'power-structured relationships whereby one group of persons is controlled by another' (p. 23) and thus sexual politics is

... like racism, or certain aspects of caste, primarily an ideology, a way of life, with influence over every other psychological and emotional facet of existence. (p. 168)

She is particularly severe on the notion that men and women are equal but different, that in effect they occupy 'separate spheres', deriding this as a deliberate strategy to stunt the growth of women's independence and intellect. In doing so, she demolishes what she sees as the unctuous condescension of John Ruskin, the chivalric excesses of Tennyson and, in particular the confusion between biology and conditioning which characterises the theories of Sigmund Freud. To bring her argument up-to-date she cites the work of Henry Miller: in fact the book begins with a devastating analysis of his 1965 novel *Sexus,* in which 'delusions about sex foster delusions of power and both depend on the reification of women' (p. 21).

Later in the year Germaine Greer published *The Female Eunuch,* a different if complementary take on the 'castration' of women. Again there is a forensic analysis of everything that is wrong with both the position of women in society and male-female relationships. Like Millett, Greer illustrates how, despite a discrepancy of just one chromosome, biology is used to exaggerate, and justify, the difference between the sexes, and she attacks Freud and his adherents like Helene Deutsch for using such shaky ground on which to build their theories of psychoanalysis – in her words, 'a farrago of moralism and fantasy unillumined by any shaft of commonsense' (p. 95). Her review of the many and varied facets of female conditioning both adds to and updates that contained in *Sexual Politics.*

But where Millett is essentially a theorist, Greer is a pragmatist and so *The Female Eunuch* offers much more in the way of practical advice, not all of it in line with contemporary feminist doctrines. She is much more upfront, for example, on the need for women to establish their own sexual identity, independent from men, and certainly from one man – 'they should be self-sufficient and consciously refrain from establishing exclusive dependencies and other kinds of neurotic symbioses' (p. 18). The result will be of benefit to women *and* men, and thus to the whole of society. With a sideswipe at Millett, she writes:

It is not necessary for feminists to prove that matriarchy is a prehistoric form of community, or that patriarchy is a capitalist perversion in order to justify our policies, because the form of life we envisage might as well be completely new as inveterately ancient. (p. 330)

Like Alvin Toffler and Charles Reich, whose work will be discussed in Chapter 8, Greer's critique of the past included a vision of the future.

Back at *Oz*, however, Greer had failed to convert her colleagues to her egalitarian philosophy. She posed nude for the magazine, for example, on the understanding that the male writers would do the same; but they demurred, and the torrent of sexism/pornography continued unchecked – that is, until 18 August 1970 when the magazine was served with a summons for obscenity. This was in respect of the April edition (Number 28), entitled 'The Schoolkids' Issue' in which input, most of it innocuous, came from a variety of minors including Charles Shaar Murray, later one of the UK's most distinguished rock critics. It also contained eight erotic photographs of a young black woman. Quite why the authorities pounced on this occasion is hard to determine – there had certainly been more explicit editions – though the involvement of children may well have been a factor. Whatever the case, they triggered one of the more colourful episodes in British legal history. The subsequent trial, the longest ever of its kind, began in June 1971. Six weeks later the magazine was fined £1,000 plus costs and Neville and his co-editors Jim Anderson and Felix Dennis received prison sentences. After protests by supporters and anti-censorship campaigners, the verdict was overturned on appeal.

But those who were disenchanted by *Oz* were not exclusively cadres of the Establishment. One of its own writers, Marsha Rowe, was so disgusted with its portrayal of women that she founded the feminist magazine *Spare Rib* with fellow underground journalist Rosie Boycott. Rampant sexism amongst apparently radical organisations was, of course, not exclusive to *Oz*. Bastions of the Left like trade unions and the International Socialists habitually relegated women to passive and menial roles. Yet somehow one expected more of a publication which in many other respects was at the cutting edge of the counterculture. The Schoolkids Issue had been a jokey response to criticism that it was losing touch with young people – ironically, however, it provided the proof.

Shortly before the magazine's obscenity summons came the London opening of *Oh! Calcutta!* – an erotic revue conceived by Kenneth Tynan and directed by Jacques Levy who, as we have seen, worked with Roger McGuinn on the country-rock opera that never was; he was later to collaborate with Bob Dylan on his 1976 album *Desire*. Despite contributions by a range of eminent writers, including Samuel Beckett, the show received a lukewarm response from the critics. It was, nevertheless, a huge commercial success with nearly 4,000 performances in London and, including a revival which lasted thirteen years, over 7,000 on Broadway. As with the *Oz* prosecution, the show created consternation among the country's moral guardians though in this case there was no legal basis for intervention. Besides, who could deny the older generation the opportunity to indulge in fantasies of their own?

★ ★ ★ ★ ★

Songs about women's liberation were few and far between in any form of music in 1970, but especially in prog rock, where attitudes tended to reflect those of the underground press. If women figured at all, they tended to be portrayed as wicked witches or idealised, docile paragons of beauty who would not be out of place in a medieval love ballad. Indeed prog – like the other forms of rock music discussed in this and the previous chapter – was now transcending the real world. Myth and legend, actual or imaginary, became standard subject-matter. To convey such visions the music should be fantastical, too – portentous in ensemble, virtuosic in solo.

All of these characteristics were prominent in the work of King Crimson. Their debut album *In The Court Of The Crimson King* was released in 1969 to great acclaim; its opening track, '21st Century Schizoid Man' was the highlight and featured bassist Greg Lake's commanding vocals, a screaming Robert Fripp guitar solo and the precise, prodigious drumming of Mike Giles. *In The Wake Of Poseidon*, released on 15 May 1970, is on similar lines: 'Pictures Of A City', for instance, with its meaty riff and high-speed instrumental interlude bears a close resemblance to '21st Century Schizoid Man'. But the album's range of sonic colour is, if anything, still greater, fulfilling the promise of Tammo De Jongh's sprawling, multi-coloured painting *12 Archetypes* that adorns its cover.

The mellotron is employed extensively on both the title track and 'The Devil's Triangle' (based on Gustav Holst's 'Mars: The Bringer of War'). Less versatile than the moog synthesiser, it is more distinctive and its gothic grandiosity gives both pieces their sense of foreboding. Acoustic guitar and flute combine for the gentle 'Cadence And Cascade' and the free jazz flourishes of pianist Keith Tippett underline the surrealism of 'Cat Food'. Peter Sinfield's lyrics are flamboyant and impressionistic and although it is not always easy to catch their exact meaning they are clearly the product of a fertile imagination and a literary sensibility. 'Pictures Of A City', for example, is a catalogue of ugly images while the contrasting 'Cadence And Cascade' contrives to make even the world of the groupie sound romantic by transposing it into a Renaissance setting. The narrative of 'In The Wake Of Poseidon' merges characters from fact and fiction – harlequins, Plato, the Midnight Queen, the Magi and bishop's kings.

By the time of the band's third album, *Lizard*, issued on 11 December, only Sinfield and Fripp remained from the original line-up. Again the cover, this time by Gini Barris, is a lavish introduction to the music: each track is illustrated in the style of a medieval manuscript with a scene from the text encased in ornate lettering. Yet while this is a useful aid to interpretation, Sinfield's lyrics are in any case less opaque than before. 'Happy Family' is clearly about the break-up of The Beatles, 'Indoor Games' a satire on selfish extravagance; the meaning of 'Cirkus' and 'Lady Of The Dancing Water' is self-evident; and the suite 'Lizard', which takes up almost all of the second side, concerns the prelude, enactment and aftermath of battle. Musically, the album is more sophisticated than its predecessors, jazzier and lighter in touch, though the mellotron again brings a sinister edge to the whirling, swirling 'Cirkus', complemented by

Fripp's nimble acoustic guitar and the silky saxophone of Mel Collins.

Other bands, lacking the varied instrumental palette of King Crimson, used more obvious strategies to distance their music from the present, one of which was to import elements of traditional folk music. Jethro Tull had always seemed other-worldly in any case: their singer, Ian Anderson, wore colourful coats, played the flute standing on one leg and grimaced at the audience from behind a mass of red hair. But on BBC TV's pop music show, *Top Of The Pops,* he exploited the commercial potential of his image with a wild-eyed performance of 'The Witch's Promise'. Entering the chart on 24 January 1970, it rose to number four, the highest position a prog rock single ever attained. It was not just Anderson's persona that accounted for its success; there was also an attractive folksy element that Jethro Tull were to follow up on their third album, *Benefit,* released on 20 April. The cover design shows the band looking through a window at cardboard cut-outs of themselves and in the sleeve note Anderson states that they are making a conscious attempt to sound English thus, by implication, avoiding the blues-rock stereotype. The plan succeeds on 'Nothing To Say', 'To Cry You A Song' and 'A Time For Everything?' where the folk influences enhance the impact of Anderson's misanthropic lyrics. Elsewhere the blend is less palatable, and one is left wanting more tracks like the complex but dramatic opener 'With You There To Help Me' or in fact 'Teacher', originally given double A-side status with 'The Witch's Promise' but actually a superior record in which frantic flute conveys the protagonist's desperate attempts to enjoy himself, the nagging guitar riffs his sense of self-doubt.

Led Zeppelin had filled the void left by Cream's demise and their first two albums were early classics of heavy metal; *Led Zeppelin III,* issued on 5 October 1970, represented a new departure. True, 'Immigrant Song', 'Celebration Day' and 'Since I've Been Loving You' all feature the familiar blend of histrionic vocals, pulverising drums and the powerful yet articulate guitar of Jimmy Page, whose solo on the latter is regarded as one of his best.

However almost all of the other tracks bear witness to the time Page and singer Robert Plant spent at a remote eighteenth century Welsh cottage, Bron-Yr-Aur, recovering from a demanding American tour. Here there was no running water and no electricity – which naturally led to the prevalence of acoustic guitar in the composition and arranging of songs for the album; in turn this allowed the duo to consider thematic areas for which this treatment was appropriate. 'That's The Way', for example, carries an environmentalist message while the misspelled 'Bron-Y-Aur Stomp' celebrates rural life. The positive message of 'Friends' is reinforced by 'Hats Off To Harper', ostensibly for the British singer-songwriter Roy Harper, but more of a tribute to the country bluesman Bukka White. But in the version of the ancient ballad 'Gallows Pole', unlike other variants of the same song, the maid does not escape her punishment.

Traffic also delved into traditional folk for the title track of their album *John Barleycorn Must Die*, released in July. Here the ending is no happier though in this case the central character is merely a personification of the crop to be harvested. Yet despite naming the record after 'John Barleycorn' and using images from the English Folk Dance and Song Society to decorate the cover, the band do not repeat the experiment: the rest of the record consists of original material showcasing the talents of, in particular, Stevie Winwood, although saxophonist Chris Wood also gets a look-in on the free-flowing instrumental, 'Glad'. Indeed their rather cosmetic approach to folk was not untypical of how, in 1970, many bands looked to folklore to give their music a new angle. Black Sabbath, for instance, marketed themselves as practitioners of the occult, a strategy which gave their debut album *Paranoid* helpful publicity when it came out on 18 September. In reality, however, their music was, in spite of the pulsating title track, orthodox heavy metal. One of the more established underground bands, Family, found a way, with 'The Weaver's Answer', of making a modern rock song sound archaic.

By this time concept albums were beginning to split opinion. Critics tended to deride them for being pretentious and self-indulgent though they continued to sell by the truckload. And, of course, they were an excellent form of escapism. But The Who's *Tommy* had shown that there were dangers, aesthetically at least, in making any allegory too specific – better to opt for an overall theme that was visible yet vague, or link together a number of tenuously related themes. The Moody Blues had actually been following these principles for some time to great commercial success and *A Question Of Balance*, released in August, repeated the formula; but this time, unusually, the single taken from the album came out four months earlier; it was also its best track, by some distance.

'Question' was, in fact, two unfinished songs merged together; as with James Taylor's 'Suite For 20G', discussed in Chapter 4, it works well, juxtaposing the political and the personal in the fast and slow sections respectively. According to its composer, Justin Hayward, it is a 'protest song about the state of the world' and so sets the tone for an album which, at a time when most bands were heading in the opposite direction, at least demonstrates commitment to the cause. Yet all too often, despite – or possibly, because of – the worthy intentions, the sentiments are trite, the lyrics hackneyed. Not that this impaired the sales of *A Question Of Balance*: it made number one in the UK and number three in the US, where The Moody Blues' tour to promote it broke box-office records.

The Pretty Things might have done likewise had their album *Parachute*, issued in June, attained the success predicted for it, but in the event it failed to chart in America and made only 43 in the UK. Still, that was an improvement on its much-lauded predecessor, *SF Sorrow*, a rock opera that predated even *Tommy*. *Parachute*, too, has a coherent storyline though its structure is slightly looser, allowing for the exploration of other topics. The central narrative concerns the impulse to flee from the impersonal and sterile confines of the city – a metaphor, perhaps, for the rejection of contemporary society endemic to the rock music of 1970 as a whole. The conclusion is that escape is well worth the risk – there will be a 'parachute' for those who dare to try. Along the way, the band touch on themes of pretence, illusion and misconception, giving the record additional dimensions and making it a work of some substance.

The Pretty Things recorded for Harvest which at that time was Britain's leading prog rock label. Ample evidence for such a claim is contained on its double-album sampler, *Picnic: A Breath Of Fresh Air,* released in May 1970. Granted, seven of the nineteen selections come from 1969, yet the 1970 material is generally superior. It comprises 'The Good Mr Square', one of the outstanding tracks on *Parachute,* and gems by such diverse outfits as Deep Purple, The Third Ear Band, Barclay James Harvest, Pete Brown and Piblokto!, The Edgar Broughton Band, Quatermass, Michael Chapman and The Greatest Show On Earth. Also included is Pink Floyd's previously unreleased 'Embryo'. But best of all is the loping 'Terrapin' by former Floyd front-man, Syd Barrett.

By the time his first solo album, *The Madcap Laughs,* came out in January 1970 Barrett had been out of the band for over eighteen months and its title can be seen as a comment on his departure. Eased out because of his unpredictability, he was now making light of it – or, in an alternative reading of the title, having the last laugh. (The words also appear in 'Octopus'.) Straight after his dismissal Barrett was in the studio recording 'Late Night', so it is no surprise to hear Floyd's trademark cosmic sound effects which he himself did so much to develop; here, they provide an arresting backdrop to what is, in effect, a tender love song. The five tracks made nearly a year later reveal how his music had developed in the interim. 'No Good Trying' and 'No Man's Land' retain a psychedelic sound but are closer to mainstream rock; 'Love You' is exultant, 'Here I Go Again', good-humoured. And the aforementioned 'Terrapin' is a masterpiece: towed along by a simple bluesy melody, it is at once childlike, whimsical and serene.

Barrett's mental state was, however, giving increasing cause for concern and shortly afterwards his former colleagues Dave Gilmour and Roger Waters took over the production duties from Malcolm Jones in an attempt to keep the album on course. The recording sessions were tortuous affairs: Barrett's instructions were incomprehensible and he would alter songs without warning each time he played them. In the end the exasperated Gilmour and Waters allowed him to do as he pleased, a decision which exposed both his flaws and his genius. For example the rambling 'If It's In You' breaks down immediately and ends in mid-air; the lyrics are incoherent and Barrett's singing is excruciating. Similarly the acoustic ballads 'She Took A Long Cold Look' and 'Feel' sound as if he is making them up on the spot. By comparison the percussive 'Octopus', its lyrics redolent of Edward Lear, is positively orderly (and thus merited release as a single) while 'Golden Hair', Barrett's adaptation of a James Joyce poem, is beautifully conceived and executed. That he himself was acutely conscious of his deteriorating condition is demonstrated by the last song to be recorded, 'Dark Globe' – the delivery is desperate, the words distressing: 'My head touched the ground, I was half the way down'. On 6 June 1970 Barrett appeared at the Kensington Olympia for his one and only solo performance: in the middle of the fourth number, 'Octopus', he took off his guitar and left the stage.

Although Syd Barrett is now viewed as one of the great innovators of the period, his approach was by no means unique. Indeed Marc Bolan, of the duo Tyrannosaurus Rex, displayed many of the same characteristics, though to a more pronounced degree. His vocal style, for example, was more mannered and his songs were more consciously poetic. And Bolan built on Barrett's excursions into the imagination by creating a fantasy world populated by gnomes, fairies and a menagerie of mythical beasts. But despite a substantial underground following, Tyrannosaurus Rex were becalmed on the periphery of commercial success – not a place Bolan wanted to be.

By the summer he had rebranded the duo T Rex and espoused mainstream rock: a few days after headlining the inaugural Pilton Festival (now better known as Glastonbury) in June 1970, they recorded 'Ride A White Swan'. While the lyrics follow the familiar formula they are set to a jaunty, danceable beat and a bouncy guitar riff – a blend that catapulted it into the UK singles chart where it eventually reached number two. December saw the release of the album *T Rex,* the cover of which has Bolan symbolically holding a Gibson Les Paul, the classic rock guitar, and like 'Ride A White Swan' it grafts the new style on to the old. So whereas 'Suneye' is Tolkienesque, the insouciant 'Beltane Walk' is based on Jimmy McCracklin's 1957 R & B hit, 'The Walk'; 'Summer Deep' is laden with hallucinogenic visions but 'Is It Love?' prefigures 'Hot Love' both melodically and rhythmically; and all the various strands are woven together on 'The Wizard', an epic, if repetitive, climax to the record.

Bolan's change of direction was no surprise. Rock music in 1970 was central to Western popular culture: exciting, colourful and varied, it offered access to unbridled adulation and massive record sales. Even musicians from respected idioms like jazz and folk wanted a piece of it. Conversely, there were those who were finding its boundaries too restricting. Not only had the standard instrumentation and playing techniques grown stale and outmoded but the very structure of the music was inhibiting creativity. For such musicians it was time to search elsewhere for inspiration.

CHAPTER 6:

Bitches Brew

Identifying the earliest example of a musical genre is a fertile subject for debate among fans, scholars and critics, with seldom any consensus as to artist, let alone year. Contenders for the first rock and roll record, for example, include 'Rocket 88' by Jackie Brenston and his Delta Cats (aka Ike Turner and his Kings of Rhythm) from 1951; Roy Brown's 'Good Rockin' Tonight' (1948); 'Crazy Man Crazy' by Bill Haley and his Comets (1953); Elvis Presley's 'That's All Right' (1954); and Fats Domino's 'The Fat Man' (from 1949, and this writer's nomination). Equivalent disputes preoccupy devotees of glam, punk, jazz (including all its sub-styles) and rap, with the same obvious point that, in the end, no-one is right and no-one is wrong – the fascination lies in the contesting arguments.

The stage at which idioms began to mate is just as difficult to determine, but one thing we can be sure of is that the practice became widespread towards the end of the 1960s. Certainly there had been instances before then (including rock and roll itself) and pop music had always been open to external influences, usually in the interests of novelty. One classical composition, Ponchielli's 'Dance Of The Hours', was adapted twice within a year, first in late 1962 for 'Like I Do' by Maureen Evans, and then in summer 1963 for Allan Sherman's comic 'Hello Mudduh, Hello Fadduh! (A Letter From Camp)'. Pursuing loftier ideals, leading jazz artists like John Coltrane and Yusef Lateef had sourced music from around the world during the same period and, some years earlier, the composer Gunther Schuller created what he called the Third Stream by enacting a formal merger of jazz and classical music.

By 1967, fuelled by the mind-expanding ethos (and drugs) of the counterculture, such experiments were more frequent. The Beatles' *Sgt Pepper's Lonely Hearts Club Band*, released on 1 June, was a milestone in this – and almost every other – respect. Indian music ('Within You, Without You'), trad jazz ('When I'm Sixty-Four') and classical ('A Day In The Life') took their place in an alluring array of sounds, some from unusual (for pop) instruments like the harpsichord and calliope, others specially and/or spontaneously invented in the studio. In jazz, Miles Davis had, as early as 1965, employed rock rhythms on 'Eighty-one', a track from his album *ESP*, though he did not repeat the exercise for three years, by which time the vibraphonist Gary Burton was already working along similar lines.

Such innovations were perhaps to be expected given the constant pressure on pop, rock and jazz musicians to come up with something new. But in folk music the compulsion is, by definition, to do the exact opposite. To hear scions of the folk scene like singer Sandy Denny and fiddler Dave Swarbrick take on rock music was, therefore, a revelation. In effect, the group of which they were both members, Fairport Convention, created British folk-rock with their 1969 albums *Unhalfbricking* and *Liege And Lief*. On the former, Swarbrick was only a guest musician yet his thrilling duet with guitarist Richard Thompson on 'A Sailor's Life' kick-started the new genre; by the latter, now in the band, he was helping to define it.

1970 was the year when all the great rock-based fusions reached their zenith, and the music of the leading UK folk-rock groups was as creative as any. Sandy Denny had left Fairport after *Liege And Lief* but they were still market leaders, their dominance underlined by the release in July of the album *Full House*. The nine-minute 'Sloth' features a lengthy improvised interlude every bit as enthralling as 'A Sailor's Life', and 'Dirty Linen' and 'Flatback Caper' are also instrumental *tours de force*. 'Walk Awhile' exudes the feel-good factor and at the other end of the emotional spectrum is the moving arrangement, and rendition, of 'Flowers Of The Forest', a traditional lament for the Scots killed in 1513 at the Battle of Flodden Field.

As for Denny, she had formed a new band, Fotheringay, with her partner, the Australian folk singer Trevor Lucas, guitarist Jerry Donahue (son of US big band leader Sam), and the impeccable rhythm team of Pat Donaldson on bass and Gerry Conway on drums. In 1970 Fotheringay recorded two albums, their eponymous debut, issued in April, and its follow-up, not released until 2008 as *Fotheringay 2* – 22 tracks in total. Not all are excellent, but the vast majority are, especially those written by and featuring Denny.

Depending on the demands of the material, her voice ranges from delicate to intense – sometimes within the bounds of the same song, as in the stormy 'Nothing More', the opening track of *Fotheringay*. Her intonation and phrasing can also conjure up the most heart-rending effect. 'Banks Of The Nile', for instance – the story of two lovers parting on the eve of the famous naval battle – is impossible to listen to with a dry eye. Her beautiful rendition of the swaying traditional ballad 'Wild Mountain Thyme' and her quiet authority on Wanda Jackson's 'Silver Threads And Golden Needles', both from *Fotheringay 2*, confirm her status as one of the very best contemporary vocalists in any style.

At the same time Denny's own compositions are exceptional. As Rob Young has written,

> The best of Sandy Denny's music inhabits the shore or the riverbank, or drifts upon the sea in the company of its dislocated sailors ... The season is typically autumn or early winter; there is frequently a restless imagistic play of ill omens; the bailiffs are calling in the debt on summer's lease. (*Electric Eden*, p. 314)

Songs like 'The Sea', 'Winter Winds', 'The Pond And The Stream' and 'Late November' could not be more fittingly described; they contrive to be both contemporary and entirely within the folk tradition.

Yet Fotheringay was not just a showcase for Sandy Denny. Gordon Lightfoot's 'The Way I Feel' features Lucas on vocals, although the track's quality is to be found in the excellence of the musicianship, in particular Conway's dynamic drumming and Donahue's flowing guitar. On 'Late

November' Conway also gives an object lesson on how to play drums at a slow tempo.

The final track on *Fotheringay 2* is the wistful acoustic ballad 'Two Weeks Last Summer', written by Dave Cousins, with whose band, The Strawbs, Denny had recorded one of her most poignant compositions, 'Who Knows Where The Times Goes', two years previously. Now The Strawbs themselves had reached the upper echelons of British folk-rock. But whereas *Dragonfly*, released in February 1970, was largely acoustic, the acquisition of organist Rick Wakeman propelled them towards prog – his lengthy, imaginative solo on 'Where Is This Dream Of Your Youth' made it the highlight of the album *Just A Collection Of Antiques And Curios*, recorded at London's Queen Elizabeth Hall on 11 July.

Also at the rockier end of the genre were Trees, a band who, despite their failure to break through at the time, are now considered among its best exponents. Their only two albums both come from 1970. *The Garden Of Jane Delawney* was recorded in March and released the following month. The dreamlike title track is one of two compositions by bassist Bias Boshell; the other, the mournful ballad 'Epitaph' is skilfully structured to sound like a traditional piece. 'The Great Silkie', 'Lady Margaret' and 'She Moved Thro' The Fair' conform to the template created by Fairport on 'A Sailor's Life': a slow, sung introduction succeeded by a frenetic instrumental workout. Celia Humphris illuminates these pieces with her pure, clear voice though her limitations are exposed by the tricky tempo of 'Glasgerion', and the interchange between guitar and male/female vocal on 'Road' doesn't really come off. Yet the integration of folk and rock on the first track, 'Nothing Special', stands comparison with Fotheringay.

On The Shore, made six months later, was a step forward. The cover design, by the then fashionable studio Hipgnosis, sets the scene; there is something distinctly discomforting about the tinted image of a little girl in Victorian clothes playing in a modern garden – a symbol, perhaps, of the dark themes of past songs now revealed in a contemporary context. Certainly the traditional 'Soldiers Three' is an ominous opener, and the atmosphere of foreboding spills over into Boshell's 'Murdoch' with its bleak rural imagery. There are, furthermore, two songs about hanging: 'Geordie' is given a suitably morose treatment but the arrangement of 'Streets Of Derry' is another variation on 'A Sailor's Life' – as is the version of Cyril Tawney's song of betrayal, 'Sally Free And Easy'. The acoustic guitar instrumental 'Adam's Toon' and the self-consciously comic 'Little Sadie' lighten the mood somewhat though grim reality returns with 'While The Iron Is Hot' and 'Fool', two more traditional-sounding originals. The album closes with 'Polly On The Shore', another track combining the cool vocals of Humphris with Barry Clarke's resonant psychedelic guitar.

Regrettably, there were no more Trees records. Bias Boshell went on to write Kiki Dee's 'I've Got The Music In Me', a UK Top 20 hit in September 1974, and later joined The Moody Blues. Celia Humphris married the DJ Pete Drummond and became a voice-over artist: for many years her reassuring tones could be heard announcing upcoming stations on London Underground's Northern Line. Yet in 1970, Trees seemed to have a bright future – more so, perhaps, than the apparently thrown-together outfit, Steeleye Span. Over 40 years later, Steeleye Span are still in existence and have released some 30 albums.

The first of them came out in June 1970 and was called *Hark! The Village Wait*, a title that immediately conjured up rural ritual – no surprise, perhaps, since the group included two orthodox folk duos, Gay and Terry Woods and Tim Hart and Maddy Prior. However, the concept, devised by its fifth member, bassist Ashley Hutchings (late of Fairport Convention), was to unite the Irish tradition, represented by the Woodses, with the English, represented by Hart and Prior, thus creating a pan-British Isles identity greater than the sum of its individual regionalised parts. The merger is successfully realised on 'A Calling-On Song' when all four singers harmonise to great effect and the sombre 'Twa Corbies', where the twin lead vocalists Gay Woods and Maddy Prior embody the eponymous birds.

Yet the best moments result, not from any ideology, but from the now-familiar device of adding a rock beat to a folk tune; 'Lowlands Of Holland' – vocals by Gay Woods, drums by Fairport's Dave Mattacks – is as exciting as anything on *Liege And Lief*, with 'Blackleg Miner' (sung by Hart) and 'The Blacksmith' (Prior, vocals, Gerry Conway, drums) not far behind. The juxtaposition of amplified and acoustic instruments also produces some remarkable new textures. 'One Night As I Lay On My Bed', for instance, blends bluegrass banjo with electric dulcimer to give an attractive exotic feel. Indeed, *Hark! The Village Wait* – along with *Full House*, *Fotheringay* and *On The Shore* – seemed to suggest that, barely one year into its history, folk-rock could, and perhaps should, look to the future as well as the past.

★ ★ ★ ★ ★

As we have seen, the rock music of 1970 was pulling clear of its origins. Almost all of the artists whose imitation/interpretation of African-American urban blues had fashioned the music in the mid-1960s had now moved on. The Animals, Them, The Yardbirds and Cream had all disbanded; The Rolling Stones and John Mayall had diversified; The Pretty Things had transformed out of all recognition. The generation of blues-based bands who had immediately succeeded these pioneers were therefore left with a problem. After only a year or two at the top of their tree, should they stick with the style that made them famous or, like their predecessors, try something different and risk being eclipsed by those who had taken a more adventurous approach from the start?

Two of the bands who elected to stay put were Taste and Free. Released on 1 January 1970, Taste's album *On The Boards* proved to be their last: displaying an unerring sense of tidiness, their final gig took place in Belfast on 31 December. It did, though, provide the blueprint for the solo career of their songwriter, lead guitarist and singer Rory Gallagher, who continued in very much the same vein up to his death in 1995. The hallmarks of *On The Boards* are its clear, clean production (by Tony Colton) and the range of sounds and tempos the band conjure up within what was generally a somewhat restricted format. Even short tracks like 'Railway And Gun' and 'I'll Remember' are packed with variety: the former progresses from a neat acoustic opening to a slow, electric twelve-bar blues and then to a piercing, top-speed guitar solo before a reprise of the introduction; the latter blends pummelling bass and drums with jagged, jazzy guitar and wordless vocals. Gallagher takes solos on harmonica ('If The Day Was Any Longer') and alto saxophone ('On The Boards', 'It's Happened Before, It'll Happen Again') and applies psychedelic touches to the title phrase of 'If I Don't Sing I'll Cry'. The band revert to a more conventional blues-rock power trio sound on ' What's Going On', 'Eat My Words' and 'Morning Sun'.

The title track of Free's *Fire And Water*, issued on 26 June, was funky enough to be covered by Wilson Pickett while the closing 'Alright Now' became one of the dance hits of the year: commencing with an elemental guitar riff, it builds up tension through its driving rhythm and wailing guitar until the release comes with the simple, instantly memorable title-phrase chorus. Released as a single, it made the Top Five on both sides of the Atlantic.

The white American blues band Canned Heat also demonstrated that there was still a market for this kind of music by reaching number two on the UK chart in January with their stomping version of Wilbert Harrison's 1962 hit 'Let's Stick Together', renamed 'Let's Work Together'. Yet 1970 was also a sad year for the band. On 3 September, exactly one month after the release of their fourth album, *Future Blues*, their singer Al Wilson died from an overdose of barbiturates, aged just 27. There was therefore poignancy in both the title of the album, coined by Wilson to draw attention to the destruction of his beloved redwood trees, and its fourth track, his composition 'My Time Ain't Long'. Wilson's warbling vocals and accomplished harmonica-playing helped define the band's sound but here additional talents are on display: his rueful 'London Blues', for instance, uses incongruously mundane images for comic effect and on the jazzy 'Skat', he does just that (scat). Elsewhere, the gruff vocals of Bob Hite and Harvey Mandel's sinuous guitar provide a more conventional blues-rock sound: alongside 'Let's Work Together' are the slow and heavy 'That's All Right, Mama' and 'So Sad (The World's In A Tangle)', an up-beat boogie with an ecological message. The cover of *Future Blues* had the band decked out in Apollo 11 astronaut uniforms but there was nothing space-age about the music: rather like Taste and Free, Canned Heat were persevering with the style they knew best.

Other bands, having strayed from familiar waters, were reverting – or about to revert – to type. In Chapter 5, we noted how Led Zeppelin opted for an acoustic, folk-orientated approach for *Led Zeppelin III*; although they would retain some of that – notably in the opening section of their most famous track, 1971's 'Stairway To Heaven' – their stock-in-trade would continue to be heavy metal. Deep Purple flirted with classical-rock fusion for *Concerto For Group And Orchestra* but, perhaps sensing that their fan-base preferred a simpler diet, they made a spectacular return to basics in June 1970 with *Deep Purple In Rock*.

Although traces of the classical influence remain – the prelude of 'Flight Of The Rat', for example, is Nikolai Rimsky-Korsakov's 'Flight Of The Bumblebee' and there are hints of Gustav Holst's 'Mars' in 'Child In Time' – much of the album consists of unembellished heavy rock. Sometimes the structures are so brutal as to eschew melody almost entirely: 'Living Wreck' and 'Hard Lovin' Man' are little more than rather tedious thrashes built on the thinnest of riffs. In compensation, there is instrumental intricacy in the otherwise frantic 'Speed King' and on the grinding 'Into The Fire' technique is harnessed for dramatic impact. Hard on the heels of *Deep Purple In Rock* came the single, 'Black Night', based on The Blues Magoos' '(We Ain't Got) Nothin' Yet' from 1966. Again the band curb their extravagance to produce a dynamic and well-constructed record. The album remained on the UK album chart for 68 weeks, reaching number four, the single for 24 weeks, making number two. Yet neither was a hit across the Atlantic; it was to be another two years before America became seduced by the charms of Deep Purple.

Ten Years After, on the other hand, already had a strong following in the USA – much boosted by their appearance at Woodstock – and their album *Ssssh* had cracked the Top 20 there in autumn 1969. *Cricklewood Green*, released on 17 April 1970, did even better – as it did, too, in Britain; while reaching the same position (four) as *Ssssh* it stayed in the chart nine weeks longer. However it is difficult to believe that this was to do with the inherent virtues of the album – more a case, perhaps, of those beguiled by their stage-act needing a current example of their work on vinyl. For *Cricklewood Green* finds the band in that classic dilemma referred to above: feeling they had to try and progress but not sure by how much.

It also has the semblance of a rush-job: of the four songs on side one, two have the word 'road' in the title and the other two include multiples of a thousand. 'Sugar The Road' and '50,000 Miles Beneath My Brain' are an uncomfortable blend of the band's customary no-frills rock with an attempt to be more significant: the first opens with irrelevant electronic noises and in the second, mystical lyrics and sitar-like sounds sit awkwardly alongside the heavy riff and tumbling guitar solo. In 'Year 3,000 Blues' a nightmarish vision of the future is set to a chugging boogie – a clumsy stab at comedy which falls flat. The powerful 'Working On The Road' represents a return the band's standard fare, as does side two's 'Love Like A Man' with its memorable riff and lengthy if repetitive solo. But it is bracketed by two more deviations from the script: the jazzy 'Me And My Baby' and the introspective, acoustic 'Circles'. Finally comes 'As The Sun Still Burns Away', the album's only successful fusion of old and new: the meaty riff and moody melody match the theme – the dying sun and the death of mankind – and this time the sonic effects work a treat.

Cricklewood Green also features liberal lashings of Alvin Lee's jet-propelled guitar and so, together with *Deep Purple In Rock*, *Led Zeppelin III*, Taste's *On The Boards* and the release in March of *Live Cream*, represented a reminder that by 1970 blues-rock had become, like prog, a major vehicle for displays of instrumental pyrotechnics. Yet perhaps the most pronounced tendencies in that direction were shown by those musicians who were merging rock with jazz, and jazz with rock.

★ ★ ★ ★ ★

In the late summer of 1968 a jam session took place which was to have profound consequences for the music of the late 20th century. The location was Ronnie Scott's Club in London and the participants were the American drummer Jack DeJohnette and two British musicians, bass player Dave Holland and guitarist John McLaughlin. It was at the same club that Holland had been noticed by Miles Davis and shortly afterwards invited to join the trumpeter's quintet; by September he was playing on 'Frelon Brun', one of Davis's first serious attempts at integrating the pulse of rock into his music. McLaughlin, however, remained in the UK, at least for the time being. DeJohnette had taped the jam session at Scott's and on his return to the US played it to fellow drummer Tony Williams, then a member of Davis's group. Williams was so impressed with McLaughlin that he wanted him for a new band he himself was forming, Lifetime.

But McLaughlin could not afford the airfare and fell back on studio employment. It was at that point, in August 1968, that he encountered the Cream bassist Jack Bruce who, as a side project, had just begun to make a jazz record with saxophonist Dick Heckstall-Smith and drummer Jon Hiseman, former members, like Bruce and McLaughlin, of The Graham Bond Organisation. On the sleeve note to the resultant album, *Things We Like*, Bruce recalls,

> I was driving home from the studio when I spotted John McLaughlin walking down the road with a guitar in one hand and his amplifier in the other, so I stopped my Ferrari and asked him what he was doing. John had just played on a session at Decca studios in West Hampstead and was feeling pretty low ... I thought for a moment and invited him to play on my jazz record and join in on the remaining album sessions in order for him to earn enough money to get to the USA.

A few days later the album was completed but, for reasons that remain obscure, not released until late 1970. By then its mixture of hard bop and free jazz was starting to sound old-fashioned though there is no denying the spirit and verve of tracks like the Ornette Coleman-ish opener, 'Over The Cliff'. McLaughlin is not present there but the tracks on which he does appear are the best on the record. On 'Ballad For Arthur' there are no solos as such and the four musicians integrate impressively with each other, especially given the slow tempo; in contrast, 'HCHHH Blues' is an exciting number with an agile, inventive contribution by McLaughlin.

In January 1969 McLaughlin was, despite Bruce's patronage, still in London, recording his debut album, *Extrapolation*, with outstanding accompaniment from baritone saxophonist John Surman and drummer Tony Oxley. But the following month he was finally on a plane to New York to join Tony Williams, who immediately introduced him to his then employer, Miles Davis. Such was Davis's respect for Williams that, without even hearing McLaughlin, he invited the guitarist to record with him the following day, 18 February 1969, a session that produced the seminal *In A Silent Way*. This exquisite album stands comparison with anything the trumpeter ever released, on a par with *Birth Of The Cool, Sketches Of Spain* and the much-vaunted *Kind Of Blue* from ten years before. As with that record it is the subtle, at times gentle, interplay between theme and solo, ensemble and individual, that creates the atmosphere, punctured only occasionally by bursts of activity. Now, however, the music has a more restless, at times menacing, feel, and the rhythms – though often broken up – derive not from the jazz tradition, but from rock. McLaughlin plays a major role, principally by carrying the melody on the title track and weaving intricate improvisations as a prelude to Davis's stately entrance.

Three months later, he was, at long last, recording with Lifetime, a trio whose other members were Williams and the organist Larry Young, later known as Khalid Yasin. This incendiary group were still more advanced than Davis when it came to exploring new ideas: their music was uncategorisable – not jazz, not rock, but an amalgam of both. Yet this was not the style later known as fusion – conventional jazz solos over a solid 4/4 time signature. On the contrary, Lifetime opted to combine the more challenging aspects of both genres – the raw power of rock with the relentless experimentalism of free-form jazz. Their double album *Emergency!* came out around the time that Miles Davis was beginning preparations for the follow-up to *In A Silent Way,* and it is hard to believe he was unaffected by it. Both Young and McLaughlin participated in the sessions and Williams had only just left his group, much to the trumpeter's regret. It was, furthermore, a step in the direction taken by Lifetime; *In A Silent Way* had captured the pulse of rock, the new album – entitled *Bitches Brew* – added its aggression.

Davis had for some time been concerned that the appeal of music was principally to the white middle classes. As time went on, this audience was not being replenished since most such record buyers were gravitating to rock. However, simply to espouse the music of, say, The Beatles or The Rolling Stones would not help him reconnect with the African-American constituency he craved. Instead, he looked to the likes of James Brown, Jimi Hendrix and Sly Stone for inspiration; echoes of all three may be perceived in *Bitches Brew*. Yet these borrowings were anything but indiscriminate; as the unnamed author (possibly Richard Cook) of the entry for the album in *The Mojo Collection* (p. 212) states, 'Miles liked the style and the energy of rock, but he couldn't entertain any dumbing-down in his own music'.

Issued in April 1970, *Bitches Brew* spelled – at least in one dimension – the end of jazz. No longer would it be possible for those at the cutting edge of the music to ignore rock and/or the electronic instruments that went with it; jazz could no longer be preserved as a rare species with which only the cognoscenti were familiar. I well remember a conversation I had with a school friend who was heavily into contemporary rock. 'Do you like jazz?' I asked. Avoiding a direct answer, he replied, 'I like Miles Davis'. He had just bought *Bitches Brew*.

Despite enormous sales – 70,000 in the first month alone – the album was not easy listening; but although rock fans were clearly able to appreciate it, most jazz critics – often a generation or two behind in their understanding of anything new – were incapable of doing so. Even with hindsight it is hard to see why. On one level alone, it should have excited positive comment: Davis's consistently superb trumpet-playing. He comes in early on almost every track – it is as if he cannot wait to get started – and invariably produces a solo of majestic proportions, ranging up and down the instrument and alternating short stabbing phrases with sustained dramatic sweeps.

Of equal interest is the part played by the supporting cast. The opening 'Pharaoh's Dance' typifies the methodology. It features no fewer than three electric pianos (played by Young, Chick Corea and Joe Zawinul, who wrote the piece) though these are not heard in solo: instead they coalesce, meshing from time to time with McLaughlin's sparse guitar and the brooding bass clarinet of Bennie Maupin. Only the occasional ray of light from Wayne Shorter's soprano saxophone penetrates this dense thicket; Davis simply rides serenely above it. On the title track, the bass (Dave Holland, double bass, Harvey Brooks, bass guitar) is more prominent, and Jack DeJohnette's thundering drums rouse Davis to a clarion call of a solo. Other tracks are rockier – 'Spanish Key', for example, gives the electric pianos a percussive role, while the funky 'Miles Runs The Voodoo Down' was actually released as a single. 'Sanctuary' bears the enigmatic imprint of its composer, Wayne Shorter, though it begins with Davis playing the romantic ballad, 'I Fall In Love Too Easily'; the relatively brief 'John McLaughlin' omits Davis and Shorter but is, as might be expected, a feature for the guitarist whom Davis clearly now esteemed sufficiently highly to name a track after him.

Just as *Bitches Brew* was hitting the shops, Davis was changing his music once again. *Black Beauty: Miles Davis Live At Fillmore West* was recorded on 10 April 1970 at the eponymous San Francisco rock venue with a smaller band comprising Corea, Holland, DeJohnette, percussionist Airto Moreira and soprano saxophonist Steve Grossman. On *Bitches Brew* no instrument – other than Davis's trumpet – soloed for long: each came briefly to the forefront before returning to the protection of the ensemble. Here, Corea and DeJohnette are far more conspicuous and help dictate the routes the music takes.

In his sleeve note to the 1997 CD issue, Corea refers to Davis's 'constant demonstration of creative disagreement with the status quo' and it is certainly tempting to conclude that he is trying to bait the jazz critics who greeted *Bitches Brew* with disdain. 'Directions', for instance, presents throbbing bass guitar, booming drums, writhing sax, and exultant solos from Davis and Corea. The latter treats the listener to a master-class in electric piano, the sound of which epitomised the jazz of the period and was (hence) a *bête noire* to the critics. Corea explores and exploits its potential, not as a surrogate piano, but as an instrument in its own right, and unleashes a torrent of icy, spiky phrases which culminate in shuddering reverberation. 'Miles Runs The Voodoo Down' is fiercer than the studio version: its hallmarks are Davis's stamina, DeJohnette's flamboyance and a four-way, free-form conversation among the rhythm section. In the vigorous version of 'Bitches Brew' Davis shapes his solo like a rock guitarist and on 'Spanish Key' his powerhouse playing is underpinned by a jubilant riff from Corea, who brings the piece, and the concert, to a close with some spacey sound effects. No wonder the crowd, among them the poet Allen Ginsberg, respond with an ovation.

During the rest of 1970 Davis continued to appear on the rock circuit, often opening for acts on the roster of his label, Columbia, such as Blood, Sweat and Tears and Laura Nyro. In August, with a band that included keyboard player Keith Jarrett, he played the mammoth Isle of Wight Festival, sandwiched between Tiny Tim and Ten Years After. Williams, Young and McLaughlin were evidently not being missed.

By then, Lifetime's second album, *Turn It Over,* had been released. Now they had Jack Bruce in the band which should have given them additional scope, but he features on bass only – lead vocals are left to Williams whose take on jazz singing is on the brink of parody. Certainly 'Once I Loved' can only be a satire on the Frank Sinatra/Antônio Carlos Jobim version of 1967 – Williams's deadpan intoning is accompanied by an electronic whine and he ends the piece midway through a line. John Coltrane's 'Big Nick' is as close as it gets to orthodoxy, with a hard bop solo by Young and walking bass from Bruce, but McLaughlin's splattering guitar commentary shatters the cosy atmosphere. Elsewhere there is plenty of the headlong improvisation that characterised *Emergency!* The best examples are the pair of Chick Corea compositions 'To Whom It May Concern – Them' and 'To Whom It May Concern – Us' where Williams traverses the kit at lightning speed while McLaughlin howls and wails, and 'Vuelta Abajo', essentially a rock piece in which a sledgehammer riff anchors the band during a raging storm of individual and collective ferocity. When Lifetime appeared at the University of Manchester Institute of Science and Technology on 21 November 1970 the writer, like the rest of the audience, was mesmerised by their vitality, invention and sheer virtuosity.

There had never been music quite like it, though McLaughlin was to fashion an approximation with his band The Mahavishnu Orchestra. However his work away from Lifetime appeared at this stage to lack focus. In June, he released the Indian-flavoured *My Goal's Beyond*, a meditative record on which he plays only acoustic guitar. Looked at in the light of his growing spirituality, it now makes sense but at the time, given his status as one of the world's premier electric guitarists, it seemed an odd route to be taking.

September saw the issue of *Devotion*, on which he was joined by Young, rock drummer Buddy Miles and his bassist Billy Rich, both of whom had worked with Jimi Hendrix. The music therefore is much punchier and less mobile rhythmically than that of Davis, or of Lifetime. The title track, for example, is built on a simple, swaying two-note riff, reinforced with thudding drums and insistent bass, but McLaughlin still manages to squeeze out a screaming high-speed solo, much in the manner that would become familiar with Mahavishnu. Mention should also be made of Young, a self-effacing musician who specialised in supporting others; here, however, his solo is exceptional – making heavy use of sustain at the outset, his playing then becomes cool and melodious, and advances to an ethereal yet grandiose climax. The best of the rest comprises 'Marbles', a supercharged stomper with a catchy riff and the Milesian 'Purpose Of When' in which McLaughlin's machine-gun like improvisations contrast with the simple child-like melody picked out by Young on electric piano.

At times in 1970 it seemed as if every new development in jazz was linked to the Davis-Williams-McLaughlin axis, even when the methodology was very different. Davis's new pianist, Keith Jarrett, for example, teamed up with the vibraphone player Gary Burton to find other ways of integrating rock into jazz. For one thing, their use of the rock beat was more straightforward: instead of – as Davis was wont to do – treating all instruments as percussion instruments and building up, and breaking up, complex rhythmic patterns, they simply had bass and drums tow the group along in the traditional manner. For another, their interest in rock lay in what it could offer melodically.

Jarrett wrote four of the five pieces on *Gary Burton And Keith Jarrett*, recorded on 23 July 1970, and all of them have a rock feel – indeed 'Grow Your Own' and 'Fortune Smiles' are not far removed from pop – the latter doubly so, since it features a tuneful piano introduction to which lyrics could easily be added, followed by a staccato, riff-like theme. 'The Raven Speaks' is medium-paced and funky while 'Moonchild/In Your Own Quiet Place' features an intricate duet by the principals before switching to a gentle melody pushed along by a soft 4/4 pulse. Two years before Burton had been one of the first jazz musicians to experiment with rock rhythms, and so it is no surprise to hear him use them as a springboard for his fluent improvisations, nowhere more effectively than on bassist Steve Swallow's lively, Latin-flavoured 'Como En Vietnam', a title which, given the grim situation in South-East Asia, can only be interpreted as a sardonic political comment. As for Jarrett, it wasn't long before he was displaying his compositional skills and formidable piano technique on a series of albums for the German ECM label. Here, however, there was no jazz-rock to be found; this was a record company with an alternative agenda all of its own.

As we saw in Chapter 1 Manfred Eicher had founded ECM in 1969 and although most discographies state that its first records were released that year the session dates make that extremely unlikely. For example ECM 1001 – *Free At Last* by The Mal Waldron Trio – was recorded on 24 November 1969, ECM 1002 (*Just Music* by the eponymous German group) on 13 December.

From the beginning Eicher opted for a distinctive identity, tightly focussed on specific genres. ECM authority Pete Newton has analysed the first eight issues – all of which seem to come from 1970 – as falling into four categories:

- piano trio records (ECM 1001, 1003, 1006)
- collective improvisation (ECM 1002, 1004, 1005)
- European jazz (ECM 1002, 1005, 1006, 1007)
- American free jazz (ECM 1001, 1003, 1004, 1008)

None of this appeared to have any commercial potential whatsoever: nobody would have been surprised if the company, trading on what appeared to be one man's personal and very idiosyncratic taste, had promptly gone bust. Eicher, however, made two shrewd business decisions. One was to extend his house-style to the album cover art – typically minimalist, beautifully photographed, bleak landscapes. The second was to ensure that only music of the highest quality was released. Fortunately that did not prevent eccentric issues like *Output* by The Wolfgang Dauner Trio (ECM 1006) featuring the leader on ring modulator, as well as piano, and with a sleeve picture of a man with a light bulb instead of a head. But it certainly led to excellent albums like *The Paul Bley Trio With Gary Peacock* (recordings from 1964 and 1968), Marion Brown's *Afternoon Of A Georgia Faun*, and *Afric Pepperbird* by The Jan Garbarek Quartet including what was to become the house rhythm section of Arild Andersen on bass and Jon Christensen on drums. In fact many musicians on these early albums stayed with the label for many years, a reflection of Eicher's commitment to their music and the top-class working conditions he offered, rare commodities among label bosses – both then and now.

★ ★ ★ ★ ★

Rock was attractive to jazz artists for a variety of reasons, not least because it was a conduit to a younger and bigger audience and hence more cash. Strangely enough, commercial gain was also a motivation for rock musicians moving the other way. Two of the early jazz-rock (or perhaps more correctly, rock-jazz) bands – Blood, Sweat and Tears and Chicago – were both hugely successful. Though the first BS&T album, 1968's *Child Is Father To The Man* reached only 47 on the US album chart, the next two,

Blood, Sweat and Tears and *Blood, Sweat and Tears 3,* both topped the chart and stayed there for a combined total of nine weeks.

The latter, released in June 1970, demonstrated how to extract the maximum commercial potential from what was, on the face of it, a conglomeration of assorted strands – rock, jazz, blues, Renaissance music, singer/songwriter classics and a three-movement suite. Yet this apparent mishmash is in fact a deliberate strategy, aimed at impressing the listener with the the band's breadth of vision, intelligence and virtuosity. Unfortunately, all too often it comes across as mere showing-off. Steve Winwood's '40,000 Headmen' for example, contains variations on themes by Béla Bartók, Sergei Prokofiev, Thelonious Monk and Fred Lewis (who?) but to no apparent purpose. The constant switches of texture and tempo in 'Sympathy For The Devil/Symphony For The Devil' may be impressive technically yet make little sense musically and the pseudo-Shakespearean lyrics of 'The Battle' verge on the unintentionally comic. Yet audiences on both sides of the Atlantic could not, it seems, get enough of such stuff. Given the panoply of musical trickery on show, it was statistically inevitable that at least one track might work, and 'Hi-De-Ho' is that track; for once the arrangement suits the song, the interplay between organ and horn section reinforcing vocalist David Clayton-Thomas's lusty interpretation of this gospel-tinged Gerry Goffin and Carole King composition.

Chicago, at least at the outset, were more grounded, although they had their moments of bombast – take, for instance, the seven-part ballet and the two four-movement suites on their eponymous album, released on 26 January. However the pulsating '25 Or 6 To 4', with its skintight horn riffs and voluble guitar provided partial compensation; when issued in July as a single it proved an ideal follow-up to the visceral 'I'm A Man'. In fact both must be considered among the best jazz-rock singles of 1970, if not ever, but they are eclipsed – just – by the dramatic 'Vehicle', a US number two in May for The Ides of March.

In terms of jazz content, the music of these bands amounted to little more than a horn section and occasional solo grafted on to a rock structure and so it wasn't long before the novelty wore off. After their two consecutive US number ones, only three more BS&T albums made the charts, reaching numbers ten, nineteen and 32 respectively: the last of these was titled, rather desperately, *New Blood*; in the UK, there were no further hits beyond *3*. Chicago moved gradually towards MOR balladry and colossal album sales while the fortunes of The Ides of March went rapidly in the opposite direction.

1970 was therefore the high-water mark for this brand of rock-jazz, as it was, too, for the more sophisticated fusions then under way. In these cases jazz was not a separate element crudely bolted on to rock, but one of many components used to assemble each individual product. The music of The Soft Machine, for instance, lay at the intersection between rock, jazz and classical. Originally a psychedelic outfit, their leanings towards jazz became more pronounced with the departure of guitarist Kevin Ayers and the arrival of bass player Hugh Hopper in January 1969. In 1970 they were also the first rock band to appear at the BBC Proms, the long established season of classical music concerts which took place in London every summer. The organisers were no doubt attracted by the band's instrumental excellence, in particular the playing of organist Mike Ratledge, a classically-trained musician influenced by the French composer, Olivier Messiaen.

Their double album *Third* was recorded in the spring and represents a radical departure from contemporary rock. There is no sign of a guitar and precious little in the way of vocals. Instead the front-line musicians are Ratledge and the eloquent alto saxophonist Elton Dean; Hopper and drummer Robert Wyatt provide irresistible rhythmic momentum and in the background is a spectrum of instrumental colour comprising violin, trombone, flute and clarinet. Each of the band members contributes one lengthy composition, but this is music devoid of ego in which displays of bravura count less than overall shape and content. And, despite a myriad of diverse strands, its shifting, swirling structures make it entirely distinctive.

In many respects the American equivalent to The Soft Machine was to be found in the work of Frank Zappa (another disciple of a modern

French composer, in his case, Edgard Varèse). But Zappa's music was on a far grander scale, encompassing *musique concrète*, jazz, urban blues, and rock and roll from every era – all served up with a liberal helping of satire. Of the three albums he released in 1970, two consisted of material by the group he had just disbanded, The Mothers of Invention.

First, in February, came *Burnt Weeny Sandwich* which featured the rock and roll pastiches 'WPLJ' and 'Valarie', alongside brief, abstract fragments and two substantial pieces, 'Holiday In Berlin, Full Blown' and 'The Little House I Used To Live In'. The former is an episodic piece in which the sentimental saxophone and military percussion mock the German city's Nazi past; the latter is an eighteen-minute epic aimed at one of Zappa's favourite targets – the pretensions of a younger generation that sees itself as superior to the rest of the population. The clue is in the title but is reinforced by the grotesquely over-aggressive playing and, after the piece has concluded, Zappa's admonishment to a heckler, 'Everybody in this room is wearing a uniform, and don't kid yourself'.

Weasels Ripped My Flesh, released in August, encompasses recordings made by The Mothers between 1967 and 1969 and thus is even more disparate. Again, the title is significant: deriving from the name of a comic book story, it now applies to the lacerating free-form interludes that pervade the record. In between there are some sterling instrumental performances such as the trenchant violin solo by Don 'Sugarcane' Harris on Little Richard's 'Directly From My Heart To You' and the inevitable satire, this time on the juvenile lyrics of heavy rock, 'My Guitar Wants To Kill Your Mama'.

October saw the release of *Chunga's Revenge*, the first album issued under Zappa's own name but, like its two predecessors, containing outtakes from the *Hot Rats* sessions of the previous year. Now Zappa turns his wrath on the groupie – a theme he was to return to the following year in *200 Motels*. Three (possibly four) of the ten tracks are on this subject: 'Road Ladies', 'Tell Me You Love Me' and 'Would You Go All The Way?'; the pop song parody 'Sharleena' is more equivocal. 'Rudy Wants To Buy Yez A Drink' is a comic portrait of the sleazy union boss, 'Twenty Small Cigars' a gentle pastiche of cocktail jazz, while 'Transylvania Boogie', 'Nancy And Mary Music' and, especially, the title track, all offer generous portions of Zappa's cascading guitar.

Zappa recorded for his own label, Bizzare, but The Soft Machine, Blood, Sweat and Tears, Chicago and Miles Davis were all on Columbia (CBS in the UK), the first company fully to espouse jazz-rock/rock-jazz. Among their more inspired signings was the Latin fusion band Santana, who thrilled the Woodstock audience only three months after recording their eponymous debut album. The follow-up, *Abraxas*, came out in September 1970 and – predominantly instrumental – it nudged the band a little closer to the jazz influence that would become more overt on the 1973 albums *Welcome* and *Love Devotion Surrender*, the latter a collaboration between John McLaughlin and their leader and superlative guitarist, Carlos Santana.

Abraxas is, in fact, the rock equivalent of *Bitches Brew*. The two records share the same cover artist, Mati Klarwein, whose multi-coloured, multi-cultural paintings provide, in both cases, an appropriately exotic introduction to the music therein. Fuelled by a range of percussive effects, each album draws selectively from external sources in order to build up a dark, brooding atmosphere. Though where *Bitches Brew* is abstract, *Abraxas* is figurative: we really can picture the inhospitable wilderness of 'Singing Winds, Crying Beasts' and the crisis in distant Persia conveyed by 'Incident At Neshabur'; the renowned 'Black Magic Woman' is at once more vivid and more sinister than the character featured in the Fleetwood Mac original. At the same time, there are interludes of hedonistic pleasure: 'Oye Como Va', written by salsa king Tito Puente, is a dancefloor-filler, 'Se A Cabo' a slab of unrefined excitement and 'Samba Pa Ti' unashamedly romantic.

In 1970, aside from John McLaughlin and The Soft Machine, all of the major players in jazz-rock/rock jazz – Miles Davis, Tony Williams, Gary Burton, Frank Zappa, B S &T, Chicago, Santana – were American. Perhaps that was only fitting, given the origins of both genres. But when it came to merging rock with classical music, there was only one country in it.

★ ★ ★ ★ ★

Though all types of rock fusion were undertaken with an eye on the pecuniary benefits, the root of these experiments was the desire to extend the expressive range of a music that was under constant threat of banality; rock itself had grown away from commercial pop for that very reason. This was an issue both for bands and for individual musicians who were now starting to be judged on their technical ability, as in jazz. One common way of showing you were going in the right direction was to create extended works – pretty much essential for any self-respecting progressive (soon to be known as 'prog') rock band. In many cases, these were merely two or more pieces gratuitously tacked together but in time they evolved into formats borrowed from classical music – operas, suites and symphonies; some, as we shall see shortly, drew from classical compositions themselves.

Pink Floyd had been large-scale specialists since their days as an underground band but, until 1970, had produced nothing of the complexity of 'Atom Heart Mother'. In fact this new piece could not have been further thematically from such journeys into the cosmos as 'Interstellar Overdrive' and 'Set The Controls For The Heart Of The Sun': here was a composition, on the face of it, about cows in a field. And, like the beasts who adorned the (aptly-named) gatefold sleeve, it plodded along at a steady medium-to-slow tempo, never once breaking into a trot. Yet this was a work of considerable substance which betokened a new maturity both for the band and for rock music in general.

Heralded by a blast of brass, 'Atom Heart Mother' lumbers into life. The stately main theme soon gives way to a lyrical melody, played first on cello, then on slide guitar, and these motifs recur throughout the succeeding 20 minutes. In between there are two wordless choral sections – the first, pristine, the second, primordial – a languid guitar solo, and a collage of eerie sound snippets, before the full ensemble returns for a triumphant statement of the main theme. Pink Floyd have since virtually disowned 'Atom Heart Mother', possibly because they received considerable help with the orchestration from non-band member Ron Geesin, yet it emerges as a complete work, just like a piece of what was then called 'serious music' should be. Everything in the band's field of vision – rock, blues, symphonic and choral music, *musique concrète* – integrates into a unified whole. As for the cows, their presence is neatly explained by Bob Carruthers on the DVD *Inside Pink Floyd: A Critical Review 1967-1974* as an 'image that is familiar but at the same time strangely disturbing' – a metaphor, in fact, for the entire composition.

Turn the record over, and there is more programmatic music, a group of three pieces evocative of summer. 'Fat Old Sun' and 'Summer '68' make direct reference, while 'Alan's Psychedelic Breakfast', consisting mainly of bits of taped conversation concerning the eating habits of one of the band's roadies, is more oblique; yet anyone listening to the piano, acoustic guitar and full band instrumental interludes would be hard pushed not to visualise the long, hot days of August during which it was recorded. Released on 2 October 1970, the *Atom Heart Mother* album reached number one on the UK album charts, a feat Pink Floyd did not repeat for another five years. Even the multi-million selling *Dark Side Of The Moon* made only number two.

Atom Heart Mother, and the title track in particular, was tantamount to classical music for a new age, its blend of the orthodox and avant garde both radical and seamless. As such it presented a contrast to the experiments being carried out by another former underground band, The Nice, who tended to lean much harder on the celebrated composers of earlier centuries and use specific extracts from their work as separate elements within what was often a diverse mix. For example 'Rondo', from their 1967 debut album *The Thoughts Of Emerlist Davjack*, was a re-harmonisation of jazz pianist Dave Brubeck's 'Blue Rondo A La Turk' but sported a quote from Bach's *Toccata and Fugue in D minor*. The following year they used part of Dvořák's *New World* symphony on their version of Leonard Bernstein's 'America' and returned to Bach for the 'Brandenburger' section of the suite 'Ars Longa Vita Brevis' from the album of the same name.

Ars Longa Vita Brevis also included the intermezzo from the 'Karelia' suite by Jean Sibelius, a piece that featured in their most ambitious project, *Five Bridges Suite*, released in May 1970, two months after the band had broken up. Side one (comprising the eponymous work) and the first two tracks of side two were taken from a concert at the Fairfield Halls, Croydon, in which The Nice were accompanied by the Sinfonia of London, conducted by Joseph Eger. 'Five Bridges Suite' is an eighteen-minute composition commissioned by the Newcastle Arts Festival to depict, as the title suggests, the city's famous bridges over the River Tyne. These provide the inspiration for some imaginative writing: in 'High Level Fugue', for instance, the band's organist Keith Emerson tries to convey this bridge's dual function: in the album's sleeve note he states,

> It suggested to me … a certain mechanical counterpoint which when expressed musically let me divide the trains and cars between my right and left hands. Brian [Davison, the band's drummer] states a third counterpoint percussive by using cymbals, simulating the splashing water of the River Tyne which becomes more and more polluted as "progress" destroys nature herself by building more and more machines.

Elsewhere, however, the 'bridge' concept signifies the link between musical idioms, best illustrated by the rousing 'Finale' where, driven on by the pounding riff, band, orchestra and jazz horn section unite in organised chaos. 'Intermezzo: Karelia Suite' and 'Pathétique' (the third movement of Tchaikovsky's *Symphony No. 6*) are on similar lines, although the orchestra is reduced to hammering out the theme statement while Emerson and Davison step into the spotlight. Next comes another live recording featuring a medley of Bob Dylan's 'Country Pie' and Bach's *Brandenburg Concerto No. 6*, a combination so audacious and delivered with such swagger and conviction as to raise at least a smile: one can only marvel at Emerson's ebullient, virtuosic organ solo and Davison's unflaggingly propulsive drumming. A straight rock number, 'One Of Those People', rounds out the album and even this is not without interest: a (possibly unprecedented) song about a self-confessed psychopath, it is rendered still more sinister by the hissing vocals of its composer, bassist Lee Jackson.

It is hard to say why the music of The Nice is so much more compelling than, say, that of Blood, Sweat and Tears. Both bands throw in everything but the kitchen sink, resulting in a jumble that – unlike the work of Miles Davis, Lifetime and Pink Floyd, for example – is far from fully integrated. Perhaps it is because B, S & T use their source material, and their own instrumental talents, indiscriminately; The Nice, though at times equally meretricious, put it all to the service of sheer excitement. There was, however, not much more that could have been done with their crude formula of rock-plus-classical; furthermore only one of their albums, prior to *Five Bridges Suite*, had made the UK chart and none had been hits in the US (nor ever were).

Perhaps it was the combination of these two factors that led Emerson, in the spring of 1970, to form a group with drummer Carl Palmer, formerly with another organ trio, Atomic Rooster, and the ex-King Crimson bass player, Greg Lake. Emerson, Lake and Palmer appeared at the Isle of Wight festival and a few weeks later released their eponymous debut album which, despite the fanfare that greeted their arrival as the latest 'supergroup', was not dissimilar in content from something The Nice might have done. There are, for instance, the familiar adaptations of classical works. 'The Barbarian' is derived from Béla Bartók's 'Allegro Barbaro' and 'Knife Edge' employs extracts from pieces by Leoš Janáček and Johann Sebastian Bach for its theme and organ solo respectively. To these are added Emerson's pseudo-classical suite 'The Three Fates'; two lyrical compositions by Lake, 'Take A Pebble' and 'Lucky Man'; and the appropriately metallic-sounding 'Tank', a feature for Palmer.

But in terms of production and presentation *Emerson, Lake And Palmer* was superior to any Nice album. The striking cover painting (originally intended for Spirit) by Nic Darnell; the superb studio sound; and the star quality of each individual all conspired to make it a hit on both sides of the Atlantic. Lake was a better singer and composer than Jackson, Palmer as least as good a drummer as Davison, if more ostentatious, and although for many non-specialists that equates to better, there is no denying the brilliance of his playing, particularly at the climax of 'The Barbarian'. As for Emerson, his virtuosity is all over the record, whether on organ, piano, clavinet or moog synthesiser.

Emerson was, in fact, typical of a new breed of British rock musician: phenomenally gifted, he was not afraid of letting the world know it. Although this left him open to the accusation that he was pursuing technique for its own sake, rock audiences and record-buyers, particularly in the UK, loved it. The magazine *Beat Instrumental and International Recording Studio* catered for this very market, including features not just on the musicians but also all the technical aspects relevant to their output – brands of instrument, microphone, amplifier and, as its title suggests, the studios themselves. It suddenly became important which bands were choosing to record where, with smaller independent outfits like Advision, De Lane Lea and IBC attracting as much attention as the fabled Abbey Road. And recording engineers, heretofore obscure backroom staff, were now among the rock elite, sought out by bands requiring a specific sound.

The magazine's principal focus was, however, the proficiency of the individual musician. In its March 1970 edition the results were given of a poll conducted among its readers to determine the top practitioners. This sort of election had been familiar in jazz circles for a quarter of a century or more but was new to rock – an indication of where the music was now positioning itself. Five sections were devoted to instrumentalists and one to vocalists; the winners were Eric Clapton (guitar), Jack Bruce (bass), Ginger Baker (drums) – this, despite the fact that Cream had disbanded eighteen months earlier – Keith Emerson (keyboard), Dick Heckstall-Smith (brass/woodwind) and Robert Plant (vocals). Of the 60 artists who made the top ten in these categories, only six were American, of whom just two, Jimi Hendrix and Roland Kirk, were African-American.

The clear implication was that British rock, following all manner of fusions with other forms of music, was now setting its own standards. In the past it was hard to imagine the likes of Ringo Starr or Keith Richards working outside the confines of The Beatles or The Rolling Stones but such was the technique and versatility of leading players like Clapton, Bruce, Baker and Emerson that it seemed as if they could fit into any band. No-one could foresee that, in the not-too-distant future, they would acquire the name, and status, of the dinosaur.

CHAPTER 7:

Powerman And The Moneygoround

Harold Wilson had never been reluctant to be seen in the company of celebrities. As President of the Board of Trade he established close connections with the film industry and in March 1964 he laughed and joked with The Beatles during a televised Variety Club luncheon, thus reinforcing his appeal to younger voters in the run-up to the General Election. The following year, now Prime Minister, Wilson attended a similar event, fraternising with the actors Sean Connery, John Mills and Richard Todd, comedian Arthur Haynes and circus entrepreneur Billy Smart. But it was the invitation issued to footballer George Best to attend a Downing Street reception for the West German Chancellor Willy Brandt in March 1970 that perhaps excited the most comment: Best was already becoming as famous for his flamboyant social life as he was for his achievements on the pitch.

Yet now such links failed to cut the required electoral ice. The crazy days of the sixties were over and voters were more interested in the hard realities of law and order, unemployment and immigration. The advent of the Conservative government under Edward Heath also brought with it a new generation of public figures who, while they may have retained some vestiges of altruism, were much more interested in the pursuit of power and money than peace-love-and-good-vibes. Rupert Murdoch, for example, had been a Labour supporter while an Oxford undergraduate and as a newspaper magnate in his native country backed the Australian Labor Party leader, Gough Whitlam, whose programme included universal free health care, free education and the nationalisation of the oil and gas industries. Having recently acquired *The News Of The World* and *The Sun*, however, Murdoch positioned himself on the right of UK politics, a dinner-guest of Heath's and, ultimately, a devotee of Margaret Thatcher.

In 1970, while still editor of the magazine *Student* (which he had founded four years earlier, aged sixteen), Richard Branson used its pages to launch his Virgin Records Mail Order business which undercut the retail prices of singles and albums by up to 20%. As well as listing the titles available for sale the Virgin ads included a side panel with the contact details of Help International, an agency offering advice on:

> V.D., Physchiatric [*sic*] help, Pregnancy testing, Homosexuality, Lesbianism, Drugs, Abortion, Contraception, Adoption, Legal Problems, Jobs, etc.

The philanthropy continued, in proportion, naturally, to the capitalism; over the next 40 years Branson created over 400 companies within the Virgin Group and at the time of writing is the fourth richest citizen of the UK. Yet, at least in the eyes of the left wing, his image is far from untarnished. As early as January 1970 he was being pilloried in *Private Eye* for failing to pay his staff, despite receiving a retainer of £3,000 from IPC Magazines for advice on youth matters, and he subsequently became a close associate of both Edward Heath and Margaret Thatcher. The latter appointed him 'Litter Tsar' and in October 1990 Branson funded Heath's trip to Baghdad to negotiate the release of British hostages taken by Saddam Hussein – some years later, Heath returned the favour by securing the right of Virgin Airways to fly over China.

One particularly active Conservative supporter at the 1970 General Election was Ronan O'Rahilly, founder of Radio Caroline six years earlier. In 1967 Caroline had been forced off the air by the Labour Postmaster General Anthony Wedgwood-Benn and at this, the first national election since then, O'Rahilly was out for revenge. He allied himself with the Dutch pirate station Radio Nord See, later renamed Radio North Sea International and, four days before the election, Radio Caroline International. In direct contravention of the Representation of the People Act 1949, the station broadcast pro-Tory and anti-Labour propaganda, including jingles abusing Harold Wilson. The Conservatives' success on polling day was, however, something of a pyrrhic victory for O'Rahilly: the government continued to jam the station (now RNSI again) until it sailed back into Dutch waters.

In starting Radio Caroline, O'Rahilly had been keen to challenge the hegemony of the BBC and Radio Luxembourg, both of whom had refused to give air time to Georgie Fame, whom O'Rahilly was managing at the time. The same combination of independence and self-interest percolated through to the disc jockeys who worked on Caroline and on the pirate stations generally. Slowly but surely the promotion of their personality and image became more important than the records they were playing, a situation that has persisted in pop music radio to the present day. By 1970 many had transferred to the BBC's new station, Radio 1, and were tantamount to pop stars themselves.

Unlike their predecessors, this generation of DJs had no inhibitions about expressing their political views. John Peel, for instance, wore a T-shirt bearing *The Guardian* newspaper's logo and described himself as a 'wet socialist', while Tony Blackburn railed against trade unions and Kenny Everett was a Thatcher devotee. But it was as arbiters of taste rather than ideology that the Radio 1 DJs had the greater impact. Peel's endorsement was crucial for any rock act and, at the other end of the spectrum, Blackburn and Everett relentlessly promoted the sort of catchy three-minute single that had dominated the charts for the previous decade.

★ ★ ★ ★ ★

The UK mainstream pop scene was holding its own in 1970, partly due to the influence of the Radio 1 DJs, but largely because it represented a refuge for record-buyers unsympathetic to prog and all the various forms of rock fusion. However numerous singles chart hits reflected, albeit in diluted form, the concerns that permeated the allegedly more profound music of the album artists. On 10 January, for example, Blue Mink were at number three with their plea for racial harmony, 'Melting Pot', followed up in March by the self-explanatory 'Good Morning Freedom' and in September by 'Our World', another appeal for friendship between nations. Other hits with similar themes included 'Let's Work Together' by Canned Heat and The Dave Clark Five's 'Everybody Get Together', written by Dino Valente under the pseudonym Chet Powers and first recorded by The Kingston Trio in 1964. (The DC5 made a habit of looking back in 1970: as well as their two 'Good Old Rock 'N' Roll' singles referred to in Chapter 5, they revived – with added Beach Boys-style harmonies – Jerry Keller's 1959 hit, 'Here Comes Summer'.) Arrival, featuring no fewer than five vocalists, took a complementary if more personal approach on the uplifting, gospel-flavoured 'Friends' and 'I Will Survive' – not the Gloria Gaynor number but an original written by band-member Frank Collins and elegantly orchestrated by Paul Buckmaster.

The Hollies' 'Gasoline Alley Bred', and Don Fardon's 'Indian Reservation', both of which entered the charts in October, displayed a less positive view of the world. The former was by the composers of 'Melting Pot', Roger Cook and Roger Greenaway, assisted on this occasion by Tony Macaulay, and a prototype version was in fact made by Blue Mink. The tale of a couple thwarted by their humble origins, it would not have been out of place stylistically on Elton John's *Tumbleweed Connection*; it was, however, The Hollies' last Top 20 hit for nearly four years. 'Indian Reservation', written by John D Loudermilk, concerns the enforced migration of the Cherokee in the nineteenth century. It was first recorded in 1959 as 'The Pale Faced Indian' by Marvin Rainwater, himself one quarter-Cherokee; Fardon, from Coventry, had already made the US chart in 1968 with his own driving version of the song.

There was plenty of ersatz rock to choose from: at the heavier end were Canada's The Guess Who with 'American Woman', while Christie's 'Yellow

River' was more in the manner of Creedence Clearwater Revival. The intro to Shocking Blue's 'Venus' sounded exactly like The Who's 'Pinball Wizard' but it then developed into something distinctive, with exotic vocals by Mariska Veres and composer Robbie Van Leeuwen's oddly appropriate country guitar solo. A number eight hit in the UK, it reached the top of the American singles chart on 17 February; it thus provided some much-needed credibility to European pop. Shocking Blue also paved the way for the subsequent success of important Dutch bands like Focus and Bettie Serveert.

The escapism endemic among album acts also found an outlet in commercial pop. Some was geographic – Mary Hopkin's 'Temma Harbour', produced by Mickie Most, evoked the sunny shores of the Tasmanian resort, and the gentle cadences of Bobby Bloom's 'Montego Bay', co-written with Brill Building veteran Jeff Barry, gave it a suitably Caribbean flavour – some historic or, as in the case of Hotlegs' 'Neanderthal Man', prehistoric. Finally, the fusion projects of the likes of The Nice and Deep Purple had a commercial counterpart in Barry Ryan's 'Kitsch'. Written by twin brother Paul, its changes of tempo and texture, rich orchestration and futuristic lyrics made for a heady mix; in the event it was too ambitious for many record-buyers and made only number 37 on the singles chart.

Naturally enough, the leading songwriters of the day were represented in a variety of cover versions, including Paul McCartney ('Come And Get It', by Badfinger); George Harrison ('Something', by Shirley Bassey); Randy Newman (Three Dog Night's 'Mama Told Me Not To Come'); Joni Mitchell ('Both Sides Now', by Judy Collins); and Bob Dylan ('All Along The Watchtower', by The Jimi Hendrix Experience – widely considered to be the greatest-ever Dylan cover). The year also saw strong comebacks by some big names of the 1960s: John Phillips, formerly of The Mamas and The Papas, reached number 32 in the US with his exuberant 'Mississippi' yet Del Shannon's punchy, psychedelic-tinged 'Isabelle' inexplicably failed to chart on either side of the Atlantic. In contrast, two singles by new acts each made number one in the UK and number three in America and so are inextricably linked with the spring/summer of 1970.

Norman Greenbaum's 'Spirit In The Sky' was at once otherworldly and infectious: built on a riff reminiscent of Canned Heat's 'On The Road Again', it rolled along inexorably, propelled by handclaps and bluesy guitar licks. Not many smash hits have taken the after-life as their theme but 'Spirit In The Sky' transcended reality in more ways than one: fifteen years after release it was, according to *Mojo* magazine (issue 152), still providing an income for Greenbaum, (who had no further hits of any description), due to its repeated use in commercials, TV programmes and feature films. While 'Spirit In The Sky' seemed to come from nowhere, Mungo Jerry's 'In The Summertime' became ubiquitous at outdoor events, following the band's appearance in May at the Hollywood Festival, Staffordshire. Low on subtlety but high on optimism, it was jug band music for a new decade – at least so it seemed. For many, the novelty wore off in the time it had taken Ray Dorset to compose it, that is, less than ten minutes.

Those on low incomes, in particular children and young teenagers, could buy anthologies of chart hits on budget labels like Pickwick and Music for Pleasure. The only snag was that they were not the actual recordings but cover versions by uncredited singers and musicians. The results, as might be imagined, were variable. The 1970 issue of Pickwick's *Top Of The Pops* series contains some respectable efforts: 'You Can Get It If You Really Want' stands comparison with the Jimmy Cliff original, while the near-impossible task of emulating Smokey Robinson on 'Tears Of A Clown' is performed creditably. *Hot Hits*, on the other hand, is disappointing. The cover poses the challenge: 'Can you tell the difference between these and the original sounds?' Regrettably the answer is a resounding 'Yes!' MFP (parent company: EMI) simply had not invested sufficient resources in the project: the same singer is tasked with impersonating Cliff Richard, Cat Stevens and Ray Dorset and his exaggeration of the latter's already mannered vocal style sails perilously close to inadvertent parody.

One of the better tracks on *Hot Hits* is the version of The Kinks' 'Lola', the original of which made number two on 8 August and was thus the band's biggest hit for three years; the follow-up, 'Apeman', also made the

Top Five. It is tempting to think that many of those who purchased them did not see, or care about, the stereotypes they portrayed, the first, of a transvestite, the second, of the happy-go-lucky Jamaican: in 1970 sensibilities were different from what they are today and besides, both – especially 'Apeman' – were otherwise excellent records. Yet despite their inclusion, the album *Lola Versus Powerman And The Moneygoround, Part One* was a flop.

The band's leader, Ray Davies, was embroiled in a dispute with his publisher, Eddie Kassner, and by 1970 he had received no song-writing royalties for five years. His frustration now boiled over into his music with an album that attacked not only Kassner but the whole pop music industry – a worthy subject for satire, certainly, though Davies's misanthropy is so extreme as to unbalance his normally sure-footed compositional technique. Much of the writing is clumsy and too often falls back on stereotypes – the grasping Jewish agent in 'Top Of The Pops', the dictatorial union boss in 'Get Back In Line' (and, of course, the characters described in 'Lola' and 'Apeman') – while 'The Moneygoround' goes as far as naming and shaming the guilty parties, the band's former managers, Robert Wace and Grenville Collins. The real vitriol, however, is reserved for Kassner – the uncouth publisher of 'Denmark Street', the megalomaniac of 'Powerman'.

The degree of detail in these assaults perhaps explains why the record failed so conspicuously: it was simply over the heads of the vast majority of the record-buying public. Anyone wanting the two most attractive tracks could get them separately and, in any case, those who bought albums were, by and large, a different breed from those who bought singles, as one of Davies's old mod colleagues, Steve Marriott, was discovering.

The previous year Marriott had formed a supergroup, Humble Pie, with Peter Frampton, formerly of The Herd, ex-Spooky Tooth bassist Greg Ridley and the seventeen-year-old drumming prodigy, Jerry Shirley. The new band tasted instant success when their debut single, 'Natural Born Bugie' made number four on the UK singles chart in September. Yet the concomitant album, *As Safe As Yesterday Is,* did not include the single and reached only number 32. The follow-up, *Humble Pie,* released in July 1970, did not chart at all, almost certainly because it found them in a state of transition to a heavier sound. Thus Frampton's otherwise acoustic ballad 'Earth And Water Song' contains a biting guitar solo, and Shirley's country waltz, 'Only A Roach', featuring steel guitarist BJ Cole, is balanced by the hard-hitting 'One Eyed Trouser Snake Rumba' which follows it. Cole reappears on 'Skint', where this time the gentle country lilt provides an ironic backdrop to a song which chronicles the decline of the band's previous label, Immediate. But perhaps the best track is the opener, 'Live With Me', a slow-burning rocker showcasing Ridley's agile bass and Marriott's hoarse, soulful vocals. For no obvious reason the album's cover includes two Victorian paintings: on the front, *The Stomach Dance* by Aubrey Beardsley, and on the back, GF Watts's *Esperance* ('Hope'), a copy of which hung on the wall of Nelson Mandela's Robben Island prison cell.

★ ★ ★ ★ ★

Southern Africa – though perhaps not Mandela specifically – was very much on the mind of Edward Heath when he took over as Prime Minister on 19 June 1970. For one thing there was the question of what to do about Ian Smith, who back in 1965 had made a unilateral declaration of Rhodesia's independence from Britain. In response Harold Wilson had condemned the regime as racist and imposed economic sanctions, but Heath was more pragmatic. Believing that sanctions were ineffective, he was prepared to come to some sort of accommodation with Smith, especially if he were to give assurances that black majority rule would be considered at some future juncture. Yet despite a promising start to negotiations the stalemate continued.

The UK's relationship with South Africa was an even hotter political potato, largely because of the controversy surrounding the sporting links between the two countries. Two years previously, the South African Cricket Board had made it clear that an England touring team containing Basil D'Oliveira would not be welcome there. Born in Cape Town of Indian and Portuguese descent, D'Oliveira was classified by the South African government as 'coloured' and hence, under the apartheid system, not fit to play with and against white cricketers. The reaction of the MCC, the sport's governing body in England and Wales, had been to cancel the tour – though not without some regret. D'Oliveira, in spite of an outstanding performance in the final Test of the summer series, had been initially omitted from the squad, informal overtures having been made to the MCC via the then Shadow Foreign Secretary, Sir Alec Douglas-Home, that his inclusion would be an obstacle to the tour going ahead. Public opinion, however, won the day and D'Oliveira got his place following the withdrawal through injury of Tom Cartwright.

The downside was that South Africa's Prime Minister, John Vorster, was then able to claim, apparently unaware of any irony, that D'Oliveira had been selected for political reasons – a position shared by Douglas-Home, who wanted good relations with South Africa to help Britain put pressure on Rhodesia. All of this came back into focus the following year since the South African rugby team were due to tour Britain and Ireland over the winter 1969-70. By now opposition to sporting links with South Africa was more organised: the 'Stop The 70 Tour' campaign, chaired by Peter Hain, operated on a nationwide basis (Edinburgh organiser: Gordon Brown) and met the South Africans with protests at key matches including the game against England at the home of rugby, Twickenham.

Sights were then set on the South African cricket team, due to visit England in the summer of 1970. This time the campaign achieved its objective: following the intervention of the Home Secretary, James Callaghan, the tour was cancelled. Instead, a Test series took place between England and the Rest of the World, whose team of 21 included five South Africans who, in all probability, would have been chosen for the national team. One of them was Graeme Pollock, one of the best batsmen of his generation, who scored a magnificent 114 in the fifth Rest of the World match. Pollock was later to say, 'Peter Hain and his guys got it right, in that the way to bring about change was to get at South Africa through sport', and many other observers have dated the beginning of the end of apartheid to the cancellation of that 1970 tour.

This, then, was the climate in which Heath contemplated how to treat with South Africa. As in the case of Rhodesia, he did not think sanctions were the way to go and believed that the cricket tour should have gone ahead. By allowing South Africans the greatest possible access to how things were done elsewhere Heath's expectation was that they would come to see that apartheid was wrong. Arms sales to South Africa were duly resumed. But this ignited a furious response from other African nations, especially those who were members of the Commonwealth. President Kenneth Kaunda of Zambia warned that he would appeal directly to the British people to get the decision reversed while the President of Tanzania, Julius Nyrere, threatened to take his country out of the Commonwealth altogether. Nevertheless Heath remained unmoved and the crisis passed.

On the domestic scene, the biggest worry – alongside the usual governmental concerns such as the economy and industrial relations – was Northern Ireland. Heath had little knowledge of, or sympathy for, the reasons behind the conflict and seemed to regard with equal disdain extremists on both sides. He therefore tended to leave the day-to-day issues emanating from the province to the Home Secretary, Reginald Maudling; Heath's, in retrospect, somewhat naive belief was that the problems would melt away if the UK were admitted to the European Economic Community, a subject much closer to his heart and to which he preferred to devote his time.

Back in the present, however, the situation was not improving. An additional 3,500 troops were sent to deal with the increasing level of civil disobedience and were met with fierce resistance, including street barricades. At the Northern Ireland General Election of 1969, the Ulster Unionist Prime Minister, Captain Terence O'Neill, had been left without a clear majority, largely due to opposition from within his own party – many Unionists had stood on an anti-O'Neill platform, believing him too conciliatory to the Catholic minority. Indeed O'Neill was himself almost defeated by the Reverend Ian Paisley. Shortly afterwards, O'Neill resigned as Prime Minister and, in January 1970, gave up his constituency of Bannside.

At the resulting by-election on 16 April Paisley was victorious, as was his fellow Protestant Unionist, the Reverend William Beattie, in the South Antrim by-election held on the same day. This presented a serious threat to the Northern Irish Parliament at Stormont where the new Prime Minister, Major James Chichester-Clark, was currently negotiating social and policing reforms with Catholic groups. The two new MPs were implacably opposed to such measures and their arrival at Stormont would further disrupt what was already a fragmented mix of moderates and right-wingers and bring the spectre of direct rule from Westminster ever closer. A jubilant Paisley told reporters, 'The most important thing of all is this election has been won because of the intervention of Almighty God'.

One week after the British General Election, there were riots in Londonderry following the arrest of the mid-Ulster MP, Bernadette Devlin; the week after that, the Army imposed a curfew in the mainly Catholic Falls Road area of Belfast, sparking off a battle between soldiers and IRA militants. The Westminster government immediately imposed a ban on all sectarian marches in the hope that the problems associated with the parade season would thus be avoided. Nevertheless the violence continued; on 2 August the Army used rubber bullets for the first time since the troubles began.

Heath hoped he could make progress by entering into a positive dialogue with the Irish Prime Minister, Jack Lynch, when the two met in Washington in October 1970. On the face of it, it would be an uphill struggle, because at the start of the troubles Lynch had called for the reunification of Ireland. Yet he also favoured a peaceful resolution to the conflict and was unsympathetic to the Provisional IRA, who had split from the 'official' IRA in order to pursue a more militant, less politically-oriented agenda. In May Lynch dismissed two senior ministers, Neil Blaney and future Taoiseach Charles Haughey, for illegally importing arms for the Provisionals and five months later he sacked the entire board of directors at Radio Telefis Eireann for permitting a broadcast by one of their senior spokesmen. Yet not for the first time in the late 20th century, events in the province moved faster than the politicians and within a few months the violence had escalated to such an extent that the Stormont government introduced internment without trial for suspected terrorists, thus setting off a further wave of carnage.

The young songwriters of Northern Ireland were slow to respond to the troubles and when they did, it tended to be from a purely sectarian (invariably republican) standpoint. It wasn't like Vietnam where you could express a general desire for peace; any Catholic bemoaning the violence would become a target (literally) of Protestant hostility, and vice versa. Of course many in the Catholic community related to Irish traditional music, which was undergoing something of a revival through the work of The Dubliners and The Chieftains. 1970 also saw the formation of Horslips, who combined jigs and reels with contemporary rock music, and the release of 'The Farmer' – the first single by another Dublin band, Thin Lizzy. But the big story of the year in Ireland was the victory of Dana in the Eurovision Song Contest with 'All Kinds Of Everything', a sentimental romantic ballad that could not have been more remote from conditions north of the border. To prove she was made of slightly sterner stuff, Dana went on to record Paul Ryan's weird and wonderful composition 'Who Put The Lights Out'; nearly 30 years later, as Dana Rosemary Scallon, she became a Member of the European Parliament.

★ ★ ★ ★ ★

While all manner of horrendous events raged on domestically and internationally, most first-year students at the University of Manchester, of whom the author was one, began Michaelmas Term 1970 in a spirit of optimism. Of course there was concern at the state of the world: many of us had been on demos and to pop festivals, where we'd made the peace sign communally and joined in with The Edgar Broughton Band on the chorus of 'Out, Demons, Out!' Now there were regular opportunities for activism: boycotting Barclays Bank for investing in South Africa; an anti-apartheid march culminating in UMIST car park with an address by Peter

Hain; a rally protesting the publication of the right-wing Black Papers on Education by one of our own professors, Brian Cox.

Sometimes the act of demonstrating was tantamount to an end in itself. On the night of 26-27 November, for example, we participated in an all night sit-in at the Owens Building, a splendid Gothic edifice constructed in 1873 to which we were to return three years later for final exams and graduation. The occupation was an immensely pleasurable occasion, with music, good company and various stimulants in evidence, but no-one in our circle was sure exactly why we were there. Like many such demos that year, it no doubt resulted from some misdemeanour by our newly-arrived but already infamous Vice-Chancellor, Arthur Armitage.

Taking part in events like this was part of the enjoyment of being at university and symptomatic of what was, for many of us, the unprecedented freedom to think and behave as we wanted. This inevitably led to a host of new experiences and, in particular, the discovery of a wealth of new music, either live or on record. 1970 represents a high water mark in the history of student union socials, at least as far as Manchester University is concerned. The first six concerts of term were as follows:

- 3 October – Emerson, Lake and Palmer (admission 10 shillings, i.e. 50p)
- 7 October – The Who, supported by The James Gang (at the Free Trade Hall, tickets 7/6 [37 and a half pence] to £1)
- 10 October – Free (8 shillings – 40p)
- 17 October – Deep Purple (7/6)
- 24 October – Steeleye Span, supported by Trees (7/6)
- 31 October – Argent, supported by Kevin Ayers and The Whole World (7/6)

At UMIST (then a separate university), the programme was of similar calibre:

- 3 October – Colosseum

- 10 October – Fairport Convention
- 17 October – Stoneground
- 24 October – Yes
- 31 October – Fotheringay

(Sadly I have no details of ticket prices for these UMIST gigs; as noted in Chapter 6, however, Lifetime played the venue on 21 November. Admission, to hear four of the greatest musicians on the planet, was 10 shillings.)

With such riches on offer, it scarcely seemed worth exploring further afield, although there were occasional forays to Manchester Polytechnic (then in its first year of existence) or outside Manchester altogether – as in the trip to '2ⁿᵈ Sound 70', an all-night progressive music festival held on Friday 6 November at the Pavilion Gardens, Buxton. For the princely sum of 25 shillings (£1.25), we were treated to desultory performances by Ginger Baker's Air Force, Marmalade (progressive?), Fat Mattress, Black Widow and others, followed by a brief (very brief) sleep in a freezing car before heading home. One aspect of the festival was, however, brilliantly successful; for at least 20 years afterwards a poster advertising it clung to a telegraph pole near Manchester's Piccadilly railway station; slowly but surely it grew faded and tattered, a fitting symbol of an event which in many ways heralded the end of an era.

A good deal of time was also spent listening to records. Friends' collections were an endless source of fascination, especially when, as was often the case, they comprised a wide range of artists and styles. Rich Page, for example, had *Emerson, Lake And Palmer*, Love's *Forever Changes* and *Dragonfly* by The Strawbs; Linda Maddison had Rod Stewart's *Gasoline Alley*, Debussy's 'Clair De Lune' and *Crosby, Stills And Nash*; Matt Luheshi had Captain Beefheart's *Strictly Personal*, *A Question Of Balance* by The Moody Blues and the first two Soft Machine albums. Jim Rafferty's records were, however, the most diverse of all: in September 1970, he arrived in Manchester with Beethoven's 6ᵗʰ Symphony, Dylan's *Nashville Skyline*, *Folk Songs* by Alex Glasgow, Louis Armstrong's *Town Hall Concert*

1947, the *Tannhäuser* overture by Richard Wagner, Fairport's *Liege And Lief* and a 78 of Scottish bagpipe music!

Nowadays many people have varied tastes but have normally developed them over a long period of time; these were eighteen and nineteen year-olds who had nothing like the access to music now available through the internet. Perhaps that is what encouraged their curiosity; as noted in Chapter 5, the culture of the period was to try anything and everything.

★ ★ ★ ★ ★

Despite our catholicity of taste, one area of music of which most of us were almost entirely ignorant was African-American pop. This was probably because it was chart music and thus tainted by commercialism and the desire to make money (not that this wasn't a priority for many of the rock bands we were so keen on!) The Top 40 then – as ever – was riddled with inanity and so was avoided by self-respecting rock fans. Little did we know we were missing out on a golden era.

To begin with, there were The Jackson Five – even we knew them, at least the singles 'I Want You Back' and the follow-up, 'ABC', which came out on 24 February 1970 and still stands as one of the great feel-good records of all time. Propelled by a dynamic yet supple bass line, it has an irresistible swaying rhythm to which the exuberant lead vocals of Michael Jackson (then aged eleven) give additional impetus. Unsurprisingly there was nothing quite as good on the album of the same name, issued on 8 May, though 'The Love You Save' with its insistent melody and catchy chorus, and 'One More Chance', featuring some neat vocal interplay between Michael and his brothers, run it close.

All of these songs were written by The Corporation – Berry Gordy, Alphonso Mizell, Freddie Perren and Deke Richards) – who also, with the assistance of Hal Davis, produced the album, and in truth the band are less effective when taking on material from other sources. 'Don't Know Why I Love You' lacks Stevie Wonder's gravitas and 'Never Had A Dream Come

True' was not one of his better songs in the first place. The cover of Funkadelic's 'I'll Bet You', however, retains the sinister atmosphere of the original and Michael's sheer enthusiasm transcends another number with schoolroom lyrics, '2-4-6-8'. The next Jackson Five single, the ballad 'I'll Be There', gave them their fourth consecutive US number one and showed a new maturity – perhaps this was only to be expected given that on 29 August, the day after its release, Michael reached the ripe old age of twelve.

Elsewhere on Motown, The Supremes (with new lead singer Jean Terrell) had American Top Ten hits with 'Up The Ladder To The Roof' and, as discussed in Chapter 2, 'Stoned Love', while Junior Walker and The All Stars produced their most intense record to date, 'Do You See My Love (For You Growing)'. The old guard's biggest success was 'The Tears Of A Clown' by Smokey Robinson and the Miracles, a number one in Britain and America. Originally a track on the band's 1967 album, *Make It Happen*, it is one of Robinson's most literate songs; the protagonist compares himself with the characters in Ruggero Leoncavallo's opera *Pagliacci* ('Clowns') who conceal their sadness under a laughing exterior.

Robinson's 'I Second That Emotion' was one of the songs tackled by Kiki Dee on *Great Expectations,* the first-ever Motown album by a white British singer. The sleeve, plastered with Union Jacks, makes no secret of her origins yet the content is well up to the label's customary standard. In order to prove herself, Dee could easily have opted for histrionics, but her measured, restrained approach allows the songs to speak for themselves. 'You Don't Have To Say You Love Me', for example, lacks the melodrama of the Dusty Springfield original and is all the better for it; on 'For Once In My Life' she makes no attempt to emulate Stevie Wonder's effervescence and finds alternative dimensions by taking it more slowly. She can be soulful when the occasion demands it, however, as on the big-production ballad 'I Can't Give Back The Love I Feel For You'. 'The Day Will Come Between Sunday And Monday' is, as the title suggests, a rather wordy number but Dee navigates her way through it with considerable skill; it is a pity, therefore that, issued as a single, it failed to chart and, despite the great expectations, her career with Motown therefore came to an end.

The Corporation had deliberately concealed their identities under an impersonal name because, after Motown had parted company in 1967 with their celebrated writing and production team of Brian Holland, Lamont Dozier and Eddie Holland (H-D-H), label owner Berry Gordy had declared that he wanted no more 'back room superstars'. It will thus be apparent that the split was acrimonious and for some time the trio were in dispute with Motown, using, for legal reasons, the pseudonym Edythe Wayne. H-D-H started their own labels Hot Wax and Invictus, attaining immediate success with the latter. On 26 September 1970, Invictus records stood at numbers one and three (bisected by 'The Tears Of A Clown') on the UK singles chart with Freda Payne's driving 'Band Of Gold' and 'Give Me Just A Little More Time' by one of the outstanding vocal groups of the period, Chairmen Of The Board.

They were fronted by Norman 'General' Johnson, former lead singer with The Showmen, whose paean to rock and roll, 'It Will Stand', was one of the best records of 1961. Johnson's emotive, almost pained, vocal style (not unlike that of The Four Tops' Levi Stubbs) became the Chairmen's trademark and helped them reach the US Top 40 on four occasions during 1970. 'Give Me Just A Little More Time' was the biggest and best, its punchy tune underlined by a dramatic H-D-H arrangement. It was followed by the similar, but faster, '(You've Got Me) Dangling On A String', the lively 'Everything's Tuesday' and 'Pay To The Piper', a stomper reminiscent of Sly and The Family Stone.

The 'B' sides of these hits were equally strong. 'Give Me Just A Little More Time' was backed with 'Since The Days Of Pigtails (And Fairy Tales)' which despite its title is a rough, tough slice of Southern soul and the other side of 'Pay To The Piper' was 'When Will She Tell Me She Needs Me', an anguished medium-tempo thumper. Norman Johnson's weepie 'Patches' was coupled with '(You've Got Me) Dangling On A String' in the UK and with 'Everything's Tuesday' in the US; it was, however, Clarence Carter's more famous version that hit the Top Five on both sides of the Atlantic in late summer. The group's 1970 albums also feature some fine music: *Chairmen Of The Board*, for example, includes the compelling tale of a shotgun wedding, 'Tricked And Trapped (By A Tricky Trapper)' while the entreaties of *In Session*'s 'All We Need Is Understanding' make it the latter-day equivalent of 'It Will Stand'. Sadly, neither was a hit: another instance of the very different album and singles markets.

Also prominent on the pop scene were the 'De' groups: The Detroit Spinners, The Detroit Emeralds and The Delfonics (though The Dells, having made the US Top Ten in late 1969 with a remake of 'Oh, What A Night', failed to chart in 1970). The first of these were originally known in the UK as The Motown Spinners, acquiring their second forename when Motown quit Detroit in 1972. The idea was to avoid confusion with the Spinners folk group but there was no mistaking their smooth, suave sound, epitomised by 'It's A Shame', an international hit in autumn. The Emeralds were yet to break through with dancefloor classics like 1973's 'Feel The Need In Me' though were on their way with a cover of The Beatles' 'And I Love Her'. The Delfonics, on the other hand, were already a big name and scored one of their greatest successes in February with the plaintive '(Didn't I) Blow Your Mind This Time'. However the follow-up, 'Trying To Make A Fool Of Me', a much better record with deft harmonies and an imaginative arrangement, proved to be their final American hit.

Meanwhile, some of the more established African-American acts were having a vintage year. Rumours were rife that the marital and professional partnership of Ike and Tina Turner was about to dissolve but the title of their album *Working Together* showed that, for the time being, the latter at least was intact. It is probably best known for the three great cover versions: 'Let It Be' (in which Tina changes the words to 'leave me be'), a swaggering 'Get Back', and 'Proud Mary', which was to provide them with their only US Top Ten single. It begins with Ike quietly intoning the chorus and Tina stating their intent: 'We never ever do nothing thing nice and easy, we always do it nice and rough – so we're gonna take the beginning of this song and do it – easy but we're gonna do the finish – rough.' And so they gently duet over unobtrusive backing, draw to a halt, and then explode into a frantic rave-up, with blasting horns, wailing Ikettes and Tina giving it her all. Yet there are also some fine originals, notably Ike's 'Game Of Love' (which, as might be expected, has no rules) and Tina's self-explanatory 'Funkier Than A Mosquita's Tweeter'. At the same time former Ikettes Venetta Fields, Clydie King and Sherlie Matthews, now calling themselves The Blackberries, were teaming up with the white rock band Pacific Gas And Electric for the pulsating gospel-flavoured smash, 'Are You Ready?'

The excellent 'Turn Back The Hands Of Time' and 'The Thrill Is Gone' were the biggest-ever US hits for, respectively, Tyrone Davis and BB King while the equally strong 'Don't Play That Song For Me' gave Aretha Franklin her highest chart position for two years in both Britain and America. All of Dionne Warwick's US hits in 1970 were by her favoured song-writing team of Burt Bacharach and Hal David. 'I'll Never Fall In Love Again' had been a UK number one for Bobbie Gentry the previous year but Warwick contrives to make it her own. The follow-up comprised two songs of comparable quality; 'Let Me Go To Him' is a sumptuous power ballad, 'Loneliness Remembers What Happiness Forgets' a lively bossa nova with strings and choir – both are beautifully sung. Eight years before Warwick had expected to be given 'Make It Easy On Yourself' as her debut single; instead it went to Jerry Butler. Now Warwick had a hit with it, her restrained delivery contrasting with the lugubrious sentimentality in both the Butler and subsequent Walker Brothers versions. Regrettably, however, it was to be her last visit to the American singles chart for nine years.

Also of note were Sly and The Family Stone's pounding 'Thank You Falettinme Be Mice Elf Again', the soaring harmonies of The 5th Dimension on Laura Nyro's 'Save The Country', and Carlos Malcolm's 'Bustin' Outta The Ghetto', an irresistible funk instrumental with a trombone solo by the leader. But one of the best releases of all came from Clarence Carter – not 'Patches', funkier if more lachrymose than the Chairmen Of The Board original – but its 'B' side, a satisfying chunk of Alabama R&B called 'I Can't Leave You Alone'.

★ ★ ★ ★ ★

Following the successful moon landings in 1969 by American astronauts, the seventh manned spacecraft in the Apollo program, Apollo 13, was launched on 11 April 1970. This, too, was to have landed men on the moon – in this case, Jim Lovell and Fred W Haise Jr, who were accompanied by Command Module Pilot Jack Swigert, a last-minute replacement for Ken Mattingly. Two days into the mission, however, an oxygen tank exploded in the service module containing the main engines. It was Swigert who uttered the immortal phrase 'Houston, we've had a problem here', a classic understatement that entered the vernacular (via the film *Apollo 13* in which is was spoken by Lovell) as 'Houston, we have a problem'. Four days later, after a hair-raising journey back to Earth witnessed by a TV audience of hundreds of millions the crew splashed down safely in the South Pacific Ocean.

Despite this near-catastrophe, NASA pressed ahead with its program, while at the same time 1970 saw all manner of craft, and passengers, take to the skies. On 5 March a nuclear non-proliferation treaty between the US, UK and Soviet Union came into force though this did not prevent the Russians testing a new rocket launcher (later used by Iraq in the Gulf War). On a more peaceful front, trials of the Anglo-French Concorde aeroplane continued and the first Jumbo Jet flew from New York to London. But charter flights to Spain were the preferred option for a new generation of UK holiday-makers: in 1962 2.4 million Britons had taken their vacations abroad – by 1970, the figure had swollen to 5.7 million, many taking advantage of cheap package deals.

In contrast, the British yachtsman Chay Blyth set out from Southampton on 18 October to sail around the world single-handedly in the westward direction (that is, against the prevailing winds and currents), a feat never before accomplished. 292 days later he arrived back to a reception committee including the Duke of Edinburgh, Prince Charles, Princess Anne and Edward Heath, himself a first-class sailor. On 6 August 1970 Heath had opened the ten-day World Cycling Championships in Leicester, a rare moment of celebration in an otherwise gloomy year for British sport.

In the art world, Britain was in the news for two very different reasons. First, a new painting of the Queen by Pietro Annigoni was unveiled at the National Portrait Gallery. Annigoni had previously portrayed the monarch as a romantic beauty; now her glum expression and heavy red cloak suggested a much more troubled character. Though the picture provoked some debate it was nothing like the furore that accompanied John Lennon's suite of lithographs, *Bag One*. Lennon had given these as a wedding present to Yoko Ono, but when they were shown at the London Art Gallery in January 1970 they were confiscated as pornography by officers from Scotland Yard.

In New York an Andy Warhol soup can label fetched $60,000 at auction while the New York Cultural Center staged the first dedicated conceptual art exhibition, *Conceptual Art and Conceptual Aspects*. In fashion, 1970 saw the invention of the midi-skirt, championed by the publisher of *Women's Wear Daily*, John Burr Fairchild; the prestigious New York retailer Bonwit Teller instructed all its female staff to wear the midi at work and the 21 August edition of *Life* magazine ran a cover story on the new trend.

Organisers of the American pavilion at the world's fair in Osaka had, literally, higher things on their mind than the midi-skirt: they exhibited samples of moon rock brought back by Apollo 12 astronauts. This was just one of many unique features of Expo 70 which ran from 15 March to 13 September and attracted 64 million visitors. As usual, the very latest technology was on display, including early mobile phones and the premiere of the first-ever IMAX film, *Tiger Child*, directed by Donald Brittain. The theme of the event was Progress and Harmony for Mankind and as such was more of a festival, with music playing a crucially important part. For example, Iannis Xenakis composed a piece of music, *Hibiki-Hana-Ma* (Reverberation-Flower-Interval) especially for Japan's Iron and Steel Federation pavilion. It is a sonic whirlpool in which Western orchestral timbres and Japanese percussion effects are atomised, combined and electronically reprocessed. Played on a tape loop, it was transmitted through some 700 under-floor speakers and 128 surface and suspended speakers symmetrically arranged in the pavilion's amphitheatre. The West

German pavilion incorporated the world's first spherical concert hall and each day presented over five hours' music by Karlheinz Stockhausen, whose concepts had inspired its design.

These important works helped make 1970 an outstanding year for contemporary classical music. Other notable compositions to appear during the year included Morton Feldman's sparse yet absorbing *The Viola In My Life 1-3*, the surging *Continuum For Harpsichord* by György Ligeti and Luc Ferrari's *Presque rien No. 1 'Le Lever du jour au bord de la mer'*, described by John Kealy (*brainwashed.com*) as

> one of the major milestones following John Cage's *4'33"* in music
> embracing all sounds as valid ingredients for a piece. These noises are
> not just a moment in time in a sleepy village but music in and of
> themselves.

Eventually Ferrari's innovations were widely adopted and field recordings became more commonplace but one immediate link was to Pink Floyd, whose 'Alan Psychedelic Breakfast' is constructed on similar techniques.

Composers such as Ferrari, Feldman, Stockhausen and Xenakis were seldom called on for major film soundtracks, even though their work was, in general, eminently suitable. Such commissions remained the province of specialists such as Alfred Newman and, increasingly, rock musicians like his nephew Randy. After contributing to over 50 pictures, the former created his final score just before he died on 17 February 1970. This was for the film *Airport*, hardly one of the most distinguished productions he had been involved with, but the second most lucrative release of the year (eventually it grossed over $100 million) and one of the most influential. Based on the book by Arthur Hailey it was the first of the 1970s 'disaster movies' and spawned no fewer than three sequels and one spoof (though this was aimed principally at *Airport 1975*). The multiple plot strands help build up tension though this is defused by strangely detached performances by Burt Lancaster and Dean Martin; the morality of the story, too, is perplexing: anti-abortion and anti-divorce, it also seems to condone adultery.

Michelangelo Antonioni's *Zabriskie Point,* on the other hand, was an unambiguous, and unflinching, portrayal of the decaying counterculture in which violence and gratuitous sex had supplanted pacifism and free love. It also benefitted from some superb music, a rare case of a soundtrack album standing up independently of the film. Pink Floyd weighed in with three tracks though other pieces were rejected, including 'The Violent Sequence' which resurfaced as *Dark Side Of The Moon*'s 'Us And Them'; The Doors' 'L'America' was also left out. In compensation Antonioni did include Jerry Garcia's 'Love Scene', seven minutes of exquisite electric guitar used to accompany the shots of mass copulation in the desert. There were also two fine items by psychedelic string band Kaleidoscope, Patti Paige's timeless 'Tennessee Waltz', mountain music from Roscoe Holcomb and the shimmering 'Sugar Babe' by The Youngbloods. Of commensurate calibre was the soundtrack to *Performance,* discussed in Chapter 4. Conversely Blood, Sweat and Tears' music for *The Owl And The Pussycat* was obscured by the focus on co-stars Barbra Streisand and George Segal.

A dominant theme of the films of the period was the compulsion to break away from societal and, particularly, parental expectations: in 1970 it ran through pictures as diverse as *Five Easy Pieces, Ryan's Daughter* and *Love Story,* comfortably the biggest box-office success of the year and a candidate for the most sentimental film of all time. To counterbalance such lapses came a welcome crop of satirical classics. Robert Altman's *MASH,* though set in Korea, was about the dehumanising effect of the Vietnam War while *Little Big Man,* directed by Arthur Penn, overturned the myths and clichés of the Western. In Europe, Luis Buñuel's *Tristana* excoriated the Catholic Church and the fifth of Eric Rohmer's Six Moral Tales, *Le Genou De Claire,* showed how lust can masquerade as love. Jean-Pierre Melville's *Le Cercle Rouge* and René Clement's *Rider On The Rain* were even more nihilistic: in the former, everyone bears guilt for the tragic climax, whereas the latter combined rape, murder and chauvinistic attitudes to women.

But most negative of all was *Joe,* directed by John G Avildsen. A violent alternative to the *Love Story* narrative, it had the eponymous central character, a bigoted factory worker played by Peter Boyle, wreaking terrible vengeance on the hippie community in which his daughter takes refuge. Both sides were depicted unsympathetically yet there is no doubt that the film reflected a very real disjuncture in American society: ten weeks before it was issued, a railway worker named Arville Garland entered Stonehead Manor, a hippie enclave near the campus of Wayne State University, Detroit, and killed his seventeen-year-old daughter Sandra, her boyfriend Scott Kabran, and their friends Gregory Walls and Anthony Brown. Though convicted of murder, Garland received letters of support from parents across America; ten years later he was released.

★ ★ ★ ★ ★

As the year 1970 began, Merle Haggard's 'Okie From Muskogee' was slipping out of the charts. It derided, in turn, drug taking, draft card-burning, free love, hippie fashions and student protest and thus neatly encapsulated the position of America's conservative heartland – so neatly, in fact, that it can almost be seen as a satire on small-town smugness. However the follow-up, 'The Fightin' Side Of Me', displayed no such ambiguity. An uncompromising attack on the anti-War movement, it replicated the success of its predecessor and was nominated as the Country Music Single of the Year for 1970 – an award which in the end went to 'Okie From Muskogee'. In addition the CMA named Haggard Male Vocalist of the Year and Entertainer of the Year.

Expressions of dissatisfaction were endemic to country music – just like blues, it was a vehicle for confronting injustice. Until recently, however, the focus had been on the bad deal dealt by love, rather than society. Now records like Johnny Cash's *At Folsom Prison* and *At San Quentin* and Jeannie C Riley's 'Harper Valley PTA' were starting to confront the Establishment or, at least, some of the attitudes that sustained it. But nothing like the Merle Haggard records had been heard before in country music, an indication of just how deep the generation gap had become in 1970.

Elsewhere, Bobbie Gentry had a hit with 'Fancy', the tale of a young woman who escapes poverty through prostitution, but more commonly, the emphasis was on the problems of just getting by, and no-one was more skilful in articulating those than Loretta Lynn. Her albums *Loretta Lynn Writes 'Em And Sings 'Em* and *Coal Miner's Daughter* were archetypical. The first was issued on 1 June 1970 and, as the title indicates, consists entirely of her own compositions, with just one piece co-written with her sister, Peggy Sue Wells. Among the most memorable tracks are the self-explanatory 'Your Squaw Is On The Warpath' and the two songs addressed to rivals, 'You Ain't Woman Enough (To Take My Man)' and the pugilistic 'Fist City'.

Coal Miner's Daughter was recorded the following month and issued on 28 December. It is a perfect exemplar of contemporary country music in that all the thematic and emotional bases are covered – guilt, regret, assertiveness, nostalgia, prayer, homespun philosophy – but its hallmark is the way in which the sentiments are expressed, and the values conveyed, with disarming, unerring directness. The autobiographical title track became famous through the film of the same name and its simple statement of pride remains affecting. At the other extreme, it is impossible not to smile at the candour of the jaunty 'What Makes Me Tick':

The way I let you treat me, it's enough to make me sick
I'm going to have my head examined to find out what makes me tick

Though Lynn admits she is the guilty party in both 'Another Man Loved Me Last Night' and 'Any One, Any Worse, Any Where', her unvarnished sincerity immediately wins our sympathy and we fully support her assertion in 'The Man Of The House' that her partner's constant absence is 'enough to cause us women to go wrong'. Lynn also demonstrates impressive mastery of the conventional ballad – she handles Marty Robbins's 'Too Far', for example, with controlled yet profound emotion.

The album concludes with the bittersweet 'Snowbird', written by Gene MacLellan and a transatlantic hit in autumn for the Canadian, Anne Murray. It was also the opening track on Elvis Presley's *Elvis Country*, recorded in June, just two weeks before his album *On Stage – February 1970* hit the charts. Despite its title, two of the selections on the latter record, 'Runaway' and 'Yesterday', are from August 1969. The first is taken too fast to enable him to put his own stamp on it, while on the second his heavy vibrato takes the Lennon-McCartney song to the brink of schmaltz. The balance of the album, made between 17 and 19 February at the International Hotel, Las Vegas, is generally superior – especially when he is on familiar stylistic turf such as the rollicking blues, 'See See Rider' or the Southern rock trilogy of Tony Joe White's 'Polk Salad Annie', Joe South's plea for racial tolerance, 'Walk A Mile In My Shoes', and the ubiquitous 'Proud Mary', a version which matches that of Ike and Tina Turner for sheer excitement. And, no matter how one might recoil at the sentimentality of 'The Wonder Of You', it clearly hit the right note with the public: it reached number one in the US and the UK, where it stayed at the top for six weeks.

The front cover of *On Stage – February 1970* does not bear the name of the artist, a response perhaps to The Beatles, who had done the same on *Abbey Road*. It could, too, be a sign of a new-found confidence which the success of the album boosted still further: on 9 September, Presley embarked on his first concert tour since 1958.

Meanwhile *Elvis Country* was being prepared for release. This was another indication of Presley's rejuvenation. Made in Nashville, the album features the cream of Muscle Shoals session players alongside local star guitarists James Burton and Chip Young – a backing band to motivate any singer. Just as important, however, was the quality of the material – not the ultra-commercial, Vegas-oriented songs which had stifled him aesthetically but compositions by the likes of Bill Monroe, Ernest Tubb and Bob Wills – the sort of musicians whom he had idolised as a teenager. Aside from the rather odd, and irritating, idea of inserting brief extracts of 'I Was Born About Ten Thousand Years Ago' between the tracks, it is a near-faultless record with an ebullient Presley clearly enjoying himself throughout. The many highlights include 'The Fool', a hit for Sanford Clark in 1956 but here given the feel of Howlin' Wolf's 'Smokestack Lightnin''; Willie

Nelson's quintessential country ballad 'Funny How Time Slips Away'; and a thumping 'Whole Lot-ta Shakin' Goin' On' which metamorphoses from rock and roll to rock.

Elvis Country represents the peak of Presley's later output. Shortly afterwards, he reverted to the safe and predictable haven of Las Vegas. Thankfully there would be no more films but equally very few great records. On 21 December 1970 he travelled to Washington to visit President Richard Nixon – a symbolic meeting between the powermen of pop and politics. The two were ideologically identical – neither had any time for hippies, students or Black Panthers. Presley told Nixon, somewhat ironically, about his abhorrence of drugs; he also outlined his concerns about the direction America's young people were taking. It seemed that neither understood their complete inability to do anything about it.

CHAPTER 8:

Future Blues

At the turn of any decade it is customary to look back. Sometimes the previous ten years do not hang together coherently and so efforts to infer any themes, trends or overall meaning are doomed to fail. But no-one could say that of the 1960s. In terms of both artistic and scientific achievement, there has never been a decade like it, certainly not in the Western world; that it should culminate with the first manned moon landing and, less than a month later, the greatest-ever gathering of young people, was absolutely fitting. It was, of course, also a period of tragedy: the horrendous waste of human life in wars across the globe and the assassination of potential peace-makers like John and Robert Kennedy, Martin Luther King and Malcolm X. Yet the overall mood was optimistic; the explosion of creativity and technological progress promised a bright future.

Although many of the important personalities, and accomplishments, were American, one of the most notable features of the 1960s was the renaissance of Britain in key spheres of activity. Nowhere was that more evident than in pop music which for the first time transcended its traditional function of providing ephemeral entertainment for teenagers and began to exert a profound influence on social and political directions. British Prime Minister Harold Wilson was quick to recognise that the appeal of The Beatles cut across the barriers of gender, age, race and class, and when in opposition made a point of associating with them. The loosening of social mores that their appearance, behaviour and attitude represented was an important factor in his 1964 election victory and led directly to the counterculture in both the UK and US. British bands were internationally dominant for the rest of the decade.

Bridget Riley, David Hockney, John Hoyland and Peter Blake emerged as artists of international repute; British actors and films were the toast of Hollywood; and Mary Quant's designs conquered the world of fashion. Peter Higgs, Herchel Smith, James Black, Frank Partridge and Geoff Raison all made important scientific discoveries; in 1964 the crystallographer Dorothy Hodgkin received the Nobel Prize for Chemistry, the first woman to do so since Marie Curie in 1911. England's football team won the 1966 World Cup and Donald Campbell broke both the land and water speed records.

Perhaps it was the decline, or at least the levelling-off, of British achievements that made 1970 so anti-climactic. In April, The Beatles split up with no obvious successors, at least on the home front. The Isle of Wight Festival, though better attended than Woodstock, failed to recapture the magic of the American event: the performances were more uneven, the atmosphere more threatening. Within weeks, Jimi Hendrix, who had headlined both festivals and whose career had been launched in the UK, was dead. The new Conservative government, under Edward Heath, seemed unsympathetic to young people and to the arts, challenging the funding of controversial plays and exhibitions and introducing mandatory admission charges at public museums and galleries.

In the USA, while the 1960s was in many respects a golden decade, the war in Vietnam increasingly dominated political and cultural life. Everyone wanted it finished, no-one more so than President Nixon. Nonetheless, in 1970 his strategy created outrage among his opponents, polarising still further a country already deeply divided on issues such as civil rights and women's liberation. So some of the burning issues of the 1960s were, at the turn of the decade, not only unresolved but driving a wedge between young and old, black and white, the conservative right and the liberal left. No wonder that frustration and negativity frequently erupted into aggression.

In many parts of the world, particularly South America, Africa and the

Middle East, conflict was a fact of life but since the Second World War Northern Europe had been relatively tranquil. There were peaceful and constructive relationships between nations and as a further expression of co-operation nine countries were bound together in a Common Market. However violent clashes between young people and the authorities gradually became commonplace and the generation gap became a generation gulf.

Inevitably these upheavals had their effect on rock music; indeed, the music had helped create them in the first place. Some artists continued to track and comment on political events and played a full role in protesting wars and injustice. Others created their own musical world to correspond to the alternative ways of living advocated by campaigners. Often these new directions involved a complete escape from present realities, resulting on the one hand in music that was introspective and self-absorbed or, on the other, prone to instrumental and thematic fantasy.

None of this was quite what the 1960s had promised.

★ ★ ★ ★ ★

It would be a mistake, nevertheless, to see 1970 only in the context of what had gone before. Of course many good things came to an end during the year, yet in some cases that seemed not only inevitable but desirable. It could be argued, for example, that peaceful protest had proved ineffective on a number of fronts – the Vietnam War was still raging and despite legislation, genuine equality of opportunity was still a distant prospect in both the US and UK. Northern Ireland remained riven by sectarian conflict even after protracted negotiations. In all of these cases more violent action could hardly have made matters worse. At the same time, who was to say that Nixon's incursion into Cambodia would not bring the war to a conclusion or that Heath's appeasement of the South African government would not convince them of the evils of apartheid?

As far as popular culture was concerned, anyone listening to *Let It Be*, or seeing the squabbles that pervaded the film of the same name, could have had no doubt that The Beatles were right to call it a day. Add the deaths of Hendrix and Joplin and the apparent decline of Dylan and The Stones, and it was clearly time for new blood and perhaps a return to more manageable and intimate gigs: after the traumas of the Isle of Wight, who could possibly contemplate bigger pop festivals? Moreover too much emphasis on those who had quit the scene obscured the fact that artists like James Brown, Joni Mitchell and Elvis Presley were producing some of their best work. And, in any case, former Beatles John Lennon and George Harrison emerged with exceptional solo albums. However it was not so much the efforts of individual artists but the crystallisation of entire genres that distinguished the rock music scene of 1970.

Singer-songwriters, often performing solo or with the most unobtrusive accompaniment, had begun to proliferate in the early 1960s on the model established by Bob Dylan. But, again following his example, many had opted for the fashionable rock band sound in the middle of the decade. A second wave came to prominence a couple of years later, leading, in 1970, to a series of releases of unparalleled quantity and quality and creating a trend that was to continue well into the future. Among the classic singer-songwriter albums issued during the year were:

- Randy Newman – *12 Songs*
- *Stephen Stills*
- Neil Young – *After The Goldrush*
- Crosby, Stills, Nash and Young – *Déjà Vu*
- Dory Previn – *On My Way To Where*
- Joni Mitchell – *Ladies Of The Canyon*
- Melanie – *Candles In The Rain*
- Laura Nyro – *Christmas And The Beads Of Sweat*
- Nico – *Desertshore*
- James Taylor – *Sweet Baby James*
- *Loudon Wainwright III*
- Pearls Before Swine – *The Use Of Ashes*
- Simon and Garfunkel – *Bridge Over Troubled Water*

- Tim Buckley – *Lorca*
- Syd Barrett – *The Madcap Laughs*
- Van Morrison – *Moondance*
- Elton John – *Tumbleweed Connection*
- John and Beverley Martyn – *Stormbringer!*
- Nick Drake – *Bryter Later*

Plus, perhaps not strictly in the genre but exhibiting similar features:

- George Harrison – *All Things Must Pass*
- *John Lennon/Plastic Ono Band*
- Derek and The Dominos – *Layla And Other Assorted Love Songs*
- The Byrds – *Untitled*

These 23 albums constitute a major body of work, characterised by more than simply presentational format. What unites it is the overwhelming impulse to look inward at personal, often private, experiences rather than outward at the issues of the day. With only the occasional exception, the songs dwell on individual, frequently idiosyncratic, perceptions, seldom implying any claim to speak for anyone other than the writer. Naturally, each song-writer employs his or her own methods: Newman and Wainwright, for instance, tend to use a cinematic approach in which the characters depicted do not necessarily represent the composer – thus clearing the way for parody/satire; Barrett's lyrics are surreal, Previn's unflinchingly candid. Yet all of them convey their specific message direct to the listener, in a way that is often labelled 'confessional'.

In due course, singer-songwriters became known merely as solo artists and reverted to more generic rock material: it was no longer clear, or even relevant, whether their compositions were based on actual events or not. Along the way, however, they reached a stage of development quite foreign to the carefree early practitioners of pop. They were seen, and frequently saw themselves, as conscious artists – not purveyors of ephemera, but creative beings on a par with painters, sculptors, novelists and film directors.

* * * * *

No doubt many prog rock musicians put themselves in the same category. That such claims might be exaggerated is demonstrated by the very variable product of their efforts. Always prey to accusations of pretentiousness, the worst of prog justifies the charge: banal, bombastic and bathetic, it barely rises above the level of juvenilia. But at its best, it is exciting, colourful and innovatory. If, as many critics believe, the first prog rock album was The Beatles' *Sgt Pepper's Lonely Hearts Club Band* of 1967, and that it reached its most extreme form in 1973 with the triple-album set *Tales Of Topographic Oceans* by Yes, then 1970 can reasonably be considered a vintage year, a time when the music reached a pinnacle of achievement before descending the downward slope to excess.

The two albums released during the year by King Crimson, for example, are prog at its best. *In The Wake Of Poseidon* built on the band's breathtaking 1969 debut, *In The Court Of The Crimson King*, by adding some new twists, though *Lizard* raised the level of sophistication by merging allusion with illusion. The Pretty Things, too, refined the rock opera format they had pioneered with 1968's *SF Sorrow* by following a looser allegorical structure for their album *Parachute*. Other bands such as Led Zeppelin, Jethro Tull, Traffic and Family took the music forward by introducing folk elements into their music.

1970 was the year that rock fusions in general were at their height. As well as rock-folk there was folk-rock, pioneered by Fairport Convention but developed in different ways by a host of new bands including Fotheringay, Steeleye Span and Trees. Then there were the jazz musicians – Miles Davis, Tony Williams and John McLaughlin – who latched on to rock with dramatic consequences and the cooler yet no less inventive sounds of Gary Burton and Keith Jarrett. The rock acts who returned the compliment were less consistent but, at the very least, exciting, especially Chicago and The Ides of March. The Soft Machine, who displayed both classical and jazz influences, became the first rock band to play the BBC

Proms, and on the other side of the Atlantic it was a year to remember for musical alchemist Frank Zappa who released no fewer than three excellent albums.

More straightforward attempts to bring together rock and classical music were made by Deep Purple and, to much better effect, by The Nice whose 'Five Bridges Suite', from the album of the same name, drew intelligently from both sources. The rest of the record, however, verged on the outrageous in its daring but thrilling blend of prog, jazz, Dylan, Sibelius and Tchaikovsky, executed with virtuosity, humour and verve. *Emerson, Lake And Palmer* used material by Janáček and Bartók, giving it a less romantic, more contemporary feel, while Pink Floyd's *Atom Heart Mother* went one step further by incorporating *musique concrète* and field recordings into the mix of sounds and styles.

Links between rock and country music had been forged two years earlier and there were still plenty of examples on view in 1970. Big names like Elvis Presley, The Grateful Dead and The Byrds were blazing the trail; it would therefore be easy to miss the less spectacular yet equally valid efforts of Michael Nesmith and The First National Band, whose 'Silver Moon' combined Caribbean and country, or Del Shannon, the 35 year-old veteran who anticipated Presley's 'Kentucky Rain' with his own 'Colorado Rain'. The Poppy Family's 'That's Where I Went Wrong' was of commensurate quality but 'Which Way You Goin' Billy' strayed into sentimentality; it was, however, good to see another Canadian success alongside the accomplishments of Joni Mitchell, Neil Young, Anne Murray and The Guess Who.

Aspects of country music were evident, too, among those artists who plundered American history for inspiration. At its most superficial, this trend was a fashion statement with groups like The Dead, Crosby, Stills, Nash and Young and The Band decking themselves out in period costume for their album covers. But inside the record sleeves there was often to be found rock music of the highest calibre, from the historical exactitude of The Band's 'The Night They Drove Old Dixie Down' to the rich amalgam of American musical traditions that comprised Ry Cooder's eponymous debut album. Like the work of the singer-songwriters, the prog bands or the fusionists, such records spelled escape from present realities.

Most rock fans liked it all, and record companies were not slow to display the full range of their wares on the budget-price samplers they released from the late 1960s onwards, and it is highly likely that these eclectic selections encouraged breadth of taste among record-buyers. CBS had led the way with its two superb *Rock Machine* collections, swiftly followed by Island with *You Can All Join In* and *Nice Enough To Eat* and, as saw in Chapter 5, Harvest, with their double album, *Picnic*. But 1970's *The Age Of Atlantic*, compiled by Janet Martin, was exemplary. It juxtaposes, for instance, one of the most subtle rock records ever – Buffalo Springfield's 'Broken Arrow' – with one of the least subtle, a huge hunk of excitement by The Vanilla Fudge entitled 'Need Love'. Other landmark tracks include one each from debut albums by The Allman Brothers and Yes; 'Comin' Home', the only hit for Delaney and Bonnie and Friends featuring Eric Clapton; the two most famous Led Zeppelin numbers of the era, 'Communication Breakdown' and 'Whole Lotta Love'; and 'Termination', from Iron Butterfly's *In-A-Gadda-Da-Vida* album which went on to sell over 30 million copies. The latter was first released in 1968, the others in 1969, though the 1970 items on *The Age Of Atlantic* were of at least equal interest. Cold Blood's 'I'm A Good Woman' featuring the soulful vocals of Lydia Pense, has become a rock classic while there is more than a hint of impending trends in the MC5's 'Tonight'. Dada included Elkie Brooks and former member of the *Hair* cast and social campaigner Paul Korda: their frantic, stop-start version of 'The Last Time' comes from their one and only LP. Finally, Dr John's lilting, good-humoured 'Wash Mama Wash' provides a contrast with the rest of the compilation (as it did with the trippy, seventeen-minute 'Angola Anthem' on the *Remedies* album, issued on 9 April, from which it was taken).

★ ★ ★ ★ ★

In order to assess the ultimate significance of the year 1970 it is necessary to identify pointers to the future. We have already seen how the notion of the 'swinging sixties' evaporated during the year and that what filled the void was of a very different character. But how much of this was simply reactive? Were there any developments which can be seen to inform the decade ahead – and beyond?

It is tempting to conclude that it was in 1970 that people began to lose faith in their leaders, or at least begin to question their infallibility – the beginning, perhaps, of an apathetic view of politics, and politicians, that persists to this day. The Labour Government was rejected by the British electorate who wanted more done about law and order, immigration and industrial unrest, yet within four years, the Conservatives, under Edward Heath, were considered to have failed, at least with regard to the latter. After Wilson's return, there were to be two more Prime Ministers before the end of the decade, the second of whom was the deeply divisive Margaret Thatcher. By 2001, voter turnout at the General Election had slumped to 59.4%, 12.6% lower than the figure for 1970.

In the USA, Richard Nixon's approval ratings, as we have seen, fell during the year and although there were many who supported his tough stance on the Vietnam War (and on the students who were protesting it), even more were concerned that his approach was the wrong one. After the secret bombing of Cambodia, Nixon had begun to tap the telephones of journalists, and even of officials in his own administration, so concerned was he to avoid leaks; he also neglected to inform Congress immediately of the actual invasion of Cambodia. These were clear signs that he was beginning to exceed his authority and getting carried away with his personal power, a process that then began to snowball but came to a crashing halt with the Watergate scandal and Nixon's resignation. His successor, Gerald Ford, had an image problem and failed to re-ignite the nation. The turnout at US Presidential Elections dropped steadily during the 1970s and early 1980s: the figure of 50.3% in 1988 was over 10% below what it had been 20 years earlier.

In mainland Europe, violent demonstrations, the inability of governments to combat terrorism and concerns about encroachment from both the West and the East all contributed to political disengagement: the same voting patterns as those in the UK and US are discernible in France, West Germany and Italy, though the deterioration in turnout began slightly later than 1970.

Of course disillusion is harder to measure in those countries, like the Soviet Union and China, where there were no elections. Economically, Russia was booming; in 1970 the Eighth Five-Year Plan had run its course and output in the factories and the mines had increased by 138% over 1960 levels. No doubt morale in China also received a boost in April with the launch of its first space satellite, *Dong Fang Hong I*. Nonetheless, we do know that in South America there was plenty of interest in the political process, following the accession in Chile of Salvador Allende, the world's first democratically-elected Marxist Head of State. Within three years, however, General Augusto Pinochet's military junta would exact bloody retribution on Allende and his followers who, as we have seen, numbered several leading composers and musicians.

But in 1970 there were many who had even more pressing issues to deal with. The worst avalanche in history took place on 31 May. An earthquake in the Peruvian region of Ancash caused a landslide at Yungay in which 25,000 people were killed; only 92 survived. In November a cyclone in the Bay of Bengal struck East Pakistan, causing catastrophic floods and estimated fatalities of between 300,000 and 500,000. The government's failure to deal with the crisis resulted in a victory for the opposition Awami League and the war of independence that transformed the country into the sovereign state of Bangladesh. Yet it was at a terrible cost: aside from the genocide and horrific atrocities perpetrated by the Pakistan Army, over ten million refugees fled the country and over 30 million were displaced.

As part of the relief effort George Harrison and Ravi Shankar organised two concerts held at Madison Square Garden, New York City, on 1 August 1971. As well as the two principals, the concerts featured Bob Dylan, Ringo Starr and Beatle associates such as Klaus Voormann and Billy Preston, whose electrifying performance of 'That's The Way God Planned It' was one of the highlights of the subsequent film and album. This was the first major benefit concert by rock musicians and so provided the template for Live Aid, The Concert for New York City, Live 8 and many others.

Meanwhile there was no let-up in the assertion of Black Power. Violent incidents continued in the pattern set at the Marin County Courthouse, where Jonathan Jackson had taken Judge Haley hostage and demanded the release of the Soledad Brothers, including his brother George, a Black Panther. On 21 August 1971 George Jackson was shot dead during an attempted escape from San Quentin; in response, there was a riot nineteen days later at the Attica Correctional Facility, New York, in which over 1,000 inmates overpowered guards and took control of the prison. By the time it was over, 43 people died, 33 of whom were inmates. As with Soledad, Attica became a *cause célèbre* and the subject of newspaper articles, books, films, poems and songs. It was, however, the last major prison riot related directly to African-American militancy.

The Black Panther doctrine of black nationalism and its precepts of self-help and independence were more permanent features of African-American life in the late 20th century. Communities became more interested in building businesses than violent confrontation and an awareness of black history began to inform ambitions for the future. It was axiomatic that African-Americans be in control of their own destiny. Racial pride and the celebration of African-American heroes coalesced in the cultural nationalism of, for example, the film director Spike Lee whose 1992 biopic, *Malcolm X*, was an enormous aesthetic and commercial success. As for Angela Davis, fugitive from both the police and the FBI in 1970, she became a respected academic – still unafraid to speak out against injustice and discrimination especially on the subjects of ethnicity, prisoners' rights and feminism. In 2012 she received the Blue Planet Award from the German Ethecon Foundation, recognition at last for her contribution not just to the interests of African-Americans but to humanity as a whole.

★ ★ ★ ★ ★

The publication in 1970 of *Sexual Politics* and *The Female Eunuch* helped kick-start the women's movement in Britain, especially the latter which, in contrast to the academic style of Millett's book, offered ordinary women practical suggestions on how to change their lives for the better. In 1971, the first British women's liberation march was held in London and Erin Pizzey established the women's refuge centre in Chiswick; *Spare Rib* commenced publication in 1972; and 1973 saw the opening of the Rape Crisis Centre and the foundation of the Virago Press. Following the successful National Women's Liberation Conference at Ruskin College in 1970, it now became an annual event (in 1972, there were two).

But as with the drive towards race equality, there was a backlash, a sustained campaign by the mass media to belittle the struggle for women's rights and its chief proponents. As might be expected, the tabloid newspapers led the way, though there were plenty of anti-feminist quotes from more respected sources including from women themselves; many advanced the 'separate spheres' argument that Kate Millett had already ripped to shreds in *Sexual Politics*. More commonly, however, attacks on women's liberation were the business of stand-up comedians and, increasingly, TV sitcoms. It was, however, just one of many targets for Alf Garnett, the central character of the BBC's *Till Death Us Do Part*, which ran from 1965 to 1975. Garnett was a racist, chauvinist homophobe whose views should, on the face of it, have exposed him to ridicule. The problem was that, instead of laughing *at* him, many people laughed *with* him and he became something of a folk hero. Much the same can be said of Archie Bunker, protagonist of the US sitcom *All In The Family*, based on *Till Death Us Do Part* and screened for the first time on 12 January 1971. For the next five years, according to the Nielsen ratings, *All In The Family* was the most popular TV show in America and led to no fewer than five spin-offs. Although the programme purported to satirise all of the characters featured it was Archie Bunker who was by far the most sympathetic. Indeed it could be said that he represented the acceptable face of Joe, the violent bigot in the film of the same name, or of Arville Garland who murdered a group of hippies, including his daughter, and thereby attracted fan mail from parents across the country.

Till Death Us Do Part and *All In The Family* were cleverly written, brilliantly acted and often uproariously funny. They also highlighted issues which concerned the general public but were seldom discussed on television. However they opened a Pandora's Box by apparently legitimising all manner of prejudice, intolerance and narrow-mindedness and planting it in impressionable minds.

Much of the television on both sides of the Atlantic had, up to that point, been fairly uncontroversial, though campaigners like Mary Whitehouse saw broadcasters, especially the BBC, as the agents of decadence. The space race was fuelling renewed interest in what the future might look like and this was reflected in programmes like *Tomorrow's World*, which charted new developments in science and technology, and the sci-fi series *Doctor Who*, *Lost In Space* and *Star Trek*. In the cinema, *Alphaville* (1965), *Fahrenheit 451* (1966), and *2001: A Space Odyssey*, *Barbarella* and *Planet Of The Apes* (1968) all, in their various ways, painted a more worrying picture of things to come. At the same time the rapid changes taking place in contemporary society had led to a boom in the study of sociology, psychology and culture, with the publication of important new works by Michel Foucault, RD Laing and Talcott Parsons and the launch of journals like *New Society*.

The development of an academic discipline devoted to the future was, therefore, almost inevitable. The writer and lecturer Alvin Toffler was one of the first to go there with his Sociology of the Future course at the New York School for Social Research; his international bestseller, *Future Shock*, was published in 1970. The proposition of the book is that life in the modern age is speeding up to an unsustainable degree: advances in technology make even the most recent inventions obsolete; the relationship between human beings and objects, places – and each other – are growing shorter. The impact on the senses and on the brain is deleterious. Transience, novelty and diversity are proceeding at such pace that the collapse of contemporary society is on the horizon.

Having foreseen Armageddon, Toffler explains how it could be avoided. Looked at from today's perspective it is fascinating to note how many of his ideas have in fact come to pass and how many, despite their obvious good sense, remain unimplemented. He states, for example that

> We shall see many more "family" units consisting of a single unmarried adult and one or more children. Nor will all of these adults be women. (p. 227)

> ... books, magazines, newspapers, film and other media will be offered to the consumer on a design-it-yourself basis ... a consumer's profile [will be stored] on a central computer. The system could be hitched to facsimile machines and TV transmitters that would actually display or print out the material in his own living room. (p. 257)

> ... a social future assembly need not literally meet in a single room, but might simply be hooked into a communication net that straddles the globe. (p. 433)

The reference to 'social future' is very much a part of Toffler's solution; he argues for a convocation of peoples across the world with the purpose of assessing the future and planning accordingly – but not via 'top-down technocratic goal-setting procedures': ordinary people must be in control.

> To master change we shall need both a clarification of important long-range social goals and a democratization of the way in which we arrive at them. (p. 431)

In the early 21st century, we are no nearer achieving Toffler's aspiration than we were when he wrote *Future Shock*; there is no consensus on how to save the planet from global warming, never mind setting social goals. Short-term planning and untrammelled consumerism are still very much with us 44 years on.

Charles Reich's *The Greening Of America*, also published in 1970, was equally visionary and shared some of the preoccupations of *Future Shock*, in particular the need to make technology work for, rather than against, the interests of mankind. He demonstrates comprehensively that what he terms Consciousness I – the raw spirit of enterprise that made America and which has been constantly invoked as quintessentially American ever since – has proved unsuited, and in some respects positively harmful, to its development as a modern industrialised nation.

> [Consciousness I] could not understand that "private property" in the hands of a corporation was a synonym for quasi-governmental power, far different from the property of an individual. It could not understand the crucial point that collective action against corporate power would not have been a step towards collectivization, but an effort to preserve democracy in a society that had already been collectivized. Consciousness I also failed to recognize that private production was not paying its costs. For example, a manufacturer would dump wastes in a stream but pay nothing to compensate for the pollution, leaving the public to share in the costs but not in the profits. (p. 39)

But in Reich's view attempts at reform have in effect gone to the opposite extreme by creating the Corporate State – Consciousness II – whereby 'organization predominates, and the individual must make his way through a world directed by others' (p. 56). In such a world, 'the forces of technology and commodity, allowed to have their own way without guidance or control or intervening values, have created a culture which is profoundly hostile to life' (p. 160). Television provides a convenient substitute for reality while 'the aim of advertising is to create dissatisfaction … a minimum willingness to accept the drudgery of life' (p. 169). Reich could have been describing 2014.

His solution for all this, however, puts an undue reliance on the ability and capacity of young people to drive change forward. No doubt emboldened by the hippies' rejection of everything he sees as wrong with society, he over-emphasises the extent to which they could be proactive in rebuilding it – and, of course, does not allow for the constant flux of fashions among the young. Reich simply did not foresee that the spirit of the sixties would fail to survive the turn of the decade. Yet his vision of Consciousness III, though as far away as ever, still seems worth aspiring to:

> Respect for each individual, for his uniqueness and his privacy. Abstention from coercion or violence against any individual, abstention from killing or war. Respect for the natural environment … Equality of status between all individuals, so that no one is "superior" or "inferior". Genuine democracy in the making of decisions, freedom of expression and conscience. (p. 320)

These words echo the American Declaration of Independence of 1776. No-one has had the temerity to suggest that document is nonsense; Reich's 'basic laws' for a new society, formulated almost 200 years later, should perhaps merit comparable veneration.

★ ★ ★ ★ ★

In any retrospective survey of pop music, it is possible to discern signs of new trends well before shifts in taste occur. These indicators are, however, seldom so easy to spot at the time, and what made the task in 1970 doubly difficult was the amorphous mass of multi-dimensional rock music that all but smothered them. Yet to a large degree it was this very diversity which would ultimately lead to change. It was simply untenable that all of the many branches of the music could be confined within a single boundary: fragmentation was inevitable. The various types of rock fusion – jazz, blues, Latin, folk, classical – were symptomatic of the dilemma, with fans beginning to question the seemingly never-ending drive towards technical excellence that most of them seemed to involve. If you wanted, for example, the instrumental facility of jazz, why not just listen to jazz? The problem posed by travelling in the opposite direction – that is, towards greater simplicity – was that the final stop was anodyne commercial pop.

For the previous five years, The Doors had proved that a stripped-down sound need not compromise intellectual respectability and their album *Morrison Hotel*, released in February 1970, took that approach to a new level. 'Roadhouse Blues' sets the scene: a crunching guitar riff, wailing harmonica and honky-tonk piano provide the backcloth for Jim Morrison's bluesy vocal and lyrics which mix the pungent ('Woke up this morning got myself a deal, a feel') with the poetic ('Ashen lady, give up your vows'). Similarly, 'Peace Frog' intersperses verse with funk while 'Waiting For The Sun' combines whimsy with heavy metal. There is also a nod to the past: 'The Spy', with its slow, sour, insidious riff, could have featured on *Strange Days* and 'Indian Summer' recalls their *magnum opus*, 'The End'. But lest there be any doubt about the direction they are now heading in, the album closes with the walloping 'Maggie McGill'. *Morrison Hotel* made number four in America and number twelve in Britain, The Doors' highest chart placings to date. The incomparable *LA Woman* was around the corner and would refine still further the blend of brains and bite. Both albums were, to a degree, harbingers of the future, yet it was Morrison's persona that would prove equally significant to the new music being forged not in LA, but 2,000 miles away in Detroit.

Slowly but surely, the big stars had grown remote from the fans. The singer-songwriters came from an environment physically and socially removed from the day-to-day lives of most listeners; on the sunny shores of California they wrote about their personal neuroses, and about each other. The luminaries of fusion and prog rock distanced themselves by their virtuosity and the complexity of their compositions. At the same time there was never any suggestion of antipathy. When James Newell Osterberg Jr, later known as Iggy Pop, went to see The Doors he was impressed both with Jim Morrison's proximity to the audience and his behaviour towards them. In 2011 he told Jeb Wright of *classicrockrevisited.com*:

So, here's this guy, out of his head on acid, dressed in leather with his hair all oiled and curled. The stage was tiny and it was really low. It got confrontational. I found it really interesting. I loved the performance ... Part of me was like, "Wow, this is great. He's really pissing people off and he's lurching around making these guys angry." The other half of it was that I thought, "If they've got a hit record out and they can get away with this, then I have no fucking excuse not to get out on stage with my band."

The attitude described here was all over the music of Detroit. The first band to make an impression in 1970 were Frijid Pink, whose 'House Of The Rising Sun' reached number seven on the US singles chart and number four in the UK. The label bore the accreditation 'Trad. arr. Price' but there is no further sign of reverence for the Animals' 1964 chart-topper: this up-tempo version was laden with rasping vocals, wah-wah guitar and frenetic drumming and one could only marvel at its effrontery. Regrettably Frijid Pink disappeared from view as precipitously as they had arrived.

It was reasonable to assume that The MC5 might fill the gap. After all, their debut album *Kick Out The Jams* had been a Top 30 hit the previous year. But they had attracted notoriety, too, for the virulent message it contained – propaganda, in effect, for the far-left White Panther Party led by John Sinclair, the band's manager. So in order to make a fresh start, The MC5 signed with Atlantic Records and set to work on a follow-up entitled *Back In The USA*.

Kick Out The Jams had drawn from a number of sources including the earthy blues of fellow Detroiter John Lee Hooker and the avant garde jazz of Sun Ra. *Back In The USA*, however, is a reaffirmation of rock and roll, a riposte to the British Invasion bands who had appropriated American music for their own use. Yet that is the point at which the patriotism ends. 'The American Ruse', for example, is a vitriolic condemnation of the country's capitalist ethic with its 'crummy cars' and 'cheap guitars': 'I'm sick to my guts of the American ruse'; it also invokes Malcolm X's infamous assessment of the murder of John F Kennedy, 'chickens coming home to roost'.

But the most striking aspect of *Back In The USA* is its crisp, no-nonsense efficiency: indeed, with eleven tracks and a total of only 28 minutes' duration, it seems to anticipate The Ramones' maxim of playing faster to get their sets over with as soon as possible. As a statement of intent, the originals are bookended by Little Richard's 'Tutti Frutti' and the title track, a hit for its composer, Chuck Berry, eleven years earlier. Though the resemblance between 'Tonight' and the Spinal Tap parody 'Tonight I'm Gonna Rock You Tonight' might alarm some listeners, 'Call Me Animal', 'Teenage Lust' and 'The Human Being Lawnmower' are clear precursors of punk – the latter seeming to lead direct to The Adverts' 'Gary Gilmore's Eyes'. Rob Tyner's clipped, double-tracked vocals, the incisive guitar-playing of Fred 'Sonic' Smith and Wayne Kramer, and Dennis Thompson's powerhouse drumming just about define the sound that a new wave band would aim for – their effect much enhanced by Jon Landau's production in which the 'boxed in' effect makes it seem like the band are about to explode at any instant. Yet after all this, the album was a commercial flop.

The same fate befell another 1970 album by a visionary Detroit band, The Stooges. *Fun House* was recorded in May with the intention of recreating the band's live performances. Consequently there is a big, booming sound with no overdubs, but it soon becomes evident that it is, nevertheless, carefully layered. Bassist Dave Alexander provides the bedrock for Steve Asheton's thunderous drumming; then comes brother Ron Asheton's ferocious if elemental guitar; Iggy Pop's yelping, ranting vocals exude all the attitude absorbed from Jim Morrison and the final component is the wildly improvising tenor saxophone of Steven Mackay. Only on the closing free-form holocaust, 'LA Blues', does the discipline disintegrate. As for the lyrics, they are largely a grotesque parody of the love song with any vestiges of sentimentality mercilessly burnt away.

On the face of it, this may seem like the recipe for the average heavy metal band, and in truth there are common characteristics. Yet *Fun House* goes well beyond the limits of any known genre of rock. What makes it different is the sheer reckless disregard for anything approximating finesse, instrumental proficiency or good taste. It all seems to come from being – in the words of the devastating '1970' – 'outta my mind on a Saturday night'. The Stooges' stance and their wailing, howling sound became a model for acts as diverse as Nick Cave, The Fall, John Zorn and The White Stripes. By 2005 *Fun House* was sufficiently well-regarded to be ranked in the top 200 of *Rolling Stone's 500 Greatest Albums Of All Time*.

But in 1970 not everyone was alive to its qualities. Roy Hollingworth, in the 26 December edition of the British trade paper, *Melody Maker*, described it as 'a muddy load of sluggish, unimaginative rubbish heavily disguised by electricity' and, unsurprisingly with that kind of endorsement, it failed to chart in either the US or UK. The Stooges therefore went into a period of stagnation which only ended when it was agreed that their next album, *Raw Power*, would be co-produced by David Bowie.

By then Bowie was well on his way to becoming a superstar. He had, in fact, been on the scene since 1964 but did not break through until five years later when his single 'Space Oddity', inspired by the Apollo 11 moon landing, reached the UK Top Five. Yet this was no routine cash-in: haunting and melancholic, 'Space Oddity' took the mundane conversation between astronaut and mission control to the level of drama, bordering on poetry. His next album was, therefore, eagerly awaited.

The Man Who Sold The World, recorded in April and May and released in the US on 4 November, not only matched those expectations but became one of the key records of 1970. Though entirely contemporary, it anticipates both his own musical direction and the new sub-culture in which he would play the leading role. 'All The Madmen', for example, reflects the singer-songwriters' predisposition for personal revelations. It is widely believed to be about his half-brother Terry, a patient of the Cane Hill Psychiatric Hospital which, indeed, is pictured on the album cover; Bowie divulges that he is happy to associate with the 'madmen': 'they're all as sane as me'. 'Running Gun Blues' is a none-too-subtle anti-war piece; 'Black Country Rock' and 'She Shook Me Cold' are heavy metal parodies; and the extraordinary eight-minute opener, 'The Width Of A Circle', is unadulterated prog – a dreamlike composition in which a narrator of indeterminate gender has sex with God.

With 'Saviour Machine' and its message that organised religion offers much but delivers little, we start to approach the essence of the record, and its vision of the future – for what will fill the spiritual vacuum for the next generation? The answer lies in Bowie's interest in the philosopher Friedrich Nietzsche and the mystic Aleister Crowley. Nietzsche declared that 'God is dead' and created the concept of the Übermensch, a super-being who sets aside sentiment, conscience and morals to exploit the latent potential of mankind. The album's closing track 'The Supermen' echoes these ideas and also refers back to the notion of rebirth, introduced at the end of Side One with 'After All'. In fact the line in the latter 'live till your rebirth and do what you will' alludes both to Nietzsche and Crowley whose dictum in its original form, 'Do as thou wilt', was becoming *de rigueur* in 1970. In addition to appearing on Bowie's album, it was inscribed into the vinyl of *Led Zeppelin III* and Germaine Greer referred to it in *The Female Eunuch*, explaining that it is 'a warning not to delude yourself that you can do otherwise, and to take full responsibility to yourself for what you can do' (p. 152). In the context of 'After All', however, the sense is that following 'rebirth', namely freedom from constraint, one should return to the innocence of childhood – an interpretation reinforced by the child-like melody of the song. That this is the reading Bowie intended is confirmed by the album's title track in which the protagonist meets his alter-ego who regrets that he 'sold the world' by failing to give up control and lose his inhibitions.

Two years later that hedonistic message became the guiding principle of glam rock and in fact it was only then that *The Man Who Sold The World* got into the British chart. By that time Bowie was the guru of the whole movement though it was typical of him that he should cast an analytical eye on the scene with *The Rise And Fall Of Ziggy Stardust And The Spiders From Mars*. From there he would move to the contrasting climes of Philadelphia for his *Young Americans* album and his first US number one, 'Fame'. The relentless staccato funk of this track, written with John Lennon and guitarist Carlos Alomar, derived straight from James Brown who had perfected the idiom five years earlier. By denouncing the trappings of success the song also links to *Ziggy Stardust*, though no-one seemed to see the unintended irony of the fact that in 1975 Brown himself could have done with a dose of fame: that year he had no national hits on either side of the Atlantic. Perhaps he consoled himself, however, by reflecting on the creative impulse which had so radically changed the course of African-American music and, now it would appear, all pop music, back in 1970.

★ ★ ★ ★ ★

It is often said that if you remember the sixties you weren't really there, but while it is true that the memories of many veterans are befuddled by sex, drugs and rock and roll, most of us who can recollect even a small portion of the decade do so with a warm glow. For everyone else this apparently halcyon era has come to life in a series of unforgettable images. Though some of these come from the end of the period – the moon landing, hippies idiot-dancing – most are earlier. Footage of Beatlemania, the miniskirt, the mini-car, the 1966 World Cup, Cassius Clay and James Bond leads us to believe that this was a time when all was well with the world.

Reality was, of course, more complicated, though there was no denying that towards the end of the 1960s things were going sour. In 1968 the Russians invaded Czechoslovakia, there were riots at the Sorbonne and Martin Luther King and Robert Kennedy were shot dead. 1969 saw the Manson murders, Chappaquiddick, Altamont and the first death from HIV/AIDS.

1970 put paid to the sixties chronologically, culturally and communally. During the year the ethos of working together for the common good finally unravelled. Some individuals and groups made violent demands for what *they* wanted; others, for whom this was a step too far, withdrew from the fray and began to concentrate on themselves. Politicians were making no headway in solving the problems of the day but were endorsed anyway by the silent majority in the hope that, if things couldn't get better, at least they might not get worse. Young people seemed to be out of control and those who might provide leadership were conspicuous by their absence.

Yet if we permeate an unremittingly negative view of the year 1970 we will make an error of judgement. Yes, many things came to an end, but many things started, too. Those young people alienated by violence began to explore alternative ways of living, encouraged by a wave of inspiring publications which mapped out what the future might hold. The giants of rock departed but new names came to the fore and a variety of sub-styles hit a peak of creativity; the whole basis on which the music was created and consumed began to change.

These were different tracks and destined to lead to very different destinations.

Bibliography

Stefan Aust – *The Baader-Meinhof Complex* (The Bodley Head 2008 edition cited in this book)

Steve Barrow and Peter Dalton – *Reggae: The Rough Guide* (Rough Guides Ltd, 1998)

British Hit Singles And Albums, 19th Edition (Guinness World Records Limited, 2006)

James Brown with Bruce Tucker – *The Godfather Of Soul* (Sidgwick and Jackson Ltd, 1987)

Kevin Courrier – *Randy Newman's American Dreams* (ECW, Toronto, 2005)

Régis Debray – *Conversations With Allende* (NLB, 1971)

Jonathon Green – *All Dressed Up* (Pimlico, 1999)

Germaine Greer – *The Female Eunuch* (Paladin 1971 edition cited in this book)

Michael Haralambos – *Right On: From Blues To Soul In Black America* (Eddison Press, London, 1974)

Christopher Hitchens – *The Trial Of Henry Kissinger* (Atlantic Books 2012 edition cited in this book)

Jim Irvin (editor) – *The Mojo Collection: The Ultimate Music Companion* (Mojo Books, 2000)

Stanley Karnow – *Vietnam: A History* (The Viking Press, New York, 1983)

Nick Knight – *Skinhead* (Omnibus Press, 1982)

Joe Levy (editor) – *Rolling Stone: The 500 Greatest Albums Of All Time* (Wenner Books, 2005)

Mark Lewisohn – *The Complete Beatles Chronicle* (Pyramid, London, 1992)

Ian MacDonald – *Revolution In The Head: The Beatles' Records And The Sixties* (Pimlico, 1998)

Martin Meredith – *The State Of Africa* (The Free Press, 2006)

Kate Millett – *Sexual Politics* (Virago 1989 edition cited in this book)

Robin Oakley and Peter Rose – *The Political Year 1970* (Pitman, 1970)

Charles Reich – *The Greening Of America* (Penguin 1971 edition cited in this book)

David E Stanley with Frank Coffey – *The Elvis Encyclopedia* (Virgin Books, 1998)

Alvin Toffler – *Future Shock* (Pan 1971 edition cited in this book)
Joel Whitburn – *The Billboard Book Of Top 40 Hits* (Guinness Superlatives, 1983)
Rob Young – *Electric Eden* (Faber, London, 2011)

Acknowledgements

At various points in this book I have quoted from other authors, giving the name of the work concerned and the page number of the edition I have used. Publication details of these works can be found in the Bibliography. The sources of other material are as follows:

Chapter 1

Some of the information on the Isle of Wight Festival comes from the review in the 5 September, 1970 edition of *Melody Maker*. The reviewers were Richard Williams, Chris Welch, Michael Watts and Mark Plummer.

Details of Richard Nixon's career are derived in part from the Thames Television series, *Nixon*, first broadcast in October 1990, and the accompanying study guide, written by Roger Diski.

Chapter 2

Quotes from speeches by Stokely Carmichael come from the DVD *Black Power Mixtape 1967-1975* (Soda Pictures Ltd).

Chapter 5

Material regarding On The Eighth Day was obtained from interviews carried out in May 2013 with Jenny Slaughter, Nicky Crewe and Tim Gausden.

Information on the representation of women in the underground press comes from Matthew Millward's unpublished dissertation *What Was The Relationship Between The Underground Press And The Women's Liberation Movement In Britain During The Period 1966-73?*

Chapter 7

The comment John Peel's political views comes from the website www.thequietus.com.

Information on the cancelled England cricket tour to South Africa in 1968 and the quote from Graeme Pollock come from the 2004 documentary *Not Cricket: The Basil d'Oliveira Conspiracy*, directed by Paul Yule.

Information on records, when not obtained directly from the releases themselves, comes from:

- the Joel Whitburn and Guinness World Records books cited in the Bibliography
- www.discogs.com
- www.wikipedia.org
- www.officialcharts.com

As regards song lyrics, permission to quote has been obtained from the song publishers listed below. The publishers of the remaining songs from which I quote in this book have not responded to contact or cannot be traced.

'Old Kentucky Home'
By Randy Newman
© Unichappell Music Inc. (BMI)
All rights reserved

'(Don't Worry) If There's A Hell Below We're All Going To Go'
Music by Curtis Mayfield
©1970 (renewed) Warner-Tamerlane Publishing Corp. (BMI)
All rights reserved

'What Makes Me Tick'
Written by Loretta Lynn
©1970 Sure Fire Music Company Inc. (BMI) – Administered by Bluewater Music Services Corp.
Used by permission
All rights reserved

Index

Names in parentheses are those to which the person or organisation are referred elsewhere. Page references in italics denote use in a quotation.

Cook, Roger, 171
Cooke, Sam, 40
Coolidge, Rita, 70
Corea, Chick, 153,154
Corporation, The, 182,184
Cousins, Dave, 144
Cox, Billy, 1
Cox, Brian, 180
Cream, vii, 6,48,106,107,115,135,146,150,1
66
Cream (film), 84
Creedence Clearwater Revival, 116,172
Creek, Hilary, 71
Crewe, Nicky, viii, 127
Crosby, David, 67,68,70,93
Crosby, Stills and Nash, vii,67,93
Crosby, Stills, Nash and Young (CSNY), 8,67-68,69,70,93,94,123,198,201
Cross, James, 73
Crowley, Aleister, 215
Cullmann, Brian, *111*
Curie, Marie, 196
Curtom Records, 42
Czukay, Holger, 7,83,84

Dada, 202
Dana (Dana Rosemary Scallon), 18,179
Darnell, Nic, 165
Darrell, Johnny, 120
Dave Clark Five, The (The DC5), 113,171
David, Hal, 186
Davies, John, 72
Davies, Ray, 174

Davis, Angela, 46,47,66,205
Davis, Hal, 182
Davis, Miles, 8,14,142,150,151,152-154,155,161,165,200
Davis, Richard, 106
Davis, Tyrone, 186
Davison, Brian, 164,166
De Araújo, Hélio Carvalho, 73
De Gaulle, Charles 11,74
De Jongh, Tammo, 134
De la Halle, Adam, 7
De Lane Lea Studios, 86,166
Deadlock (film), 84
Dean, Elton, 159
Debray, Régis, 37,78
Debussy, Claude, 181
Decca Studios, 150
Dee, Kiki, 145,183
Deep End (film), 84
Deep Purple, 5,106,138,148,172,180,201
DeJohnette, Jack, 150,153,154
Delaney and Bonnie, 107
– Delaney and Bonnie and Friends, 107,202
Delfonics, The, 185
Dells, The, 185
Democratic Party (USA), 13,19,47,62,70
Dennis, Felix, 132
Denny, Sandy, 142-144
Derek and The Dominos, vii,108,199
Detroit Emeralds, The, 185
Deutsch, Helene, 131
Devlin, Bernadette, 10,178
Diddley, Bo, 49,114

Index

Family, 6,136,200
Fardon, Don, 171
Farrell, Joe, 95
Farrow, Mia, 99
Fat Mattress, 181
Fatah (faction of the Palestine
    Liberation Organisation), 78
Feldman, Morton, 189
Female Eunuch, The (book),
    131,206,215
Feminine Mystique, The (book), 130
Ferguson, Jay, 24
Ferrari, Luc, 189
Ferré, Léo, 73
Fields, Venetta, 186
Fiery Creations, 13,14
First Of May Group (Spanish
    anarchist group), 71,72
Fisher, Nigel, 88
Five Easy Pieces (film), 190
Fleetwood Mac, 161
Fly, Claude, 73
Flying Burrito Brothers, The,
    121,124
Flying Machine, The, 97,98
Focus, 172
Fonda, Jane, 46,66
Ford, Gerald, 203
'Forgiven' (poem), 95
Foster, Stephen, 98,103,119
Fotheringay, 142-144,181,200
Foucault, Michel, 207
Four Tops, The, 184
Fox, James, 104
Frampton, Peter, 174
Franklin, Aretha, 186
Free, 14,146,147,148,180
Free Democrats (West Germany) 3

Free Syrian Army, 31
Freek Press (newsletter), 14
Frei, Eduardo, 3,33
Freiberg, David, 70
Freud, Sigmund, 131
Friedan, Betty, 130
Friends (magazine) 14
Frijid Pink, 212
Fripp, Robert, 133,135
Frondizi, Arturo, 32
Funk Brothers, The, 41
Funkadelic, 48,183
Future Shock (book), 207-208

Gaddafi, Muammar, 31
Gallagher, Rory, 146,147
Ganjavi, Nizami, 108
Garbarek, Jan, 7
    – The Jan Garbarek Quartet,
    157
Garcia, Jerry, 70,123,190
Garfunkel, Art, 23,24
Garland, Arville, 191,206
Garland, Sandra, 191
Gates, David, 105
Gaynor, Gloria, 171
Gedeck, Martina, 80
Geesin, Ron, 163
Gene Tryp (stage show), 121
Gentry, Bobbie, 186,191
George, Lowell, 120
George, Sidney, 69
Gibb, Maurice, 9
Gibbs, Phillip Lafayette, 66
Giles, Mike, 134
Gilmour, Dave, 138
Ginsberg, Allen, 46,154
Gismonti, Egberto, 7

229

Poppy Family, The, 201
Popular Front for the Liberation of
   Palestine (PFLP), 73
Popular Unity (coalition – Chile)
   33,34
Powder Ridge (festival), 94
Powell, Enoch, 12,87,88
Powers, Gary, 3
Prescott, Jake, 71
Presley, Elvis, 113,141,192-
   194,198,201
Preston, Billy, 18,204
Pretty Things, The, 7,137,146,200
Previn, André, 99
Previn, Dory, 99-100,198,199
Price, Alan, 104,212
Prince Charles, 187
Prince Norodom Sihanouk,
   21,22,31
Princess Anne, 187
Prior, Maddy, 145
Private Eye (magazine), 169
Procol Harum, 5
Prokofiev, Sergei, 158
Protestant Unionist Party, 178
Provisional IRA, 178
Puente, Tito, 161

Q (magazine), 84
Quant, Mary, 196
Quatermass, 138
Quest, Dan, 53
Quilapayún, 35
Quintessence, 5
Queen Elizabeth II, 188

RCA Studios (Chicago), 42
Rackley, Alex, 47

Radio Caroline, 169-170
Radio Luxembourg, 170
Radio Nord See (Radio North Sea
   International, Radio Caroline
   International), 170
Radio Telefis Eireann, 178
Radiohead, 17
Rafferty, Jim, viii,181
Rainwater, Marvin, 171
Raison, Geoff, 196
Ramones, The, 213
Randy's Studio 17, 92
Rapp, Elisabeth, 105
Rapp, Tom, 104-105
Raspe, Jan-Carl, 79
Ratledge, Mike, 159
Rau, Fritz, 115
Rawlinson, Peter, 71
Reagan, Ronald, 46
Rebel Armed Forces (Guatemalan
   guerrilla group), 72
Red Army Faction (RAF) (Baader-
   Meinhof Group), 76, 78-81
Redding, Noel, 1
Redding, Otis, 14,92
Reed, Blind Alfred, 119
Reggae: The Rough Guide (book),
   90
Reich, Charles, 132,208-210
Reid, Duke, *90*
Renaissance, 5
Republican Party (USA), 19,62
Rhodes, Jim, 62
Rhodes, Red, 125
Rich, Billy, 155
Richard, Cliff, 173
Richards, Deke, 182
Richards, Keith, 122,166

Music Index

The following records are referred to in this book. Albums are in italics.

DIFFERENT TRACKS